Too Big To Fail

Too Big To Fail

Olympia & York:
The Story Behind the Headlines

by

Walter Stewart

M&S

Canadian Cataloguing in Publication Data

Stewart, Walter, 1931-

Too big to fail: Olympia & York: the story behind the headlines

Includes bibliographical references and index.

ISBN 0-7710-0177-0

1. Olympia & York Developments.   I. Title.

HD316.S84 1993   338.8'6'0971   C93-094840-8

The support of the Government of Ontario through the Ministry of Culture, Tourism and Recreation is acknowledged.

Printed and bound in Canada on acid-free paper.

McClelland & Stewart Inc.
The Canadian Publishers
481 University Avenue
Toronto, Ontario
M5G 2E9

1 2 3 4 5   97 96 95 94 93

For Barbara Barnum, with love

Contents

Death-Watch Beetles
in Courtroom 6-1

If, like some banks, a real estate company can be "too big to fail," O&Y appears to be that company.
— *Wall Street Journal*, March 14, 1992

$

Courtroom 6-1 of the Court of Ontario, General Division, is, appropriately, on the sixth floor of the General Division courtroom building on University Avenue in Toronto. The matter before us on this May morning in 1992, a series of nineteen motions in the case of Olympia & York Developments Limited and the Companies' Creditors Arrangement Act (CCAA), had to be moved here from another, smaller courtroom, because of the shoals of lawyers involved. They overflow two rows of tables at the front of the chamber, and spill out into the jury box, the witness area, and the pews where the spectators sit. Some even intrude into the rows where the journalists perch, straining, with growing incomprehension, to make sense of the legal babble before them. A cowboy who attended a banquet in New York once

1

commented, "I et for three hours, and the only thing I recognized was a olive." This is like that.

Away up at the very front, surrounded by the comforting symbols of regal ritual that bedeck every Canadian courtroom, sits a bearded Mr. Justice Robert Blair, in his black robes and red sash, elevated two tiers above us mere mortals, protected by piles of documents, attended by his clerks, and hustled by the lawyers. "Not that page, your lordship, page 66." "Not that document, your lordship; I believe you will find the document my learned friend referred to in the pile to your right."

The proceedings are already under way as I slip into a seat at the back of the room. I am late for the ten o'clock kick-off, in part because I went to another courtroom, in quite another building, on Queen Street, where I had been directed by a clerk in the Bankruptcy Court office, and in part because I stopped to talk to a man on the street outside. He was wearing a hand-lettered sign around his neck that read, "No job, three children. Can pay rent. Need money for food." I told him that if he wanted to see someone with real money problems, all he had to do was follow the line of lawyers recently debouched from their limousines up to Courtroom 6-1. The man said "Huh?"

After an hour or so, I begin to get some of the drift of the legal babble. The lawyers here gathered represent various interests in the complicated affairs of the Reichmann brothers, Canada's – and probably the world's – largest private-property developers, who own Olympia & York Developments Limited and its host of subsidiaries. There are whole posses of creditors, all represented by their lawyers, and foremost in battle are the lawyers of the "Gang of Four." The Gang of Four are the large Canadian banks – the Royal Bank, the Bank of Nova Scotia, the Canadian Imperial Bank of Commerce, and the National Bank – who led many of the syndicates that rounded up the loans to Olympia & York that have so recently gone sour. The lawyers from some of the other banks are contending, in delicate legal language, that the Gang of Four led them up the O&Y garden path, which came to its end, not in a greenhouse, but in a financial slaughterhouse. Failing that – because we always want a fall-back position in court – the other banks claim the Gang of Four acted the role of Judas goat; once arrived at the slaughterhouse, the Gang slipped out the side door to safety, while the other banks took the main hit.

The Gang of Four lawyers do not take these accusations kindly. Their clients lost more, and stand to lose more, than all the others. Whatever actions they took were quite proper actions in support of their own interests. They are banks of the highest integrity and soundest judgement; they wound up in the soup with all the others through a chain of circumstances for which there is either no one to blame, or lots of blame for everyone.

This back and forth is all performed with the best humour. No shouts or waved arms, no theatrics, no Perry Mason stuff, just the kind of friendly badinage you might expect from black-robed and white-dickied lads and lasses who are pulling down $3,500 a day or so, no matter what happens to the case, and who can comfort themselves with the knowledge that this will go on for months, and that all the money will come from Olympia & York's cash flow. The legal help will probably pull in $150,000 today, less GST and stamps. Why should they be cranky?

Those who might be out of sorts are the Reichmanns, along with the shareholders of the banks, trust companies, pension funds, and insurance firms who loaned them the money, the contractors who find themselves staring at job orders that have just turned to wallpaper in their fingers, and the thousands of ordinary workers who have lost, or will shortly lose, their jobs – 2,500 will be shaved from the staff of the Canadian Imperial Bank of Commerce alone,[1] none of them in the ranks of those who made the decisions that led to this mess. That'll teach 'em. Oh, yes, and among the other losers this day are the thousands, here and abroad, who previously benefited from the Reichmann charities, from hospitals to synagogues and schools, who will benefit no longer. The taxpayer, too, is entitled to wear the mask of tragedy. As part of their hymn to free enterprise, the Reichmanns accumulated debt to the Ontario government, which backed a loan of $14.9 million, secured by assets that are now gone where the woodbine twineth. The whole amount will have to be written off.[2]

The Reichmanns are not on hand to cast a pall of gloom. They are back down on King Street, at company headquarters, trying to hold up the walls while keeping several dozen balls in the air at once. No easy feat. As for the other losers, they are probably out scrabbling through their savings accounts, looking for jobs, or hand-lettering begging signs for the day when their unemployment insurance runs out.

One of the things we learn here is that there is broke, and there is *broke.* For the Reichmanns, broke is when there is a little less lavishness in the offering from the private corporate kitchen, or when the company jet goes on the block; for others, broke is sitting on the front step of a small house on the Isle of Dogs, in East London, waiting for the next bit of dole money, or folding up the plans of a nice bit of contracting in the Yerba Buena project in San Francisco, or clearing out a desk at one of the stricken lending banks, or wandering through one of the abandoned offices of O&Y itself and taking a kick at a packing crate that holds the memories of a decade or more of work.

One of the motions before us can be dealt with easily. A contractor who is owed a mere $19,500 for windows he put into an O&Y building in downtown Toronto wants to be "carved out" of the general mob.

You see, when the court stepped into the financial affairs of the development company every form of legal action against it was frozen. That is why the Companies' Creditors Arrangement Act[3] was passed, at the height of the Depression. Under the Bankruptcy Act a company could go into receivership, but there was almost no way, at that time, for it to emerge and go into business once again, short of liquidation. This created a hardship not only for the firm and its owners, but also for employees and even creditors, so a law was passed which said, in an astonishingly brief eight pages, that, where a debtor company has "secured or unsecured bonds," either the company or a creditor or the trustee in bankruptcy can go to court and have the court approve an arrangement which will allow the company to continue, provided that a majority of the creditors, representing three-quarters of the debts, sanctions the deal in a recorded vote. And, if it does, the arrangement is binding on all the creditors, whether they approve or not.[4] If most creditors want to keep a debtor going, the argument runs, it would be unfair to let a single lender force the firm into liquidation. The idea is that the company can be reorganized under court supervision, over time, rather than having to go bankrupt.

In the meantime – and this is the key point – the court may make an order staying, "until such time as the court may proscribe or until any further order, all proceedings taken or that might be taken in respect of the company under the *Bankruptcy Act* and the *Winding-up Act* or either of them."[5] The law applies only to a company that has issued bonds as a means of borrowing money. Moreover, as a practical matter, the law applies only to very large companies, because it costs so much to administer. There are all the lawyers and accountants to pay, to say nothing of court charges, witness fees, transcripts, and God knows what all.

But, not only can the (very large) company that has sought protection keep a creditor from seizing the collateral put up to back a loan, or its assets to repay a note, it can also escape interest and principal payments as long as the court protection lasts. (Under the more-generous, and even-more-bizarre, terms of Chapter 11 in the United States, the interest payments are usually gone for ever; in Canada, they just pile up until the protection ends, or the company goes entirely bankrupt.) The court will decide who gets how much of whatever money flows through the distressed company, if and when the court and administration costs are covered. The shortage will be divided equally among the peasants.

The debtors are in sanctuary. We used to call it "Safies" in the street game of kick-the-can; as long as I am standing behind the goal, you cannot tag me. The Reichmanns and their companies are standing behind Mr. Justice Blair and the other judges who will oversee bits and pieces of the action; they will huddle there for most of a year.

Thus, in the motion before us today, and referred to above, the contractor whose payroll may depend upon his being paid for the windows cannot collect unless His Lordship waves a wand and exempts his claim from the CCAA action.

"We can deal with this one rather quickly," a lawyer says, "and get on to something more substantial." All the other lawyers chuckle. Mr. Justice Blair scribbles and, *voila!*, a cheque for $19,500 will emerge further down the line. We are not going to waste serious time on such chicken feed.

The other motions, alas, are not so easily dealt with. They are all attempts to carve out various loans from the wreckage. Among the gaggle of ninety-one creditors[6] represented in court are two main groups, the secured and the unsecured. The secured creditors, which include banks, insurance companies, trust firms, and pension funds, loaned money to the developer against a specific security, such as a mortgage on a specific building, either here, or in New York, Calgary, Chicago, London, or wherever. The unsecured creditors, mostly banks (who are often both secured and unsecured creditors to the same company), loaned money on the general good name of O&Y or because, as one close observer of the development industry later tells me, "the banks are sheep; one leads, they all follow."

The secured creditors think it would be nice if they could, now that the money has stopped coming in to repay them, simply seize the assets against which they hold a pledge, but of course they can't do that while O&Y are in Safies behind Mr. Justice Blair. They must be carved out of the general action.

It is, in fact, the overwhelming advantage of the secured creditors, especially the banks, that has brought about the revival of the CCAA. In cases where this law does not apply, Uwe Manski, president of the Canadian Insolvency Practitioners' Association, comments:

Secured creditors are often reluctant to participate in the bankruptcy process, finding it simpler to appoint a receiver to seize the business and assets of the debtor and sell for the best price available. While they are entitled to claim in the bankruptcy for any shortfall they may incur, it is often pointless to do so, because there is no money.[7]

Under the CCAA, the secured creditors are subject to the same stay as other lenders; it is not surprising that they want to get out from under.

On the other side, the unsecured creditors have a sneaking suspicion, which in this case will later harden to a certainty, that, if the secured creditors scoop up enough assets to cover their security, there will be nothing left for them. It doesn't seem right. Moreover, some of the secured creditors on one loan, most notably some of the banks, are also unsecured on other loans; they hold bonds and mortgages, but they also hold short-term notes, commercial IOUs, with nothing behind them but a smile and a promise. Their feelings on the subject of carve-outs are somewhat mixed. Nothing much will happen today; all the motions will be put back, and back, as the tortuous proceedings wind on.

What the company is asking for, stripped down to essentials, is a five-year breathing space. Let the creditors step back for a bit, accept what can be paid on account, and let Olympia & York rise again. Snowballs will be reconstituted in hell before this proposal is accepted, and if that isn't clear yet, it is already clear that at least some of the creditors represented in court today feel a sense of betrayal that will prevent any outcome that does not punish the Reichmanns in some way. The Reichmanns do not, will not, begin to understand this bitterness towards them. They were only doing their best, they believe.

We are death-watch beetles here, clicking away as we bore through the wood of what was once one of the finest, largest, best-run development companies in the world. We are not here to lament, but to learn, and to make what we can of it along the way. Indeed, we take a certain amount of shameful pleasure from the Reichmanns' downfall. They were so big, so exclusive, so seemingly arrogant. When rumours first began to circulate that the company was having a tough time coming up with enough money to pay its bills, Paul Reichmann, the family strategist, told the *New York Times* that only "children who don't know what they are talking about"[8] would speculate that O&Y could be strapped for cash. Appears the kids had it right, but, until recently, who would have believed them?

In the 1991 listing of "The Billionaires," in *Fortune* magazine, the Reichmann brothers ranked Number 4 on the planet, with a wealth estimated at $12.8 billion in U.S. funds. The Queen, poor thing, dragged in in sixth place, with a mere $10.7 billion.[9] The Reichmanns could do no wrong. Buildings sprouted where they strolled, full-blown developments appeared at their command – and immediately began to spew out profits. Reporters hung on their every word at their rare public appearances, and hastened to polish up the required adjectives, "brilliant," "daring," "legendary," and, of course, "reclusive" and "mysterious." There is not much joy in the overthrow of the ordinary, but "I am Ozymandias, King of Kings. Look on my works, ye mighty, and despair" – that's the chap we want to see get his tit caught in the wringer.

My first contact with the three Reichmann brothers came when I was assigned to do a story on them for *Weekend* magazine, back in 1979. John Macfarlane, then the editor of *Weekend,* was tired of reading what a wonderful bunch the Reichmanns were. They were still celebrating their triumph in Manhattan at the time (see Chapter Four), and every business journalist in the country was strewing roses in their path. Macfarlane, a contrarian, thought it might be worthwhile to probe for feet of clay, and called me in. He did not exactly say "Sic 'em," but the thought was there.

The Reichmanns do not give interviews, except when they can control the outcome, more or less, either by laying down ground rules or by talking to journalists for whom no ground rules are necessary. I therefore did not waste my time telephoning for an interview, but walked over to First Canadian Place, rode the elevator to the thirty-second floor, then entered the executive offices of O&Y. Pretty intimidating. Oceans of carpet, doors with polished brass, dark, rich-looking furniture, and, on the wall next to the elevator, an inscription from the Old Testament. Gulping several times, I hoofed it across the thick carpeting and greeted a secretary who had a smile that would freeze fish.

I asked for a Reichmann, any Reichmann, and was told that Albert, Paul, and Ralph, the brothers in descending order of age, were all occupied. I said I would wait. How long was I prepared to wait?, the fish-freezing secretary asked. I said that, after six weeks, I would begin to get anxious, so she engaged in a low-voiced conversation with someone on the telephone – who no doubt told her to get rid of the bum – and then ensconced me in a straight-backed chair beside her desk.

There was a waiting room just around the corner, redolent of coffee and fresh muffins and festooned with chairs and couches and with a place to hang your hat, but that was for people with appointments. For me, a wooden chair would do. It worked out wonderfully well. Proper people, with appointments, would come in to see a Reichmann, get ushered into the waiting room, and begin talking about the brothers, while I hung from my chair with my ears flapping and my pen scratching.

"When these people built the Shell Centre in Calgary, it was three-quarters done before there was a contract."

"We did a $60-million deal in New York, with never a difference of opinion. These are very efficient people."

"We had a handshake deal and then prices changed, but they kept their word. Even though it cost them money."

I thought then and I think now that the reclusiveness of the Reichmanns is a handicap to them, because it is accompanied by a basic politeness; they will try to freeze you out, but never throw you out. Because I wasn't dropped down an elevator shaft, I was in my chair about half an hour later when two businessmen, one in his sixties, the other in his thirties, and both from New York, were ushered into the waiting room for a meeting scheduled with Albert Reichmann. They were soon joined by a Toronto colleague who had never met the brothers, and, over muffins and coffee, he was put on his best behaviour.

"This is a most unusual man you're going to meet," the younger man said. "I've been dealing with these people for four years, and he operates without contracts. He'll just shake hands, but he'll never double-cross you, and he'll never make a mistake about what was agreed."

The elder man was worried. "These people are Orthodox Jews. They don't just pretend. He'll be wearing a skullcap. For God's sake, don't look surprised."

When Albert Reichmann appeared a few minutes later, a burly, bearded, smiling man, wearing a grey suit, white shirt, and narrow, black tie, the forewarned Toronto man shoved out his hand and stared fixedly at the floor, for fear of being caught sneaking a peek at his yarmulke.

Not long after this, a tall, slender, bearded man loomed up beside my chair and introduced himself as Simha Fordsham. He, too, wore a skullcap, and I stared at it. (Journalists are not as sensitive as businessmen.) He said he was "handling communications for Olympia & York," but he didn't look like a flack, he looked like a Talmudic scholar who had just misplaced one of the scrolls. He asked me dolefully if I had an appointment, and grew even sadder when I confirmed his worst suspicions. He took me into a private conference room and subjected me to the politest brush-off I have ever received in a long life of dodging insults, boots, and writs from those who resent the prying press.

"The Reichmanns would very much like not to have a story done on them," he said.

I replied that, in the *Pogo* comic strip, when his pals decided to run Pogo for president and he demurred, Albert the Alligator said, "Son, when the public decides to pay you an honour, it doesn't consult your personal taste." Simha looked even gloomier. Pogo appears nowhere in the scrolls.

In the end, after six weeks of poking around the Reichmann empire, talking to their friends and foes, I came away with a story that *Weekend* titled "Good and Rich." The title was John Macfarlane's, not mine, but it fairly reflected the story. I noted that, in one deal, Paul

Reichmann agreed to rent space to a client for $12 a square foot, but nothing was signed. By the time the building was up, space was going for $15 a square foot, but the Reichmanns did not change their price, and the industry was astonished. Keeping their word seemed to make them some sort of freak in the development business. "The notion that a developer who gave his word kept it, without being forced into a courtroom by a posse of lawyers, should not astound anyone," I wrote. "The fact that it does says as much about the development industry as it does about the Reichmanns." [10]

Well, those were the good old days, when the Reichmanns were beyond reach and reproach, instead of, as today, merely beyond reach. They are still, in my judgement, among the most ethical developers – if the term is not an oxymoron – in business, but they have picked up a few blots on the company escutcheon over the years, and it is hard to escape the conclusion that their collapse was richly deserved.

Today's O&Y flacks are a much slicker, hardier breed than Simha Fordsham, but they have a much tougher task to perform. One of the firm's public-relations men, when I was angling, in vain, for an interview with Paul or Albert Reichmann for this book, told me that "if the brothers give your project their blessing, doors will open." When I said I didn't want the brothers' blessing, didn't want anybody's blessing, come to that, doors closed.

The Reichmanns are no innocents in these matters; they have used their power, and money, to block the publication of material they didn't like by lawsuits or the threat of legal action, including in the case of this book, and distrust the entire tribe of journalists.

This distrust creates an impasse. On the one hand, the family complains that journalists can never get things right; on the other, they will not provide the access that might set the record straight. From time to time, they have tried to make sure that only positive reports about their companies appeared by granting access to selected journalists under ground rules laid down before the interviews. The technique has blown up in their faces on more than one occasion, and it has now been replaced by a stony-faced refusal to talk, except through the medium of press agents who explain that the Reichmanns have no need to account for themselves, because their companies are privately held. In fact, they owned large shares in a number of public companies. Moreover, their activities, public and private, have had significant impact on the general welfare, and the economies, of a number of countries, and have been supported by huge investments of public money.

I was unable to solve this difficulty. Although I made every attempt to ensure that Olympia & York and the Reichmanns had the chance to tell their side of the story, I was met by what Douglas Gibson, the publisher of this book, and its originator, calls "an unbroken wall of brass." Accordingly, you will not find here any coy references to unnamed high sources within the Reichmann empire, or secrets poured privily into my shell-like ear. I have gone to the record, on the theory that, if you look hard enough, in the modern world, you will find most of what you need to know. I. F. Stone taught that lesson to my generation of journalists.

In Courtroom 6-1, while drawing rude pictures of the lawyers, I begin to reflect on these astonishing brothers; their family's remarkable rise, from dealing eggs in Hungary to dealing city blocks in London, Toronto, and New York, the empire they built, and the astonishing speed with which it came apart in their hands.

We do not know, in Courtroom 6-1, how much Olympia & York owes, or owns, or when it is likely to be able to pay back (we can guess, though: a lot,[11] not much, and probably never). We are staring at what might be the largest bankruptcy on record; or, perhaps not. Olympia & York is currently showing an exact balance of $14.6 billion in assets and liabilities, which caused Rick Salutin, a cynical chap, some pain. He wrote in the *Globe and Mail* that it made him think of "Frank the Pirate, my old used-car dealer. ('How many miles has it got on it, Frank?' 'How many do you want?')."[12] Actually, there is nothing sinister here; assets and liabilities are *supposed* to be the same on any well-regulated balance sheet; that is why it is called a balance sheet. How they get there is up to the accountants; whether they are believed is up to the auditors. Let us say that the company is, in fact, several billion dollars in the hole, as well as being unable to meet its current obligations. Otherwise, why would we be here?

The one thing we do know is that O&Y will not be allowed to collapse entirely, because they are too big to fail. If you or I missed a number of payments on the car, it would be hauled off with little ceremony and sold out from under us. Not O&Y. They are in default, at the moment, on $1.4 billion in various payments,[13] and they are still hugging everything they own. If you or I had been nailed in court, as O&Y has, twice, for failure to fulfil the terms of a contract, and soaked millions of dollars,[14] we would be down to our skivvies as fast as the bailiffs could strip us. Not O&Y. If we couldn't pony up the money for the mortgage, or meet dozens of IOUs as they came due, our irritated creditors would have us upside down and be shaking the change out of our pockets in short order, unless, as with O&Y and other giant firms, we owed so much that sinking us might sink them, too. The man with a hand grenade in a small room is not someone we want to push into precipitate action.

The banks, in general, are not pleased with O&Y; but if they call in the bailiffs the moment the company emerges from Safies, there is a good chance that in the scramble most of the assets will vanish or be whisked off by the wrong parties. And so, the quality of mercy is not strained; it is rented, in legal fees, at about $1 million a month.

There is also the undeniable fact that O&Y are wonderful managers, superior builders, and all-around worthwhile people. Their buildings are among the finest business complexes in the world, and the buildings they manage are always clean, well-kept, maintained to the highest standards. Their creditors, who are often their tenants as well, don't *want* them to fail when all is said and done; they just want to extract as much blood as they can from the stone without turning it into rubble.

A few months before this court action began, the Reichmanns appeared to bestride the world. They were not only the pride of

Toronto, where their buildings dot the landscape like raisins in a pudding, they were also the largest private landlords in Manhattan, substantial property developers in Ottawa, Calgary, Chicago, and Los Angeles, and they were about to embark on gigantic projects in Tokyo, San Francisco, and Moscow. They even had a joint project under way in Budapest, Hungary, within a few miles of where Poppa Reichmann began business. They were building a paper mill in Australia and drilling for oil off Indonesia. They owned Gulf Canada Resources Ltd., one of our largest oil companies, Abitibi-Price Inc., the largest paper-products company on earth, and shares of dozens of other firms. (A chart of the empire at its height appears in Appendix III.) Their holding company owned a substantial share of Trizec Corporation Limited, their real-estate rivals in Canada, along with chunks of Santa Fe Southern Pacific Corporation, Trilon Financial Corporation, a handful of property companies, and Campeau Corporation, now reborn as Camdev Corporation. In turn, GW Utilities Limited, a holding company held by the holding company, owned nearly all of Consumers' Gas Company, 10 per cent of Allied-Lyons plc, the British food-and-booze conglomerate, and nearly half of Interhome Energy, which, in its turn (a holding company holding a holding company holding a holding company) owned 100 per cent of Home Oil Canada Limited and Interprovincial Pipeline Incorporated. If you could live in it, work in it, write on it, ride on it, heat with it, eat it, or drink it, chances were, not long ago, that O&Y had a piece of it.

The *New York Times* put the company's assets at "perhaps $30 billion," just a tad more than Canada's federal deficit in 1989.[15] If that were right, in 1990 the Reichmann companies had assets worth nearly one and a half times the gross national product of Hungary, the family homeland.[16] They had a company jet and one of the finest corporate kitchens in downtown Toronto, along with fleets of cars and other executive toys. But they were not only rich, which is rare enough, they were richly respectable, which is rarer still.

They were renowned for their donations to charities, and saluted for the quality of their buildings. Deservedly so. Their World Financial

Center in New York, an eight-million-square-foot masterpiece of urban design, was widely recognized as one of the finest developments of its kind, anywhere; their Queen's Quay Terminal, a one-million-square-foot waterfront complex in Toronto, was named Best Building in the Commonwealth for 1984;[17] and Canary Wharf, the partially built complex on the Isle of Dogs in East London, was described by Dr. Brian Edwards, senior lecturer in urban design at the University of Strathclyde, as a development "of breathtaking beauty."[18]

That was then, this is now. Now their assets are frozen, their shares of outside firms sold or for sale. In a few short months, the entire edifice has cracked, and now hangs on the brink of bankruptcy; the Reichmann fortunes have dwindled, sucked into the black hole of debt created by Olympia & York. Not that they are paupers, but they are down, according to one of their closest friends and financial advisers, to perhaps 10 per cent of what they were worth before the trumpet sounded. More importantly – much more importantly to the brothers – they are the object of scorn and ridicule in the eyes of many.

"What is Paul Reichmann's personal reaction to all this?" I asked Andrew Sarlos, a Toronto financial guru and Reichmann ally.

"Embarrassment, I think," Sarlos replied.

The men whose name stood for quality and integrity are now lumped in with the developers whose crassness made them cringe. Henry Gonzales, chairman of the U.S. House of Representatives Banking Committee, administered the unkindest cut: "I look on this as a sort of high-level Donald Trump operation. These old boys are just more sophisticated and worked to a much broader international scale, but essentially the same."[19]

Robert Campeau, the Ottawa builder who ruptured himself trying to swallow two huge U.S. department-store chains, once capered fawningly around the Reichmanns; now he is suing them, and the National Bank, for $1.25 billion. Oh, no, they will not fail – but they will, as this case drags on and on, go through one form of exquisite humiliation after another, until the court removes its blessing and the creditors grab what they can, while the Reichmanns begin again, as managers of the buildings they erected. From giants to janitors – in less than a year.

What went so drastically wrong, and how did it come apart so fast? This book will attempt to answer these questions, but it will deal with some other issues, too, with a wider bearing on the world than the fate of the brothers. We will find that although the Canary Wharf development was the straw – some straw – that broke O&Y's back, it was only the last in a catalogue of disasters that began breaking around the company as far back as 1987. One of the most astonishing feats of the brothers was the way they were able to go on, as if nothing had happened, while catastrophe piled upon calamity, and no one the wiser.

We will find that, just as they say, the Reichmanns were not entirely the authors of their own misfortune, but they certainly put a word in, here and there. They are a family steeped in ironies, not the least of which is that, unlike most developers, they believed in – and worked for – the long term, and got clobbered in the short term just the same. We will learn something of the strange laws that govern the business of going broke, here, in the United States, and in England, and how they bear on all of us. And we will learn something of the limitations of the development business, and how Olympia & York, merely going about its own trade in its own way, first privatized and then distorted the planning process in Britain, demolishing, along the way, the comfortable and dim-witted Thatcherite dream that a deregulated economy would bring excellence and social progress together, with no cost to the taxpayer and plenty of profits for investors.

There are many lessons to be learned from the O&Y story, but the key lesson has more to do with politics than finance. When governments let the private priorities of developers determine policy in the name of market freedom, they will get not merely bad politics, but bad economics.

This is the story of how decent men, remarkable builders, outstanding citizens, screwed up. And what it means to thee and me.

PART I

Beginnings

If not the largest, certainly one of the most respected real estate firms in the world is Olympia & York Developments Ltd. Olympia & York (O&Y) is the privately held creation of three brothers named Reichmann, and it has been at the forefront of large-scale office development for decades. The Reichmann brothers have assembled a staggering collection of the world's finest office towers and a fair number of Canada's leading industrial corporations as well, all the while maintaining a reputation for honesty and a passion for privacy unusual in the world of big-time real estate.

– Jonathan Miller, 1992 [1]

CHAPTER ONE

Flight into Danger

The tragedy for Hungarian Jews was greater than the violence of the months of "White Terror": the blood lust nurtured in that period animated a Hungarian fascist movement that ultimately had a significant role in the Holocaust.

– E. Garrison Walters, 1988 [2]

$

The scene that comes to mind is the one from *Fiddler on the Roof*, where Topol sings about the irreplaceable, implacable, immovable role of tradition in the life of the family. To begin to get the slightest glimmerings of what makes the Reichmanns tick, it is necessary to go back to Beled, a small town about ninety miles west of Budapest and fifty miles southeast of Vienna (and thus actually closer to the Austrian capital than the Hungarian one) and to Samuel Reichmann. The patriarch.

Samuel was born of a strictly Orthodox, middle-class Jewish family on February 11, 1898, and grew up in a world that combined equal parts of terror, tradition, and uncertainty. Some background will help us to understand a little of that world.

Hungary at that time was part of the Austro-Hungarian Empire, and its head of state was the Emperor of Austria, who was, in a dual monarchy, King of Hungary. There were no borders between Austria and Hungary and, although the two nations had separate legislatures and separate armies, they had only one diplomatic corps, and were run, in most important matters, by imperial decree. Hungary was better off than Austria in this regard; the Hungarian parliament had to be consulted on matters of concern to Hungary alone, but the Imperial administration ran foreign affairs, military and financial affairs, and the ten-year plans that were supposed to govern the economy. The Hapsburgs had created a government which Robert Kann once called "a standing army of soldiers, a sitting army of bureaucrats, a kneeling army of worshippers, and a sneaking army of informers."[3]

When Samuel Reichmann was born, the Jewish population of Hungary was growing rapidly, at about four times the rate of the general population, because of the Declaration of Tolerance, which Emperor Franz-Joseph II had promulgated at the time of the Constitution of 1867. Until this Declaration, Jews had been forbidden to settle in towns,[4] join the army, own land, or transgress any of a score of other regulations designed to keep them isolated and inferior. Most of them lived on the estates of nobles and earned their keep by running the landlord's inn or shops, or acting as his agent. They were not actively persecuted, except from time to time, but they were not part, and not intended to be part, of the society around them. The Declaration of Tolerance brought the Jews officially into Hungarian society for the first time. Their religion was recognized and a school system established, although it had to conform to the Austro-Hungarian system. This was all very well for the mainstream Jews, but of less use to the ultra-Orthodox, like the Reichmanns, who did not want their children educated by the State, or involved in any way, beyond the minimum unavoidable contacts, with the secular world. The Jewish community was split, with the Orthodox barely acknowledging their co-religion-ists, the "Neologues," as Jews.

The Declaration of Tolerance set off a large-scale immigration of both kinds of Jews from Galicia, then a Crownland of Austria and later a part of southern Poland, into the eastern European nations, along an immigration route that moved roughly from northwest to southeast. In 1787, the Jewish population of Hungary had been estimated at 93,000.[5] By 1869, it had grown to 542,000, and by 1910, to 909,500. This meant that roughly one in twenty of the total 1910 population of eigh-teen million was Jewish.[6]

By the first decade of this century, all of the legal restrictions were abolished, at least for the time being, and the Jews were beginning to move from the country to the towns and cities – Budapest contained a Jewish population of 200,000. The counties of the northeast, in the area known as the "Burgenland," including the area around Beled, had vibrant Jewish communities, and the highest proportion of Jews in the general population, because these areas marked the first stage along the immigration route. Seven villages along the rich alluvial plain of the Danube, on either side of the border between Austria and Hungary, had substantial Orthodox synagogues. Beled was one of these.

Religion governed everything these people did, said, read, or ate; it instructed them, among other things, to hold themselves aloof from the secular world and from others, even Jews, who did not share their views. It taught them the hundreds of laws to be obeyed and the cus-toms to be followed – girls were to be separated from boys at age three, for educational purposes; the head was to be covered at all times; a man did not shake hands with a woman – and it taught them, correctly if you think about it, that contact with those outside this narrow faith would inevitably erode the framework of traditions that supported them. Moses Sofer, the most influential of the Orthodox rabbis, took as his motto, "No change at all."[7]

Just the same, the Jews were finding their feet, working hard, becoming prosperous in the slightly more open atmosphere of the first part of the century. They worked in all sorts of jobs, from agricultural labour to mining and industry, from domestic service to commerce.

Then came the First World War, a conflict in which Hungary found itself on the wrong side; along with Germany, Austria-Hungary formed the Central Powers. The disintegration of the Austro-Hungarian Empire left the nation with no effective leadership of her own at war's end. Hungary was thrown into chaos, with massive unemployment, and even starvation. Her neighbours marched in to grab what they could, and the Treaty of Trianon, in 1920, would later legalize these seizures; Romania grabbed Transylvania, Yugoslavia took Croatia and Bacska, and the newly created state of Czechoslovakia seized Carpatho-Ruthenia.[8] Hungary was reduced to about 36,000 square miles, less than the province of Nova Scotia.

The monarchy was swept away when the last emperor, Charles I, was deposed and exiled by the Allies. He was replaced by a provisional president, Count Michael Károlyi, who was in turn overthrown by Béla Kun, the thirty-four-year-old son of a town clerk from Transylvania.[9] He set up a "dictatorship of the proletariat." It didn't work any better than the Soviet dictatorship of the proletariat, but at least it didn't last so long.

The threat of a Bolshevist takeover was enough to drive much of the remaining capital out of Hungary; it also brought the Romanians marching in. Kun fled to Vienna on August 4, 1919. The Austrian authorities promptly interned him and later dispatched him to Russia, where he was named a political commissar in the Red Army. (He was tried for "disrespect" to Stalin in 1937, and was murdered in 1939.)[10]

The Allies installed a puppet president, K. Huszár, in 1920, but he was soon ousted by Admiral Nicholas Horthy de Nagybanya. Horthy had been commander-in-chief of the Hungarian navy, but had decamped to Vienna after the Kun coup. There, he helped to form an "anti-bolshevik committee" and a small "national army"[11] to restore order. Horthy was named Regent of Hungary by parliament, and surrounded himself with other former officers, spear-carriers in the rightist reign of terror. [12] The fact that Kun was Jewish lent a racist element to the revenge they exacted.

The Allies, who had never recognized Kun, promptly acknowledged Horthy, whose right-wing leanings would shortly blossom into full-blown fascism. He would rule Hungary for twenty-five years, in a regime marked by brutality and anti-semitism, and he started by conducting his own reign of terror against anyone who had been connected with Kun. To distinguish the reigns of terror, Kun's was known as the Red Terror and Horthy's as the White. Not that it made much difference to the victims.

This brief summary suggests that in Hungary as in Germany, Jews had always lived under various forms of repression, which must have reinforced the sense of exclusiveness, mistrust of the outside world, and respect for tradition and family values that were the hallmarks of the Orthodox grouping of which the Reichmanns were a part. Keeping kosher, respecting the Sabbath, honouring the parents, were important as religious rules but equally important as social conventions that drew the Jews more closely together for mutual support against an outside world that was always hostile and untrustworthy, even when it wore a friendly face.

It was against this background of chaos, prejudice, and uncertainty that Samuel Reichmann grew up. The only sure rock in his life was his religion, the only things he could count on were his own acumen and the small group of like-minded people in his own class and group. It was this legacy, at least as important as the money he made and the plans he laid, that he would pass on to his children.

In 1921, the stern-looking, brown-haired Samuel Reichmann married Renée Gestetner (whose cousin David would move to England and invent the first stencil machine), a dark-eyed, handsome woman of twenty-two from Győr, on the Danube just west of Beled. By this time, Samuel had probably already had his fill of prejudice and economic chaos, had probably already begun – for he was always a

far-sighted man – to think his way towards an escape from the mael-
strom that was Eastern Europe.

Samuel Reichmann described himself as an egg merchant, but he
was a little more than that. He and one of his brothers bought eggs
from all over the Burgenland to sell in the cities. He was one of the first
to use cold storage to keep eggs for longer periods by storing them in
calcium, a process that allowed him to sell them in winter for as much
as four times the summer price.[13] He sent to England for an egg-grad-
ing machine that put him ahead of his trade rivals, and he established,
even as a young man, a reputation for shrewdness. For eight years he
worked steadily amid the chaos to build an egg-exporting business
that spread across Europe, and he spent a good deal of his increasing
wealth, in accordance with his religious custom, on charities.

He and Renée had three children while they lived in Beled: Eva,
born in 1923, Edward in 1925, and Louis in 1927. His family, religion,
charities, and expanding business occupied him fully, but he could
hardly fail to observe the rising tide of intolerance against Jews that was
permitted, if not actively promulgated, by Admiral Horthy's government, as well as the business opportunities that awaited outside
Hungary.

In 1928,[14] the family moved to an apartment in Vienna, where
Samuel had been trading for years. It was in Vienna that the next three
children, the Olympia & York trio, were born: Albert in 1929, Paul in
1930, and Ralph in 1933. During the next decade, Samuel expanded his
business, while living beneath the volcano of anti-semitism about to
erupt once more over Europe. They moved to a better apartment, on
Rembrandtstrasse, and then to a still better one on Hafnergasse, in the
high-rent district. They attended a synagogue for Hungarian Orthodox Jews. Samuel ran his poultry and expanding egg-exporting business, built a large warehouse and cold-storage depot, prospered and
worried and planned.

Then came the ascension of Hitler, in 1933, the passage of
the Nuremberg Laws, virtually isolating German Jews, in 1935, the

remilitarization of the Rhineland, in March 1936 – and Germany's frantic rearmament. These were not far-off events, they were happening all around. Austria was becoming as dangerous as, more dangerous than, Hungary had been. Austrian chancellor Kurt von Schuschnigg was bullied by Hitler into releasing Nazis who had been arrested for various crimes – including the murder of Engelbert Dollfuss, his predecessor – then into bringing Nazis into his cabinet, and finally into resigning. It still wasn't enough, and German troops marched into Austria, unopposed, on March 12, 1938. This was the *Anschluss,* and the Nazis were turned loose to seize the property of rich Jews all over the country.[15]

By a fluke the Reichmanns were out of Vienna when the huge crowds thundered their support of Hitler in the Burgplatz, not far from the family's Vienna apartment. They had gone back to Beled to celebrate Edward's bar mitzvah, because his grandfather, David Reichmann, was too ill to travel.[16]

The Reichmanns would not wait for the appeasement of the Munich Pact in September, or for *Kristallnacht,* the night of broken glass, on November 9-10. The three middle boys, Louis, Albert, and Paul, were left with their grandparents in Beled, where Edward was enrolled in a yeshiva, a religious school. Sometime soon after August 11,[17] Renée, Samuel, Eva, then fifteen, and Ralph, then four, cleared out, to a temporary haven in Paris.

They moved into the Hotel Montholon, and Renée gave French lessons in order to help Samuel start his business again in France. But Samuel was already planning to move once more; he expected a war – soon. Renée went back to Hungary to pick up the four boys left in Beled and brought them back to Paris just before the Second World War broke out, in September 1939.

When the German armies poured through Belgium – where Allied strategy said they were not supposed to go – the Reichmanns fled again. They went by rented truck to Orléans, on traffic-clogged roads occasionally strafed by German planes. At one point they took shelter from an air raid in a small hut at an airport, and discovered that they were sheltering among full tanks of aviation fuel. From Orléans, they took a train to Biarritz.

"We thought we were safe," Edward Reichmann told Elaine Dewar.[18] Then, of course, Marshal Philippe Pétain cut a deal with Hitler, and the Nazis gained effective control of France. The Spanish, for a wonder, opened the border temporarily to refugees fleeing from France, and the Reichmanns were able to dash across Spain to Madrid. From there, they decided to go Spanish Morocco, to Tangier, on the northwest coast of Africa opposite Gibraltar, which had a substantial Jewish population. With the help of the chief rabbi of Spanish Morocco, they got a visa quite quickly, and arrived in Tangier in late 1940.

Morocco was effectively divided between the French and the Spanish, but, in 1923, the Statute of Tangier created an international zone of 140 square miles, embracing the city and the trading zone around it. It was an open port, a trading centre at the top of Africa.

When war broke out, Spain tore up the Statute of Tangier and, in June 1940, sent in troops from Spanish Morocco "to restore order." The Reichmanns were out of the European frying pan, but it would not be much cooler where they landed. The Spanish soon began to apply some of the then-standard restrictions against Jews, but this process had not gone far when the Americans in turn invaded, with comparatively little resistance, in November 1942. Tangier was an international port once again, restrictions against Jews were removed, and money-making opportunities, in a neutral, free port on the edge of both Europe and Africa, abounded. There was still turmoil, but it was profitable turmoil for some. *Fortune* magazine described Tangier as a "no man's land" which had "no national anthem other than the sweet melody of hard cash."[19]

The Reichmanns moved into a large, comfortable apartment at No. 25 rue Molière, and Samuel went back into business. Soon, he was joined by Edward, who started in a chocolate factory and then went into the import-export business, before establishing a bank. Samuel, with his money and business connections throughout Europe, also set up a bank, the Bank Samuel Reichmann, which was a merchant bank and currency dealership. (Small banks of this sort are common in many countries, although not in Canada.) Soon the family was in construction, real estate, merchandising, and finance, with two banks, the Bank Samuel Reichmann and the Real Estate and Commercial Bank, run by Edward, on the third and fourth floors of the building where they lived.[20] The ground floor was the Bolsa, or exchange, for Tangier, and the living quarters were on the second floor. Albert worked with his father, while Paul and Ralph were at yeshiva.

Renée Reichmann became active in the Va'ad Hatzalah, a committee devoted to rescuing Jews trapped by the Nazis, and was involved in the dangerous business of helping to smuggle Jews out of Nazi-occupied lands. According to Edward's reconstruction of the story for Elaine Dewar, there was an arrest warrant out for Renée in Hungary, but she was never captured. She became the Tangier agent of the committee, sent packages of food and clothing to refugees who were prisoners in the concentration camps, and wrote countless letters around the world on behalf of trapped Jews. Agonizingly, she could find no trace of her own nine brothers and sisters and their children, who had all been deported. She wrote to one of her contacts in New York, in March 1945, in a letter asking for help with shipping food into the camps:

> My own affairs are also very wrong. I could not learn where are my 9 brothers and sisters, the 82-year-old mother of my husband and his 8 brothers and sisters. One of my sisters has 9 little children, all under 14 years, the other has 8 and the third has 5. All have been deported and there is no news about them. In spite of my greatest effort I could not learn where they are, to send them a piece of bread and warm clothes.[21]

Her brother, Layush Gestetner, was caught smuggling food to Jews in Győr, and executed. Her daughter, Eva, was also active, gathering money, food, and clothes in Tangier, as well as in the Spanish cities of Barcelona, Madrid, and Tetuán.

A memoir prepared by Rives Childs, who had been in the U.S. legation in Tangier during the war, detailed how Renée got him to go to the Spanish governor and obtain 1,200 Spanish visas, which were used to protect 500 children and 700 adults in safe houses run by the Red Cross in Budapest.[22] Some of the children smuggled out of Europe were housed in the Reichmann apartment in Tangier, which became a haven and orphanage combined. Every member of the family became involved, perforce, and the mind reels at the thought of Samuel Reichmann, bearded, correct, polite, and private, dealing with the gaggle of children his wife had gathered into their home. An astonishing woman.

After the war, Paul and Ralph were sent to England to attend Gateshead, the major Orthodox yeshiva there. Their sister, Eva, and brother Louis would go to England, too. Eva married an English merchant banker, Louis worked in the industrial diamond business, before moving on. Edward, Albert, and their parents stayed in Tangier. In 1945, Samuel and Renée made a trip to New York to see if it was a possible place to set up, at last, a permanent residence. But the Americans were not welcoming; it was not a place the Reichmanns wanted to live. Neither, for the long term, was Morocco; things there were heating up.

As part of the peace settlement, Morocco came squarely under the thumb of France, and became part of that nation's aggressive empire building, along with neighbouring Algeria. When an independence movement began in 1947, it was brutally put down, and when the sultan, Sidi Mohammed, embraced the principle of an autonomous Morocco, he was ordered to abdicate by the current French resident general, General Guillaume. The sultan refused, and was bundled aboard a Dakota aircraft, with two of his sons, and flown off to Corsica. His uncle, Moulay Arafa, an enfeebled man who wanted nothing more than to be left in peace, was thrust onto the throne in his place.

This set off a storm of protest, not only in Morocco, but in France, and then in the United Nations. There were riots, and repression – on one occasion, according to Gavin Maxwell, who wrote a fascinating book about this period,[23] French troops machine-gunned a crowd of protestors, killing at least five hundred. As they did in Algeria, the French managed to unite a badly divided populace in hatred of themselves.

Tangier was comparatively calm at this time, but it was obvious that independence must come eventually. It was time to move, but where? Hungary was under the Soviet heel, most of the rest of Europe was unstable, England was an economic wasteland, and America, from what the Reichmanns had seen of it, was a decidedly unfriendly place for them.

In 1954, in the midst of the turmoil, Samuel Reichmann told his oldest son, Edward, "Go look in the world for another place, because we may all have to leave."[24] Armed with an Austrian passport, obtained because the family had permanent residence there before the war, Edward went to Paris and got visas for Canada, the United States, Mexico, Venezuela, Brazil, and Uruguay.

They had come a long way from Beled; they had succeeded beyond any measure they might have expected when they first fled the Nazi onslaught, but they were still under threat. Everything that had happened to them had reinforced the feeling that they must cling to their own ways, their own kind, their own traditions, and the certainty that no government, anywhere, was to be trusted.

So Edward was off to find a permanent home for a family that wanted nothing more than stability, opportunity, and a chance to practise its own religion in its own way.

That refuge turned out to be in Canada.

CHAPTER TWO

The Sons Also Rise

$

The roots of their success were remarkably simple: the Reichmanns
simply pursued excellence in all they did.
    – Peter Foster, 1987 [1]

Edward Reichmann had wanted to go to Israel in 1954, not roam the
world, but, even at the age of twenty-nine, no Reichmann son would
disobey a parental decree. Israel was still in its birth-throes, and in the
control of a socialist party. Edward was an active Zionist, but, as a family, the Reichmanns did not want anything to do with a socialist government. Thus he found himself, in December 1954, in New York City.
Yes, his parents had already visited here, but that was nine years before,
and New York was the centre of growth, expansion, and opportunity.
The family had bonds of business and friendship here, and Edward,
who had dabbled in cotton futures, knew some of the commodity
dealers. It was worth a look. But it was also, alas, the financial centre of
a nation in the grip of an hysterical anti-Communist crusade led by
Senator Joseph Raymond McCarthy. Not that the Reichmanns had

anything to fear on that score, but the place gave off a stench of intolerance and fear that turned Edward off. As he told Elaine Dewar,[2] "I didn't have English, but I read the foreign papers and could follow the headlines." They were enough.

Edward decided to do a little exploring farther north, in Canada, and flew to Montreal. He spoke fluent French and had contacts from the Parisian refugee community, now living in the affluent suburb of Outremont. It was a friendly enough place, and had a stability the Reichmanns had never known. The prime minister was a man called Louis St. Laurent, whose party had been in power since 1935, and the nation next door was not strife-torn Algeria, but the United States; you could do business in that intolerant land from here. A single trip to the Montreal library, where he looked at trade statistics and figures on the Canadian economy, convinced Edward that this was the place. On January 10, 1955, he applied to exchange his tourist visa for landed-immigrant status, indicating that he wanted to settle permanently in Canada. Four weeks later, he was issued with an order of expulsion. He had thirty days to get out.

Canadian immigration practice has always been marked by hypocrisy and racism. During the war thousands of refugees were refused entry, even though they faced certain death, because they were Jewish. There seems little doubt that Edward Reichmann's refusal was based on the same grounds. But it is one thing to turn back a penniless, powerless refugee from an internment camp, quite another to try to rebuff a rich, well-connected, brash and bullheaded man like Edward Reichmann.

He had already transferred a large sum of money into a Canadian bank, had rented office space on Craig Street, and had written to dozens of overseas companies in the export and import business to find out if they would use his services as a Canadian agent. He had also bought a new car, which he drove the 120 miles down to Ottawa, where he soon connected with Leon Crestohl, a Jewish MP from Montreal, who introduced him to J. W. Pickersgill, then minister of immigration. Not long after, he got the papers he needed to bring his wife and two children over. (His wife was a refugee whom the Reichmanns had helped to get out of Hungary. They were married in Tangier.) Visas for Louis, Paul, and Ralph followed. But what were they to do?

Edward began importing goods from Europe to sell in Canada, and formed a company for this purpose. Part of setting up a company involves a check to make sure that any proposed name has not already been chosen, but all the names he put forward, such as "Canadian Import Export" or "North American Importers," were in use. One day, while he was discussing the problem with his lawyer over the telephone from his downtown Montreal hotel room, Edward idly picked up a pair of new socks from his suitcase. The manufacturer's label read "Olympia." He told the lawyer to try "Olympia Trading Company." It went through;[3] the Olympia Trading Company was in the export-import business.

There was a growing demand, in Canada's burgeoning economy, for floor and wall tiles, and Edward soon found himself buying and selling tiles, from Spain, Japan, and Italy. He saw an ad under "Companies for Sale" in the *Wall Street Journal*,[4] and this led to the purchase of Montreal Floor and Wall Tile – then the largest Canadian importer – and of Pilkington Tile, which manufactured tiles in Montreal. The companies were put together as Olympia Floor & Wall Tile.

Edward joined an Orthodox synagogue, built a comfortable house for his family, and sent for his brothers to help in the new business. Louis came first, in 1955, but he showed little interest and moved on to New York and, later, Israel. Ralph, still a bachelor, came in 1956, followed later that year by Paul, who had married in Tangier in 1955. Albert, who had married in Jerusalem in 1954, stayed with his parents in Tangier for the time being.

The most outgoing, and restless, of the Reichmann sons, Edward became active both in Liberal politics and in the construction business. He felt he owed the Liberals for helping him to get into Canada, and he knew the construction business from his days in Tangier. He worked in Leon Crestohl's election campaigns and built Place Crémazie in north Montreal. For the official opening of this fourteen-storey office-and-retail complex, he drew people like Eric Kierans and René Lévesque, then provincial Liberal cabinet ministers, and Liberal MP Guy Rouleau (later to achieve infamy in the Rivard scandals). Place Crémazie was built through a company called Three Star Construction, which occupied more and more of Edward's time, while Paul and Ralph got on with the tile business.

They decided to move the company to Toronto, where they were already doing much of their business, and where the younger brothers, who spoke more English than French, felt more comfortable. Paul and Ralph established Olympia Floor & Wall Tile Company (Ontario) in 1956, with a paid-in capital of $50,000. This was raised to $70,000 in 1958, and remained at that level. The brothers established a line of credit with the Royal Bank, amounting to $75,000. When they asked for this to be raised to $100,000, the local bank manager demurred, so they switched accounts to what was then the Imperial Bank, later the Canadian Imperial Bank of Commerce. If any more proof were needed that there were no illicit millions behind the firm, this surely is it. Who, with millions to draw on, would go through the torture of having a bank manager peer down his nose at him over a $25,000 extension in a line of credit?

The first building they bought, a four-thousand-square-foot warehouse on Densley Avenue in northwest Toronto, proved too small for their booming business almost from the day they moved in. So the two brothers bought land close by on Colville Road, and sent out for bids on a larger warehouse, based on architectural plans drawn up on nights and weekends by a freelance architect who worked days for one of the Toronto banks.[5]

When the bids came in, the lowest was $125,000, $25,000 more than the $100,000 they had budgeted. They consulted Samuel, back in Tangier, and made a decision. They would build the warehouse themselves, with Paul in charge. Why not? He was a brilliant Talmudic scholar, a slender, grave, polite twenty-six-year-old with a good deal of energy and even more of self-confidence, and the family had some experience with construction. What more could you want? The warehouse went up, on schedule, for $70,000. It was neat, spare, and efficient, and soon the brothers were deluged with requests from others anxious to explore the possibilities of having a factory built in the same efficient style.

By now, it had become clear that Canada was the stable, prosperous land of opportunity that Edward had spoken about in 1954. Accordingly, in 1959, Samuel, Renée, and Albert, the son who had stayed to help in Tangier, moved to Toronto. They went into the factory business. York Factory Developments Limited was founded by Samuel and Albert Reichmann, with a paid-in capital of $40,000. The "York" came from the county, the "Factory Developments" from the work it did.

Later, it would come to be received wisdom that the Reichmanns arrived in Canada with millions, and that their empire was founded on this fortune. Peter Newman wrote, in *The Canadian Establishment*, "Rumours persist that the elder Reichmann arrived with at least $30 million, plus much valuable jewelry. Other stories claim that the seed money really came from the English branch of the Rothschild family."[6] Rumours also persist that Elvis is still alive. Other stories claim that Hilary Clinton has adopted an infant from outer space.

In fact, Samuel and Renée Reichmann were required to make a declaration, on entering Canada in 1959, of their net worth at that time. They were worth $410,000. When he died in 1975, Samuel Reichmann's will was probated, and the application for probate shows that his estate amounted to $2,184,773. A comfortable amount, but no vast fortune. The fortune was made here.

The company began putting up small, one- and two-storey warehouse-cum-office buildings along highways 400 and 401. These were mostly "turn-key" operations; the Reichmanns would oversee the building until the moment they were ready to hand the keys over to the owner, for a contracted price. And guess where the tiles came from.

At first, the family lived in small apartments in the Bloor–Palmerston area, west of downtown – the lower-rent district – but soon moved into middle-class country on the western fringe of Forest Hill. Samuel and Renée had a small, two-storey house; Ralph and Paul lived in apartments nearby, and Albert bought a house on Bathurst Street. They were still operating at a very modest level. Although a number of other firms were set up, usually for building a single project, none of these had a paid-in capital of more than $200. As late as April 23, 1963, the combined balance sheet of all the Reichmann companies showed a paid-in capital of $110,924. There were, in addition, advances from the family of $534,720, nearly all of it from the profits of the various company ventures. The total family-provided funding at this point was $677,358, of which Samuel Reichmann had advanced $107,183.[7] With the buildings they owned, they now had total assets worth $3,665,131.77, but most of that was tied up in property.

The Toronto the Reichmanns came to was quite a different city from the Toronto of today. It was smaller, more parochial, less multinational, and a good deal less tolerant. The subway had opened in 1956, but most minds were still closed. The Orange Day Parade was still big stuff, and if Toronto had a Jewish mayor, Nathan Phillips, he was certainly not a Reichmann kind of Jew. He was chummy, noisy, and sometimes embarrassing – as when he called the Russian ambassador to Canada, whose name was Aroutinian, "Mr. Rootin' Tootin'."

The banking business, Samuel Reichmann's business, was not one that welcomed Jews to its seats of power in Canada, whether they had money or not; indeed, Jews found it harder to borrow money than other segments of the population. Though nothing overt was said, of course. It was not until Walter Gordon, a former finance minister, made a speech in 1970 lamenting the fact that so many bright ideas died aborning because of the closed, Wasp, old-boy network that ran the banks, that the subject was even raised in polite society.[8] Gordon's speech inspired the founding of Unity Bank, Canada's first "ethnic" bank, which ran into serious trouble launching a share issue when the head of a major investment house snapped that he was not about to start raising money for a Jew.

None of this could have surprised the Reichmanns; nor is it surprising that, given their background, the Reichmanns clung protectively together. They would live, according to tradition, within walking distance of their place of worship, which would be of the most Orthodox kind. They would observe the 613 duties, or *mitsvoth,* of Jewish life; they would expose their children as little as possible to secular education, follow kosher food rules, celebrate the three daily prayers with proper solemnity, and, of course, observe the Sabbath, from sundown Friday to sundown Saturday, in the strictest way, shutting down every aspect of business, not just the salesrooms, but the tile-manufacturing plant as well. Under the rules of observance, an Orthodox Jew cannot, during the Sabbath, drive or use public transportation or carry anything from the public domain into the private one, where family worship is conducted, or vice versa. There were religious quotations on plaques on the office walls, and there was a clause in every contract they drew up forbidding their subcontractors, of whatever religion, to work on the Jewish Sabbath.

Tradition. Also, inevitably, segregation, stratification, and a certain amount of stultification.

The family building firm was not, at least not yet, really a development company. What had attracted Paul Reichmann to the business was the fact that, with proper planning and hard work, you could make a quick, fat profit. The brothers had budgeted $100,000 for their warehouse; the lowest tender was for $125,000, but the actual cost had been $70,000. The difference between $70,000 and $125,000 suggested a possible profit margin of close to 80 per cent, if Paul Reichmann had done the job for someone else. Paul could undercut other bidders and still make good money.

This is not the same thing as developing, going through the whole process of assembling land, dancing through the fields of forms to get permissions, serving the selected block with roads and water, sewers and power, finding the financing – which must mean, in turn, lining someone up to buy or rent enough of the project in advance to convince your backers to come up with the money – and designing, building, and finishing the project. The development industry, in this sense, was in its infancy in Canada at this time. Robert Campeau was putting up frame houses outside Ottawa; William Teron was working as a draughtsman; Trizec, Marathon Realty, Cadillac Fairview, and their kin were not even a gleam in anyone's eye. But there was one big, brash developer at work in Montreal who would have an enormous impact on the Reichmanns. His name was William Zeckendorf.

Zeckendorf's autobiography, while somewhat wonky – he skips lightly over his own bankruptcy, leaving the reader to wonder why he keeps muttering about the forces of evil that brought him down, without saying very much about being down – is nonetheless an illuminating read.[9] The son of the owner of a general store in Paris, Illinois, he went to New York to attend university but dropped out before graduation to go to work for his uncle, in the real-estate business. Then, at the age of thirty-three, he went to work for Webb & Knapp, a large, conservative realty company started by a Rockefeller connection. He later bought control and made it much larger and much less conservative. During the Second World War, he managed a $50-million estate for Vincent Astor while the millionaire served in the navy. Zeckendorf earned a profit of $15 million on this nest egg, and sent Astor an accounting of it, along with a bill for $350,000 for his services. He was decidedly nervous about how Astor would treat the bill, since he was known for his tightness with a dollar, but the millionaire simply told an aide, "Pay him, and send a bunch of flowers from me."[10] Seed money for the capture of Webb & Knapp.

Zeckendorf assembled the seventeen-acre block of land that became the site of the United Nations, along the East River in Manhattan, and sold it to John D. Rockefeller. The French architect who designed the building drew up the first plans from a rough sketch made in Zeckendorf's New York apartment. When the proposal was accepted, Zeckendorf told his wife, "We have just moved the capital of the world."

Not a Reichmann sort of thing to say, but then he was not at all like the studious, quiet, unassuming Reichmanns. He was a large – 250 pounds – loud, garrulous, and flamboyant man, whose favourite hobby was eating, and who boasted of his twenty-four-thousand-bottle wine cellar. He liked to show off. He and his wife paraded a toy Dobermann pinscher with silk bow tie at New York parties. He would show visitors his trophy photos, including the Chase Manhattan Plaza and a *New Yorker* cartoon depicting a man pointing to the Manhattan skyline and saying to his son, "Someday, my boy, all of this will belong to William Zeckendorf."[11] Only the fact that he ran out of money stopped him from building his dream, the Zeckendorf Hotel. He was also superstitious, and demanded that every Webb & Knapp subsidiary – they were numbered companies – be registered containing the number thirteen or a multiple thereof.[12]

But what Zeckendorf had, in common with the Reichmanns, was intelligence of a very high order, vast amounts of energy, a gambler's instinct, and absolute single-mindedness. What he thought he had – congratulated himself for having – was "imagination" and "vision," which are the words most developers use when they have fired up a plan to knock down a dozen or so city blocks of housing and stick up a tower. "If I am a maverick in my business, it's because other people work only with money. I employ imagination,"[13] he said. Hard to say exactly how much imagination is required, if you are in the business of covering several city blocks with really big buildings, to draw up a plan for covering more blocks with really huge ones. Developers sometimes like to kid themselves. And us.

Zeckendorf put up ever-larger developments in Denver, Washington, Chicago, and Philadelphia. In 1953, in a manoeuvre the Reichmanns would follow two decades later, he bought up a package of skyscrapers, including the Chrysler Building, for $53 million, in what was the largest real-estate transaction in New York City history.

He was lured to Canada by Donald Gordon, the undisputed king of the CNR, who wanted a new office building around the railway terminal in midtown Montreal and couldn't find a developer at home big enough to finance it. Zeckendorf flew up to look at the seven-acre site, where a building for the same purpose had actually been started thirty-four years earlier, although all that project had accomplished was to remove four million cubic feet of earth and leave behind a giant, costly hole.

Montreal's colourful mayor, Jean Drapeau, welcomed the developer to the city, and in December 1957, Zeckendorf signed a $105 million deal to build the Place Ville Marie on land owned by the CNR. Up to that time, the largest private office project in downtown Montreal had contained 383,000 square feet; the Place Ville Marie would be more than ten times that size, at 4.2 million square feet. It also introduced another concept that would be copied by the Reichmanns, among others: it was to include extensive and expensive retail stores with office space, restaurants, and even theatres, to say nothing of the giant railway station in the basement.

If you want to find the prototype of the huge, classy, city-shaking developments the Reichmanns would put up in Toronto, New York, and London, you need go no further than the Place Ville Marie. You will also find in that building's history one of the tricks used by the Reichmanns to assure not only the financing but also the leasing of their projects. The main financial backing for Place Ville Marie came from the Royal Bank of Canada, whose irascible and bullying president, James Muir, was willing to lend money, but not to move into the complex.

Zeckendorf was having trouble finding companies willing to sign long-term leases and, according to his autobiography, he called Muir at home one weekend and told him so.

"Jim, you know we are not getting anywhere with this damn renting."

He roared back, "Why the hell should you get anywhere. That goddamn Chinaman [I. M. Pei, the project designer] is stopping you."

"No, you're stopping us . . . Jim, your enemies, the ones who hate you, won't take space here. . . . There is a gang-up on the part of the other banks. . . ."

He said, "You're crazy."

"I'm not crazy."

Then he said, "Well, what do you want me to do about it?"

"Move."

"I should move? You're mad."

"Move, Jim. We'll call the new tower the Royal Bank of Canada Building in Place Ville Marie. You will be king of the hill...."

"You're out of your mind. We have the biggest bank in Canada in the biggest bank building in Canada."

I said, "I'll buy it from you."

"You've got no money to buy it, you ———— Jew." [It was Zeckendorf who daintily deleted the expletive.]

"Now look here, Jim. Think this over. I'm coming up tomorrow."[14]

And it came to pass. In a pattern that would be repeated by O&Y, the bank sold its own building to Zeckendorf and moved into a tower, named for it, in Place Ville Marie, signing a long-term lease. Now the bank was not only a brand-name tenant with a tower named after it, it had the motive, and the muscle, to ensure that other corporations trooped in behind it. Which they did.

As James Lorimer notes in *The Developers*,[15] Place Ville Marie combined the four key elements that would make it the model for future corporate ventures of this sort: it was large-scale, grand enough to dominate the area around it, as well as drastically affecting the supply of office space (the Reichmanns would call this "creating an address"); it had the developer as owner, not merely builder, with the businesses as tenants on long-term leases; it combined office with retail space; and it was built in the heart of the city, where government departments, large corporations, accountants, lawyers, and consultants could meet and mingle. Cost is not the key in these matters, convenience and prestige are what count. All of these elements had been present in earlier developments, but never on this scale. That's vision, I guess.

While Zeckendorf was raising the Place Ville Marie and such other Canadian projects as the Yorkdale Shopping Centre in Toronto and the Halifax Shopping Centre, the Reichmanns were quietly putting up more buildings, making more money, and building a reputation for quality, integrity, and efficiency. They kept to the deals they made and the timetables they projected – which was almost unheard of. They had no visible vices, beyond Paul's habit of smoking American cigarettes; they didn't even play golf. If they had any hobby, it was work.

"They were very hands-on," says Fred Beer, who did a number of concrete and marble contracting projects for the Reichmanns. "They did not just sign a deal and turn it over to others. They managed it, every step of the way. They listened to the client, and they went over the plans, inch by inch. An architect who worked for them, worked for them; he didn't just produce a batch of plans. And they produced first-class, good-looking buildings, very cheap." [16] When you consider that Fred Beer ended up suing the Reichmanns, as we will find later in this chapter, this is high praise indeed.

Word of mouth got them more business, and each completed job became an advertisement for the next. The turn-key, or "package," arrangements that they preferred meant that their increasing expertise gave them an advantage, as well as a higher margin. In the more traditional tender approach, the landowner invites bids from contractors, with the lowest bid winning. A chancy business, especially when it involves subcontractors whose costs are usually not certain until the last minute. The winning bid may well be a loser, as the contractor cuts costs to beat the competition only to discover that he has cut out his own profit. Instead, the Reichmanns went looking for customers who needed office space and presented them with a plan, and a cost, for a complete building. By the mid-sixties, they had built warehouses and factories, for others, all over the Toronto region.

That was when Zeckendorf did his bellyflop.

Zeckendorf led Webb & Knapp into more and more rapid expansion, all over Canada and the United States, with sometimes half a dozen huge projects under way at once. In 1958, in concert with the Rubin brothers of Toronto, he had bought a five-hundred-acre block of land at the corner of Don Mills Road and Eglinton Avenue, which he planned to develop into a massive commercial and office complex – as soon as he got around to it. But his habit of using the money as it flowed in for one project to launch others instead, got him into trouble. The first $25 million that was put up for Place Ville Marie, for example, he used to buy 177 Petro-Canada gas stations. That left him short, so he borrowed more. He kept borrowing at higher and higher rates, but never stopped expanding.

In 1960, to get cash fast, he made a deal with Philip Hill, a British merchant-banking firm, to create a company, half of which would be owned by Webb & Knapp (Canada). The other half would be owned jointly by two British companies, Eagle Star Insurance and Second Covent Garden Property, which had a sister real-estate company called English Property Corporation; we will meet it again in Chapter Five. He called the new creation Trizec, the "Tri" to commemorate the three firms and the "zec" to commemorate himself. We will meet it again, too.

The infusion of cash from his new partners kept Zeckendorf going, but nothing could induce him to cut back, or slow down, and when the economy went soft, it was all over. Among the hotels, suburban malls, and office complexes that he built was a huge amusement park, Freedomland, in the middle of the Bronx in New York City. He got the rides up, but never got them going. Webb & Knapp was leaking money at every seam; the firm lost an astounding $70 million between 1959 and 1965[17] and could no longer pay its bills. In May 1965, U.S. creditors forced Webb & Knapp into bankruptcy.

In Canada there was a firesale of Webb & Knapp properties to raise cash, and a Swiss creditor who had advanced some of the money on Place Ville Marie seized Flemingdon Park in Toronto and put it on the market. The Toronto development was partially under way, a combined housing-office-and-industrial complex next to what would be the Don Valley Parkway, but it was nowhere near finished, and it could only be guessed whether it would ever be a success. Paul Reichmann guessed that it would. Most other potential buyers shied away, since the development was away from downtown, in the boondocks. Every developer knows the three prime requirements for any real-estate investment: location, location, location. But Paul Reichmann could only see that a block of five hundred acres, with many of the services in place, was going at a bargain-basement price. Peter Foster quotes him as saying to Gil Newman, then the company accountant, later a vice-president in charge of finance, "There's gold on the table and nobody wants to pick it up. Are we making a mistake somewhere? Am I missing something?"[18] The answers were No and No. The Reichmann brothers bought Flemingdon Park, in great secrecy, for $17.8 million, every penny of it borrowed. The Bank of Nova Scotia, which was one of the Zeckendorf lenders, backed about half the amount, and the rest came from the Oelbaums, another Toronto Jewish family prominent in the development business. Peter Foster says that the final deal "was signed in the vaults of the downtown offices of the Bank of Nova Scotia."[19] The Reichmanns didn't pay anything; the bank itself transferred a debt from one debtor to another, and got the rest from the Oelbaums. The money came streaming back within six months as the family sold off parts of the parcel and began their first really large and challenging development.

In addition to several thousand rental and condominium apartments, the Reichmanns built thirteen office buildings in Flemingdon Park. Their first multi-storey structure was the MonyLife Insurance building, into a floor of which they moved York Developments Limited. Later they built a data centre for Bell Canada, which led to their building the Place Bell Canada in Ottawa. They also put up a head office for Shell Canada, which led to a thirty-three-storey development for Shell in Calgary. After the triumph of Olympia Square, as the development came to be called, the Reichmanns could pick and choose their projects. They were still known only within a narrow circle, but it was the circle with the cheque-books. I talked to a rival of the Reichmanns about this time, and he pointed to the crucial importance of word-of-mouth boosts in the development business.

> You don't go out and hustle this kind of business. You don't put an ad in the paper saying you want to build an office building. It all works through the banks. IBM is looking for new office space, and the president mentions it at some luncheon to a banker. The banker, who has done a lot of business with the Reichmanns, says, "They're good people." That's all there is to it.[20]

Paul Reichmann became more and more involved in the development side of the business, and dropped out of active participation in the tile firm. They made a lot of money, and gained a number of valuable clients while constructing the largest suburban office centre in Canada, and soon they were active in a number of developments in downtown Toronto. They built the *Toronto Star* building at the foot of Yonge Street, and when in 1969 they set up a new company, Olympia & York Developments Limited, they came downtown themselves. Olympia & York's head office was in the *Star* building. They also built York Centre, Global House, and a new downtown building for the Ontario Ministry of Consumer and Commercial Relations.

Everything did not go smoothly all the time, but one of the few serious imbroglios into which they got themselves reveals a good deal about the Reichmanns: the two brothers who sued them for failing to live up to a contract hold them in the highest regard, to this day.

Fred and Doug Beer, owners of what was then Canada's largest precast concrete firm, Beer Precast Concrete Limited, signed a contract on February 5, 1973, to provide precast concrete walls, faced with marble, for L'Esplanade Laurier, a large Reichmann complex at the corner of Bank and Laurier in Ottawa. The job was to be completed by June 1, 1974, and the contract laid great emphasis on the necessity of sticking to the schedules that O&Y was setting with great precision.

Olympia & York would provide the Carrara marble, in a grade known as Edward White, through two Italian companies, Freda S.p.A. of Querceta and A. Bufalina Succ. ri. [21] The Beers would fasten the marble to the concrete in large panels, and install it on the project. But, not long after work started, at a hundred-thousand-square-foot facility set up for the purpose in Ottawa, the Beer brothers, waiting for the next shipment of marble from Italy, were looking at each other and muttering, "He cometh not." Or, if the shipment did come, it was not of the quality specified. (You first use the A, or finest marble, closest to the ground, B next, and C at the top of the building. If you get C before A and B, you can't do much but stack the stuff and wait.)

Fred Beer spoke to Albert Reichmann about the delays. Albert was very attentive and polite, but nothing changed. In addition to problems of grade, they ran into increasing difficulty getting marble that matched in colour. In the end, it took months longer than expected and tied up the Beers' equipment; instead of making money on the contract, they lost. So they put in a bill, and Olympia & York, in the politest way possible, told them to drop dead. In 1976, the incensed Beer brothers launched a lawsuit that dragged on and on until it was settled at the courtroom door in February 1987. Olympia & York paid the Beers $500,000. [22]

"Boy," I said to the brothers, sitting in Fred Beer's mammoth den at his home near Claremont, northeast of Toronto, "I guess you guys are really ticked off at the Reichmanns." Fred looked at Doug, Doug looked at me. "Finest people we ever worked for," said Doug.

Fred, the elder brother, said, "Of course they tried to screw you down. It's that kind of business. They're marvellous builders."

Doug said, "They were innovators, not afraid to try something new. And, something else unusual, they were highly principled."

So, despite suing them, the Beer Brothers have nothing but praise for the Reichmann brothers.

They never did learn exactly what caused the delays that plagued the Laurier complex, because O&Y, once the writ dropped, would never admit there were any delays, much less discuss what caused them. Both Fred and Doug suspect that their marble had gone instead to the tangled and triumphant construction of the biggest, boldest, and best O&Y project ever, the centrepiece of the Olympia & York empire, First Canadian Place.

CHAPTER THREE

Once I Built a Tower

I cannot now walk past Toronto's First Canadian Place, the tallest
office building in this country, without regretting the Reichmanns'
fate. They have been exemplary ambassadors of innovative design and
construction techniques.

    – David Olive, August 1992 [1]

Sometime when you have nothing better to do, and you happen to be
in downtown Toronto, wearing a hat fastened down with staples and
glue, stroll over to the corner of King and Bay streets and look up. You
need the staples and glue because the bank towers that surround you
here create their own microclimate, marked by a wind that howls up
Bay Street from the Lake Ontario waterfront, sending smaller cyclones
left and right as it hits King, and genuflecting as it passes all the money.

If you are standing on the northwest corner, facing south, you will
have the whitish granite of a Bank of Nova Scotia building on your left,
directly across Bay street on the northeast corner. Not very impressive,
but behind it you can see the red richness of Scotia Plaza, rising

sixty-eight storeys, and up to its hamhocks in debt. It was built by Robert Campeau, seized by the Reichmanns, and is in the process of being seized from them, by, among others, the Bank of Nova Scotia, which is owed $98 million on its own head office. The BNS is not in trouble, just the building.

Across from Scotia, and therefore kitty-corner from you, are the towers of the Canadian Imperial Bank of Commerce, a glassy-eyed, grey monolith. Dead ahead of you, on the southwest corner, the Toronto-Dominion Centre marches in serried ranks of towers off to the west. There used to be a touch of humour here, a group of cows sculpted by Joe Fafard of Saskatchewan, life-sized, and chewing their metal cud on a small knoll put there for the purpose. They have been banished down to Wellington Street, and robbed of their knoll.

Immediately beside you is No. 1, First Canadian Place, 1.6 million square feet of office tower, clad in white marble, looming seventy-two storeys overhead.

Up on the thirty-fourth floor there is a plaque on the marble that reads, "These stones were brought over by Otto, Patricia's father, with sweat and tears, Anno 1975." This human touch shows, I think, what decent people the Reichmanns are, and why employees like Otto Blau, a senior vice-president of O&Y, remain loyal to them.

If you go across the street to the T-D Centre and look back at First Canadian Place, you will notice, up there on the seventy-second floor, along with the huge blue Bank of Montreal logo – twenty feet high, it is, a stylized M which stands for Montreal, but might just as well stand for Mulholland, for reasons that will soon become clear – that the tower is not square. Each corner has a notch cut out of it, so that, from the top, the building must look like a cross, with very short arms. These little dents create extra corner offices on every floor. You can rent corner offices for more money; you can also satisfy more status-hungry exec- utives by giving them corner offices. Clever, eh?

First Canadian Place was the first giant, recognized triumph of the Reichmanns. I happen to think it is a disaster, and that plunking huge bank towers of granite, marble, and glass cheek by jowl in the centre of the town may "create an address," but not an address where anyone wants to live. It also creates a windy mess. But, if you are going to do it, this is the way to do it. And nobody listens to me.

First Canadian Place was, like so many office towers, mainly the giant symbol of a giant ego, in this case that of William Mulholland, then chairman of the Bank of Montreal. The building the bank already owned on this corner was dwarfed by the T-D Centre across the way, and by Commerce Court. Mulholland wanted a head-office building to outdo these giants, dammit. He wanted, and he got, the tallest office building in the Commonwealth, the tallest bank building in the world, with his penthouse right at the top. And, of all the proposals that came before him to make it happen, the most impressive was the one submitted by Olympia & York, a company with a growing reputation and a track record that suggested that they would do whatever they said they would do, on time – which would be a novelty.

After protracted negotiations, they got the job. They would build a pair of massive towers in a project that would cover 90 per cent of the block bounded by Bay and York streets, from Adelaide to King. It would be built in two stages, with the Bank of Montreal slab to go up first, and to be completed between 1973 and 1978, and the second tower to follow once the City of Toronto had given its approval.

This was not as easy, in those days, as it would become in our own day. There had been a time when developers were the undisputed kings of the city, and the first part of the plan received approval in 1971, while these beneficent conditions still prevailed. But the election in 1972 of David Crombie, the tiny, perfect mayor, signalled a sea-change. Crombie ran on a platform of restoring the downtown area, saving it from the kind of unchecked development that had thrust the T-D Centre and Commerce Court into place, and bringing down the density, the number of times a square foot of space can be covered – high density equals profit, for a building – in the city's core. Very soon Crombie had a city planner, Ron Soskolne, and a housing chief, Michael Dennis, both young, abrasive, confident, and committed, and a by-law that they could use to beat the developers about the head. Not that it was ever put so crudely, of course. The by-law stated that no new building in the Central Area Plan could exceed forty-five feet in height without receiving a waiver from the city. The idea was not to bring building to a halt, as the developers wailed at the time; it was to make developers negotiate with the city for the projects they wanted to build, by adding low-cost housing, or more parks, or whatever. They would be made to give up something to the area plan to get the densities they wanted.

Needless to say, Soskolne, the city planner, and the Reichmanns were soon engaged in dubious battle. The opening skirmish was over a street and a lane the Reichmanns wanted to close off, and three historic buildings: the lovely old *Toronto Star* building; the *Globe and Mail* building (on a site chosen in 1861 by George Brown, the *Globe* founder); and the Bank of Montreal's former Toronto headquarters. Soskolne said they could have the street closings if they preserved the historic buildings, but Paul Reichmann told him that this wouldn't do; they already had a legal commitment to the *Globe* to demolish the building. The *Globe* had moved into what looks like an insurance office, down on Front Street; why that made them want to tear down the lovely old building, I don't know. There is an accepted response to the sort of gambit O&Y was using to hang on to its right to smash down perfectly fine buildings already in place, and that is to say, So, you have a legal commitment, so what? But Soskolne did not use it. He found the Reichmanns reasonable men, courteous, attentive to the City's demands, and not at all like the knee-jerk reactionaries he had met elsewhere among developers.

In the end, O&Y did get to knock down the historic buildings, and did get the streets closed. Peter Foster, in *The Master Builders*, his first book on the Reichmanns, says, "They quickly came up with compromise plans."[2] Actually, most of the compromise was to do it the O&Y way. The city did, however, win a few points. The original scheme called for a solid block of office-and-commercial space along King Street; the Reichmanns were persuaded to break this for a small park, where you can go and sit down for a few minutes before the wind comes along and blows you to Barrie. The Bank of Montreal tower was reconfigured to keep the "canyon effect" along Bay Street. It is not an accident that the street looks that way; the city cyclones were destined to be. And the second phase of First Canadian Place was to be redesigned so that it would not be another tower twinned to the Bank of Montreal slab. There would be two buildings in this phase, neither of them as tall as No. 1. The end result was, essentially, what the Reichmanns wanted.

Now to build it.

The story of the building of First Canadian Place has been told elsewhere, over and over – Peter Foster follows the thing up floor by floor, almost – and that is because, for people who are fascinated by these things, it was full of innovative and impressive efficiencies. By this time the Reichmanns had put up 120 office and warehouse buildings, some of them – like York Centre, just a block from First Canadian Place, and the *Star* building, just down Yonge Street – in the mini-skyscraper class. They had learned that what slowed building most were the delays caused because the right materials were not available on site when needed and the endless time wasted on site by all the workmen trudging up and down ladders.

They had also learned that it is hard to lease space in an office building ahead of time – and that is essential, to get the money flowing – when all you have to show is a hollow shell, junked up with construction debris, and a pretty little model. ("This will be your office, Al, right here, beside the pencil.") What if you worked out a plan that had all the subcontractors delivering their materials to a schedule, laid out on a computer and rigidly enforced? What if the elevators went up with the building? And what if you finished as you went, from the bottom up, so that you could show a gleaming lobby and suites to prospective lessees? And what if you used huge elevators to get all the materials where they were needed fast, and then jumped the hoisting machinery up the elevator shafts, floor by floor, as you went, instead of doing everything from outside, by cranes? And what if you used double-deck elevators, so they could serve two floors at the same time?

You would get, it turned out, a saving of 1.3 million work-hours compared to the original estimate, and a building that would go up in less than three years, instead of five. You would also get a building with the first twenty-two storeys finished, leased, and advertising for you, while you went on with the upper floors. The building cost $200 million U.S.,[3] about $250 million Canadian; no firm estimate was ever released, but whatever it was, the Reichmanns apparently beat it.

In one of the neater tricks devised by Keith Roberts, O&Y's construction chief, a freight elevator stationed at ground level with a capacity of forty-five tons lowered the trucks bringing materials in, to a turntable in the basement which would spin them to one of eleven bays where they would be unloaded and the materials whisked up one of the other elevators to where they were needed. The freight elevator became part of the building.[4] New techniques were designed to deliver concrete to the location at which it was needed, through radio-controlled hoppers, at up to 130 tons an hour, and to attach the marble facing using a double tier of scaffolds; the first scaffold was used to put in the brackets for the marble slabs, the second to install the slabs.

The subcontractors, incredulous at first, were given huge briefing books to guide them, and found themselves grudgingly impressed by both the speed and the quality of the work. There were problems, of course; there are always problems. We have had the hint of one of them in the last chapter, a delay caused by a shortage of the right grade of marble in Italy. For a time it seemed that the building would be white up to about the twentieth floor, and then go whitish grey. Paul Reichmann wouldn't have it; the colour had to be the same all the way up, all sixteen miles of the stuff.[5] Otto Blau was sent over to Italy to search out new supplies, and solve the problem. He did, although there was a five-month delay, without which the building would have been finished even faster than it was.

Another problem was harder to deal with; a dispute with William Mulholland, beside whom marble seems more like chalk. Mulholland found out that the second tower would have Sun Life Assurance

Company of Canada as its principal tenant, occupying four hundred thousand of the one million rentable square feet. That was all right. But the building would also house a branch of the National Bank. That was not all right. Mulholland couldn't do anything about all the other banks around him, but he saw no reason to put up with the National Bank on his side of the street, in his own block, Mulholland and discuss the issue, but the infuriated bank chief refused to see him, and lined up his lawyers. There was a clause in the agreement between O&Y and the Bank of Montreal to freeze other banks out of the project. But should the second phase be considered the same project, or another one? Did the clause apply? Lawyers put in tennis courts on the proceeds from questions like this, but it never came to court. The National Bank was scratched, Sun Life pulled back, and the Toronto Stock Exchange moved in. The shorter of the two buildings in the second phase became the TSE itself, and the taller one, the Exchange Tower. (The National Bank got in later, and now sits smugly on the first floor of the Exchange Tower.)

While First Canadian Place was going up, there was a small sag in the Toronto rental market, and No. 1 filled slowly, so that Olympia & York lost about $20 million in the first full year of leasing. The company refused to lower rents, however, and lived with the empty space, until it could be filled, as the market came back, with leases at much higher rates. The first lessees were paying about $12 a square foot annually, the last ones more than three times that. This would teach the Reichmanns a lesson – don't lose your nerve, higher rents are bound to come back soon – that was entirely misleading, and would prove damaging later on.

For the time, though, everything was coming up roses. First Canadian Place went into the *Guinness Book of Records* as the world's tallest bank building, at 935 feet, and Mulholland's big M made it as the highest advertising sign in creation. Everybody who counted praised the building, including the retailers on the lower levels and the crowds who wandered through, and the tenants loved it. The finishings were of the finest materials and workmanship, the design was effective and workmanlike, with more open space than other comparable structures, and O&Y, as landlord, kept everything clean and in good order and responded quickly to any complaints.

By this time Ralph, the youngest brother, was almost entirely occupied with Olympia Floor & Wall Tile, which was also doing well, with sales of over $100 million annually. In fact, O&Y was, really, Paul and Albert: Albert was the president, Paul the executive vice-president, but they were almost interchangeable. They wandered constantly in and out of each other's offices, which were now on the thirty-second floor of First Canadian Place; they consulted each other continually, and either of them could make a decision, on the spot, on issues which, in any other corporation of comparable size, might take weeks to work their way through a board of directors.

If they wanted to talk something over in the presence of other businessmen, they would either switch to Hungarian, or leave the room for a few minutes to hold a "directors' meeting," returning with a decision. Samuel Reichmann was the titular chairman of the company and, after his death in 1975, Renée held the post, but the effective decision-making power rested with Paul and Albert. And increasingly it was the brilliant, ascetic, younger brother, Paul, who laid down the company strategy. As the company grew, this single line of command would show some built-in drawbacks, as we shall see, but at the time it was accepted as part of the awesome efficiency of the Reichmann brothers.

The company was run on a strict operational formula laid out in a series of one hundred manuals in loose-leaf binders (later, all would be moved to computer), with hundreds of control forms covering almost every conceivable problem that could come up. The rules were not ironclad, but you'd better have a good reason for making a change.

One of those who dealt with the Reichmanns for years is Ken Field, who was, for eleven years, president of Bramalea Limited, the now-foundering real-estate firm. A slim, boyish-looking and energetic man of forty-nine, Field was wearing an extensive wire-and-plaster sling arrangement, the outcome of a skiing accident in Vail, Colorado, when we had lunch in the Daily Planet restaurant, near his consulting firm's office on Eglinton Avenue in Toronto. It is not unfair to say that Field appears himself a little wired up, full of stories, good humour, and an almost-visible abundance of energy. His first dealings with the Reichmanns came while he was vice-president of Bramalea, when he was assigned to buy the old *Toronto Star* building on Yonge Street for his firm, after O&Y moved into First Canadian Place.

Field made an appointment and went to it with a certain amount of apprehension. "I was just a kid, really, with very little experience, and expecting to be dealing with a whole gang of executives. I was very nervous. But there was just Paul. I had heard of the Reichmanns, but never met one. They were said to be very upright, and you could count on their word. Not always the case in this business."

He rolls his eyes.

"I had an idea of what we should be paying for the building, and he had an idea of what they should be getting, and they weren't the same. I also had a list of things we wanted done to the building before we took it over, which would cost something. I gave him my figure and he gave me his figure and I said I didn't think that was the right figure, so we agreed to think it over and meet again.

"The second time, he started out by looking at me, very grave, the way he is, and saying that he had been thinking it over and he thought perhaps I had made some good points, and we could probably do a deal at the figure I had mentioned.

"'If you're comfortable with that figure, Mr. Field,' he said, 'I think we can do something.'

"Well, I went on with my list of all the things that needed to be done, and with each one, he would nod very courteously and say, 'If you're comfortable with that, so are we.'

"I was expecting to pay his price, but to get all these things done, and by the time it was over, I was paying my price and still getting these things done. He just kept saying, 'Well, if you're comfortable with that,' until I wasn't sure I *was* comfortable any more."[6]

Field was pleased with the deal, which certainly impressed his bosses at Bramalea, but he suspects that it was probably a good deal for

O&Y too, or Paul Reichmann would never have agreed. He came away deeply impressed with the grave, courteous man.

By the time First Canadian Place was under way, the family had moved again, from the outskirts of Forest Hill to the area around Lawrence and Bathurst, in Toronto's northwest, where there is a substantial Jewish population. All three brothers, and their parents, had large, comfortable, but unspectacular homes close to each other and close to the synagogue they established in the district. The synagogue, known as the "Boat Shul," is located in what was once a grocery store. It is, needless to say, Orthodox to the core.

The completion of First Canadian Place, ahead of time, the cleverness of the design, and the fact that it began, in its second year of operation, to generate a profit that would rise over the coming years, profoundly affected the company's fortunes. They were recognized, at least in Toronto, as the finest, smartest, most-efficient developer around, and the first stories about their polite, secretive way of doing things began to appear in print. They would never use such an expression, of course, but they had it made.

What is more, they began to give the development industry a good name. In Canada, developers have been the guys in the black hats for a long time. They get a fawning press in the real-estate pages – what company doesn't? – but elsewhere they are regarded with the natural distrust that flows to landlords, wheeler-dealers, and those who rake in huge profits by gambling. Entrepreneurs at the leading edge of the economy always go through this. There was a time when fur traders were set down as robber barons, then lumber kings, then railway men, then mining bosses and oil magnates and packing-house tycoons and stock manipulators. In every case there has been a kind of transmutation of the risk-takers. They begin as hustlers (George Simpson, in the early days of the Hudson's Bay Company, stealing the Indians blind); they develop their holdings with ruthless skill (Robert Dunsmuir working Chinese coolies to death in his British Columbia mines); they jostle for position with their fellow tycoons (the lumber kings of the

Ottawa Valley hiring gangs of thugs to raid each other's rafts); and then they emerge, rich, cleansed, and respectable. George Stephen, the railway tycoon and early president of the Bank of Montreal, should have gone to jail; instead, he went to the House of Lords. As Lord Mount Stephen, he could never have been blamed for the wicked things that mere George Stephen might have done in an earlier life.

The development industry, like its predecessors atop the economic pile, provides a real service. In the past we needed railways and timber and coal and oil, and now we add to the list subdivisions and shopping plazas and the remoulding of our cities. But there have been payoffs and other scandals in the development industry, and a rising suspicion that city councillors and planners, in too many cases, were more responsive to the special interests of the chaps who came up with a cheque at election time than to the public interest. No one is more conscious than the developers that they are not loved. "We're just trying to do the best job we know how," one complained to me. "But make a buck and you're a crook."

Mind you, he said this from behind a desk you could use for a ping-pong table. It's a tough life. Enter the Reichmanns. Unlike the usual image of the developer – loud, profane, and pushy, like Zeckendorf – they are discreet, soft-spoken, and shy. Instead of thumping themselves on the chest, they pat their employees on the back. Instead of trying to bully, or buy, city employees, they sit down with them, fold their hands and say, "Gentlemen, what can we do for you?" And, with it, they build fine buildings, on time, under cost. It was not only the part of the press that was paid to sing hosannas to tycoons that was impressed; we all were. First Canadian Place might distort the planning priorities of downtown Toronto, together with the gangs of towers around it, but almost no one was saying so at the time, including Ron Soskolne and Michael Dennis, the mayor's pit bulls.

The irony of it all is that it is this project, the one that launched the Reichmanns into the big time, that would precipitate their crash into insolvency seventeen years later. The financing was, as always, complex, but not nearly as complex as it would become later. The land under the project was owned 50 per cent by Olympia & York, which assembled the *Star* and *Globe* blocks for demolition, and 25 per cent each by the Bank of Montreal and North American Life. The building was financed partly out of money O & Y had from its other successful ventures, but also by a $70-million mortgage advanced by Canada Trust Company, which issued the long-term mortgage to replace shorter-term loans advanced during building – as is usually done. Thus, O & Y owned the building, but only part of the land beneath it, leasing the rest. At that time the Reichmanns had a rule never to mortgage more than half the value of their properties, so that no one else could control them. But the building, once completed, was worth a great deal more than its construction cost. They could borrow money against the increase in value, and by 1988 First Canadian Place was appraised at just under $1 billion;[7] Olympia & York replaced the $70-million mortgage with $475 million in bonds, secured in part by a first mortgage and in part by an assignment of rents from the building. Then there was another $10 million ranked ahead of these bonds; then another $131 million against four O & Y buildings, including this one. By late 1991 there would be close to $600 million in debt against the building, as money poured out to other projects, especially Canary Wharf in England, but it was no longer worth that much. The First Canadian Place bonds were trading only rarely by this time, at a discounted rate of 79 cents on the dollar, and the interest charges could no longer be met. It was a missed bond payment on these notes that would put the bondholders in a position to foreclose and plunge the company into the arms of the Companies' Creditors Arrangement Act.

But all of that was far in the future; in 1975 and 1976 the Reichmanns were the talk of the town. They would shortly become the talk of another town, New York City, when they took a giant gamble that first aroused the scorn, and later the admiration, of just about everybody in the real-estate business. They were about to push the Rockefellers aside as the largest commercial landlords in New York City. They'd turn Manhattan into an isle of joy.

PART II

The Reichmann Empire

How is the Empire?

– Last words of George V

CHAPTER FOUR

Wonderful Town

I have never been afraid of debt, because debt is what gives you
leverage.
– William Zeckendorf, 1970 [1]

$

The Big Apple was full of worms. Dirty, depressed, and bedraggled,
New York City in the early 1970s was deep in debt and going deeper,
and the economic malaise that had settled over the country was pinch-
ing hard here, at the centre of the universe – as New Yorkers saw it. The
costs of municipal services, driven upwards by aggressive public-
employee unions and a swelling of the welfare rolls, were climbing
even faster than the then-considerable rate of inflation. Local corrup-
tion cost some, too. At the same time, the state and federal governments were trying to cut back, curbing their support of municipalities
(does this have a familiar ring to it?). The city had dug itself into a hole
by issuing municipal bonds in ever larger amounts just to get the
money to meet the payroll; the spiral downwards could only get worse.
Mayor Abe Beame, an accountant, was spending $12.8 billion a year

and taking in $10.9 billion, and bankruptcy loomed.[2] The city turned to Washington for help, and the reply given by President Gerald Ford was summed up in a headline in the *Daily News*: "FORD TO NEW YORK – DROP DEAD!" It was the teachers and sanitation unions that rode to the rescue, with last-minute loans that allowed the paycheques to go out.

Finally, a new body was set up, the Municipal Assistance Corporation, also known as Big MAC, to oversee city finances. Washington was reluctantly persuaded to make a short-term loan of $2.5 billion, but at the same time made it clear that the bailout would not be repeated. Translation, for anyone with the wit to read a balance sheet: higher taxes. As services dwindled and rates climbed, many corporations in the heart of Manhattan began to vote with their moving vans; they sought cheaper pastures across the river in New Jersey, or just farther north, in southern New York State or Connecticut, tore up their leases, turned off the lights, and moved out.

As they left, vacancy rates soared, and the price of office leases drooped, inevitably. Offices that had been going for $20 a square foot in annual rent were available for $12. That meant that the buildings themselves were worth less, which made the taxes, proportionately, that much more of a burden, and the further pastures that much greener. The circle was getting vicious. Into the middle of it stepped the Reichmann brothers, who bought eight skyscrapers at one swoop. Everybody who knew anything knew they had to be crackers. For one thing, the buildings contained 11.5 millions square feet of space,[3] more than ten times the area of First Canadian Place; for another, what sane person would buy what amounted to 4 per cent of all the office space in Manhattan when it appeared the island was about to sink into the Hudson River?

The New York buildings were called the "Uris Package," after Harold and Percy Uris, two brothers who had flourished in the early part of the century, had gone bankrupt in the Great Depression, and had returned to become major builders and owners of office complexes in the late 1960s. In 1973 they decided to retire, and sold their holdings to the National Kinney Corporation, then controlled by Warner Communications.

Warner's chief, Steven Ross, decided to get rid of the Uris Package, which could only continue to decline in value, as everybody knew. A number of real-estate corporations were contacted, and some sent representatives to look over the properties, which constituted some of the best real estate in the world. There were, for example, two buildings on Park Avenue, America's most prestigious address, including one cheek by jowl with the Helmsley Building, almost astride Central Station. Leona Helmsley would be a neighbour. This one, at 245 Park Avenue, had American Brands as its chief tenant; ITT were the big lodgers at 320 Park Avenue. There was also 10 East 53rd Street, where Harper & Row, the publishers, hung out. But probably the pick of the crop was the fifty-two-storey mammoth at 55 Water Street, overlooking the river, and just around the corner from the New York Stock Exchange on Wall Street. With 3.6 million square feet of office space – more than twice the capacity of First Canadian Place – in central Manhattan, and with tenants like Citibank, Goldman Sachs & Co., and the Chemical Bank, it looked as if it might make money for somebody, if it could be snatched up for the right price.

But the Uris brothers had not kept their properties up, and anyone who bought them was going to have to invest millions in repairs, upgrading, and maintenance. The general consensus of potential buyers from Chicago to Hong Kong was thanks, but no thanks.

By this time the Reichmanns were beginning to move away from home base, and were exploring building projects in Dallas, Los Angeles, and Chicago, as well as in Ottawa, and, in the small world of real-estate dealers, they were becoming known. Thus it was that one morning in 1976, a real-estate broker named Edward Minskoff turned up on the Reichmanns' thirty-second-storey doorstep with a strange tale to tell, and a commission to earn, if he brought it off. There were these buildings for sale in New York, Minskoff said, which could probably be had for a price far under what it would cost to replace them, and which carried a series of mortgages at very low rates, between 5.25 and 8.75 per cent. How about it?

The Reichmanns were no fools. If the Uris Package was such a good deal, why wasn't someone in New York grabbing it? Still, it was tempting. The Reichmanns were now in a position where the banks, once uncertain, coy, and hard to please, were practically begging them to borrow money, whatever amount they wanted. The friendship of the banks, especially the Canadian banks, gave them an advantage in the United States, where most banks are limited, by state law, in the amount they can lend to any one borrower – usually 10 per cent of the capital investment in the bank. (After the collapse of a couple of Canadian banks in the 1980s, our financial institutions finally got around to putting a curb on themselves, and now limit loans to 25 per cent of the bank's capital for any one venture. But this is not a matter of law, because it would be unheard of for Canadian governments to interfere with the right of banks to play craps with the depositors' money.) What the U.S. regulation meant at this time was that, almost any time a really big deal needed to be financed, a syndicate of banks had to be set up to handle it. There was all that paperwork, and back-and-forth. It took weeks, sometimes months, to get all the right signatures in all the right places. The Canadian banks, operating at home or abroad, were under no such strictures, and became the eager gambling partners of Canadian developers like Cadillac Fairview and Daon Development, then grabbing off deals from under the noses of their American rivals by getting in first with the cash. So finding the money would not be a problem.

Moreover, it wasn't as if a developer had to come up with the whole $300 million or so in U.S. funds that this deal would probably take. There was, at the developer's side, the magic of leverage. A lovely, though doubled-edged, sword, leverage. A corporation wanting to buy or erect a building worth $150 million doesn't have to find the entire sum, any more than a homeowner does. He puts up, say, $10 million, borrows the rest, and pays the interest on the borrowed money with the rents that come in from the tenants in the building. There is, usually, a building loan on short terms at fairly high rates, and then a long-term mortgage at lower rates. Then, if he sells the building two years later for, let us say, $200 million, he turns the mortgage over to the newcomer, and pockets the $50 million. In two years he has made $40 million on an investment of $10 million. He can use the new money to finance another four deals, and give the wheel another spin. That's leverage. The corollary is that it can work backwards, as well. If he puts up $10 million on a $150 million building, and the market goes sour, the developer won't be able to cover the mortgage with the rents. Then he will have to sell the building, worth now about $100 million, but will still owe the mortgagee $140 million, although all he invested was $10 million. The developer sells the building and still winds up in debt for $40 million, ten times what he thought he was gambling in the first place. Doesn't seem fair, somehow, when it goes that way. But screw your courage to the sticking-place, as Lady Macbeth used to put it, and we'll not fail.

Albert and Paul Reichmann flew down to New York to try to decide which side of the leverage squeeze they might find themselves on. They talked to a number of the prestigious tenants, and to the folks who ran the stores on the ground floors, and they talked to municipal officials and real-estate experts, and then they threw the dice. Very carefully.

"Manhattan is Manhattan and will remain Manhattan," is the way Albert Reichmann explained it at the time.[4] Economic cycles come and go; the downturn had come, but it would go, and when it went, the richest real estate on earth would be up again. "A boom in New York rents wasn't a hope," said Paul Reichmann, "it was a conviction."

It took almost two years to structure the deal, all of it done in secrecy. Oh, yes, the papers got onto the fact that someone was sniffing around, but no one mentioned either Olympia & York or the Reichmanns. In fact, the *New York Times* had the Uris Package on the verge of being sold to Samuel J. LeFrak, a New York developer – actually, the firm that Minskoff worked with.[5] In the end, the Reichmanns paid $50 million in U.S. funds and took over $288 million in mortgages. Just about the time the last "i" was dotted and the last "t" crossed, the city began to feel the move and stir of life along its keel again.

Not that the problems of existence were getting any easier for ordinary New Yorkers; they were getting worse. More than 65,000 workers had been cut from city payrolls; teachers, police, and firefighters had their wages frozen, and the poor were hard hit by cutbacks in basic services. But the harsh cuts inflicted by the new mayor, Ed Koch, allowed the city to repay the federal loan a year early. This, in turn, won the confidence of the money men, real-estate operators, and Wall Street. Old money came back and new money came in. And, as Olympia & York put new millions into refurbishing their buildings up to something like an O&Y standard, they became premium office space once more. As leases came due, companies that had been paying $10 a square foot were asked to pay as much as $25 a square foot. And they did. They didn't smile, but they did pay. The high vacancy rates in most of the buildings dropped sharply. Very soon O&Y was clearing something like $50 million a year on these buildings. Did they use the profits to pay down the debt? Of course not. They put it out on other investments to give leverage another chance to work its magic.

In the meantime, they must have taken some pleasure in the accolades that poured in. This is what I wrote about that New York triumph:

> It is a strange feeling for a Canadian in New York to emerge from Grand Central Station on Park Avenue at East 46th, cross to the old American Brands Building, and read, on the notice board there, the names of the three Reichmann brothers at the top of the Olympia & York roster. (They are just as unavailable here as in Toronto.) Go through this building, out onto Lexington, turn right, and there is 486 Lexington Avenue, about to undergo an Olympia & York refit. Just down the way is another string of skyscrapers that once belonged to an American firm

that thought they were a drug on the market; Olympia & York snapped them up and now such U.S. corporate fixtures as ITT and Sperry Rand Corporation have Canadian landlords. It is no big deal, really, our side has not exactly taken over Manhattan, but we are getting a little of our own back. And when the *Wall Street Journal,* that arbiter of American business affairs, devotes an awestruck feature to the Reichmanns ("It is difficult, perhaps impossible, to find anyone, even a competitor, who will say anything against them"), well, that's the tycoon's equivalent of an Olympic gold medal.[6]

At least I didn't call it "The Deal of the Century," with the century far from finished, or claim that "It would be recounted in real estate circles in the same hushed tones that Peter Minuit's original purchase of Manhattan Island for U.S.$24 was told to wide-eyed schoolchildren."[7] (I love that, "U.S.$24" – was that "Wampum$30"?) Nor did I, like the Washington *Post,* call the Reichmanns "the Rothschilds of Canadian realty."[8] (According to Peter Newman in *The Bronfman Dynasty,* the Bronfmans are the Rothschilds of Canadian realty; now the Edper Bronfmans are clinging to the cliff, too. It is best to wait a few centuries before handing out the Rothschild bouquet.) Still, it was a nice job of work, even if, unlike the Minuit purchase, it would finally come back to bite the Reichmanns on the ankle. For the time being, the Uris gamble brought nothing but wonderful news.

The increasing rents, from $7 to $13 a square foot in 1976 to from $18 to $45 a decade later, drove up the value of the buildings. In 1981 Susan Goldenberg said they were worth $1 billion.[9] The British newspaper the *Independent* saw her $1 billion and raised it. "Within five years, the value of the property increased tenfold."[10] They were worth $3.5 billion in American dollars, although the newspaper did not say where this wonderful figure came from.

The property at 55 Water Street alone – as shown on Olympia & York's own books, when the world finally got a peek at them during the Toronto bankruptcy hearings – had a 1986 market value of $792 million. The Reichmanns, remember, had put down $50 million on the entire package. Quite a lever. Like so many of the figures that would be tossed around, this was a bit chancy. A building is worth what it will fetch in the market, and if you have to sell it in a hurry in a slump, it is worth a good deal less than if you can wait for the market to perk up again. But it was the rising value of the package, on paper, that turned it into yet another lever to be prised against the backside of Fate. If buildings are worth more, you can borrow more on them, right? You would be crazy to pay off a low mortgage with money that could earn you much more in new investments, right? Before they were done, the Reichmanns would borrow $548.3 million U.S. against 55 Water Street, which, if you care to go down and wander around it today, is a very sad building indeed, and mostly empty. Dirty, blank windows peer sightlessly out onto Water Street, scrap paper rattles up against barred doors, and, when I was there, a workman was listlessly rubbing unprintable slogans off a wall. I calculated that he would have the job done about the time the market rebounds again.

Lord knows what the building is worth today. Olympia & York's own books showed the building with a "fair value" of $388,836,000 on January 31, 1991. [11] By that time the Reichmanns owned only 41.6 per cent of it, with a "book value" (an accountancy value, as opposed to the "fair value" estimate of what it might fetch on the market) of $166.5 million for their share. It all became academic when O&Y agreed to relinquish the property to the bond-holders in return for cancelling their notes, which were selling in the secondary market for sixteen to twenty cents on the dollar. [12] That would make the building worth, at twenty cents per dollar on $548.3 million, $109.6 million, which is not quite $792 million. But the point about all these wild guesses is that if you can get someone to lend you money on the basis of them, you can give the wheel another turn. This, the Reichmanns proceeded to do.

By the late 1970s, they had reason to consider themselves pretty smart fellows. Everybody had said the Flemingdon Park deal would flop; it was a complete success. All the world agreed that the Uris Package was madness; throughout the late 1970s, it was pulling in profits and gaining in capital value every day. The scoffers stopped scoffing; the O&Y anterooms began to clog with deal-makers anxious to present plans for the latest, sure-fire, can't-fail development. The Reichmanns looked them over, picked out the best, and went with them. They put up buildings in Orlando, Dallas, Los Angeles, Portland, Hartford, Springfield, and Boston, and they all started to spin out money, and the Reichmanns looked upon them, and saw that they were good.

In an interview with Susan Goldenberg, one of the rare interviews the brothers would give, Albert Reichmann, responding to the comment that neither he nor Paul had a university education, responded, "When you learn the Talmud, you learn everything." [13]

Goldenberg wrote it down, and printed it, and everybody nodded. Sounds right. The gods wait behind the door with a sockful of sand for people who say things like that. They were waiting now, although it would be some years before they would swing.

CHAPTER FIVE

Different Drummers

A corporation is just like any natural person, except that it has no
pants to kick or soul to damn.
 – An unnamed western judge, 1932

$

Olympia & York was getting to be a significant company, now, and Gil
Newman, the money man, thought it should behave like one. He went
to Paul Reichmann and told him that he had employees scattered all
over the continent whom he had barely met. They needed to be
brought in, talked to, made to feel part of the team. Reichmann told
him to arrange it. So Newman got on the telephone and, after a lot of
juggling, set up a meeting in Toronto at which all the significant managers of the various outposts of empire – all men, needless to say –
could be present. They met in the boardroom on the thirty-fourth
floor of First Canadian Place, around an impressive hardwood table,
with notepads in front of everyone, and coffee on a side table.

The managers were chatting away to each other when the door
opened and Paul and Albert Reichmann slipped into the room and

took their places at the head of the table, next to Newman. There was a silence, and then Paul Reichmann said, "Thank you all for coming." There was another silence, which grew and grew until finally Newman couldn't stand it any more. He turned to the managers and began to ask them, one by one, what they did. They went around the table that way, and when they got back to the top, Paul Reichmann thanked everybody once more – and left.

This is not, you understand, never has been, one of your ordinary companies, with small talk, doughnuts, and golf scores to make the boys feel part of the family. The employees were not part of the family. They were cherished, looked after, well paid, but they were not . . . well . . . chums.

"Paul Reichmann was always polite," says a man who attended some of these board meetings, "but you had better know what you were talking about, or you would be given very short shrift." This was not the sort of bullying common to many of our financial wizards – when William Mulholland got sore at one of his public-relations women at the Bank of Montreal, he threw an apple at her[1] – it was paternalism, in the old sense. Daddy knows best. Employees did not own stocks in the company, could not buy stocks. They were asked to do research, asked for their advice, but it did not follow that the research would be used or the advice taken. In its form, Olympia & York was a private corporation, closely held. Eaton's is a private corporation, closely held, as well. Such entities have huge advantages over an ordinary individual acting in his own name in business. The most important is limited liability. That is, the company's liability is limited to the money invested in the firm's capital; when that is gone, so is whatever chance the creditor had of collecting the debt. When O&Y applied for bankruptcy protection in the spring of 1992, its debts were estimated at more than $20 billion, when every arm of the empire was included;[2] but no one knew what its assets were worth. Considerably less, as it turned out.

Had the Reichmanns borrowed all that money on their own account, the creditors, when the cash flow stopped, could have stripped them of everything but the minimums allowed under Canadian bankruptcy law – the "necessaries of life," as defined by the judge who winds up with the case. But limited liability prevents all that. This concept was an invention of the Select Committee on the Investments for the Savings of the Middle and Working Classes, which discovered, in England in 1850, that none but the rich could afford to invest in corporations, for fear of being sued into penury on the basis of a few shares.[3] In 1855, an act was pushed through, designed to allow "men with small capitals" to invest in companies without being liable for anything more than the money they had already put into the firm when they bought its shares. That was the "limit" to limited companies. The *quid pro quo* was supposed to be that corporations, in return for this immunity, would abide by a number of strict conditions, including two that would give company directors of our own day the screaming meemies – any director who approved a dividend, knowing the company to be insolvent, or any director who approved a loan to members of the company, could be held personally liable for any subsequent debt; and the limited company could not pick its own auditors, they had to be approved by the Board of Trade.[4] However, virtually all of the responsibilities attached to the corporation in return for its limited status were dropped over time, leaving only the immunity.

Thus, the Reichmanns' liability is limited to the assets within the companies secured by their shares. Olympia Floor & Wall Tile can go on making money, and it does, while all the other parts of the empire fall to pieces around it. The brothers own it, but they didn't borrow against it to finance any of the other deals. The Reichmanns don't have to put any more money into the mess, and whatever assets form their personal fortunes remain, in the main, intact. Of course, a large part of their net worth consisted of the shares of Olympia & York Developments Limited, which are worth very little, so they have lost a great deal of paper wealth, and whatever new, personal money they put in once the roof started to buckle. This has been estimated at $5 million,[5] but there is no way of knowing if that figure is just another figment of someone's imagination. The *Wall Street Journal*, in November 1992, estimated that the Reichmanns were down to their last $400 million or so, and I asked Andrew Sarlos, a longtime ally of the family, whether he thought that was a reasonable figure.

"Ten per cent of that," he said. It was just a guess. At a guess, then, the Reichmanns have forty million or less, when they once had somewhere over $10 billion, on paper. If they had not been acting as a limited corporation they would be down to the personal property permitted by the bankruptcy law: a house, a car, clothes, enough income to support their families – and no more.

Another large advantage of incorporation is that the brothers can cause the companies to act in their names, and pay for the actions through the companies, rather than, for instance, having to take money into their own hands from the companies – thus incurring tax liabilities as the money becomes income – and spending it that way. If the brothers want to buy a city block, or hire a chauffeur to whisk them around, or order up a luncheon prepared in the company's kosher kitchens, it is looked after within the corporation, and, not so incidentally, written off against Olympia & York's income when tax time rolls around. The taxpayer picks up a portion of the tab, every time. The Reichmanns made personal donations to charity; they also made many donations that were funnelled through their companies.

In the same way, the company is the body – which is what incorporation really means – that engages in business, and, when things go wrong, it is the corporation that pays for the ensuing lawsuits, unless the directors have misbehaved themselves in so blatant a manner as to destroy their immunity. Corporation law has developed in such a way that the people who make the decisions are, by and large, rendered harmless from the evil consequences of bad decisions, while benefiting from the good ones. The law presumes that it was the tobacco companies that did all the damage to our health; if you get cancer, you can try to sue the company, and much good may it do you, but you are wasting your time trying to sue the men who actually made the decision to keep on turning the stuff out long after the link between smoking and cancer had been established to the satisfaction of everyone free of nicotine stains. They didn't do it; the company did.

Every time the corporation prospers, the managers give themselves a little reward, but few of them feel any compulsion to suffer just because the company does. When one company goes after control of another, and gets it, the directors all give themselves a bonus out of the proceeds; if the bid fails, or turns out to be a disaster, the losses are borne by the company, not the people who made the decision. In this way, the risks taken by the "risk-takers," to whom we pay such elaborate court these days, are passed on to the shareholders at large, and, in the end, when all the costs are deducted from revenue, to the taxpayers.

In fact, the company's directors and managers are so protected by the development of corporation law that they can even do their best to destroy the corporation for which they work, and get paid for it. Thus, when F. Ross Johnson and a gang of his pals worked out a deal to buy their own company, RJR Nabisco, by using its own assets to finance the junk bonds they would float to clinch the deal, and it backfired, they all made millions in profit. Johnson was ushered out the door with a pay-off of $52 million U.S.[6]

Finally, the corporation invented a way to make itself live, and grow, forever. This development was the brainchild of a "rosy little lawyer" named James Brooks Dill, who actually thought it up as a way to lure more corporations into setting up their headquarters in the state of Delaware, where he worked as a corporation counsel, and later as a judge. On April 8, 1888, Dill's invention, an act of law consisting of only 132 words, made it legal for one corporation to own the shares of another corporation.[7] Until then it was considered both unethical and illegal for one company to own another, since obviously it destroyed the whole notion of responsibility for the operations of the firm – and that is exactly the way it worked out. It was, in the phrase of Frederick Lewis Allen, "a device for the manufacture of millionaires." It was also a device for corralling competition, as J. P. Morgan, who was one of the first to put it to work, discovered.

Suppose there were ten companies in competition with each other, each with a capital base of one million dollars. A holding company would offer the owners two million dollars in shares in a new company. The purchase would be written off against future income of the new company, and gouged out of the customers easily enough, because there was now less competition. Morgan formed his steel empire that way, by taking over Andrew Carnegie's Carnegie Company and most of his other rivals with nothing more than the paper it took to issue stock certificates. Carnegie made a few hundred millions, Morgan made much more; the only losers were the public, who paid for the operation through higher prices.

The corporation had been cut loose from any sort of social, civic, or community responsibility. It remained only to cause the taxpayer to finance the process. This was accomplished in Canada by the amusingly entitled "Tax Reform" legislation of 1971. Under that law, which still applies, corporations are entitled to deduct against profits the entire costs of interest paid on the money to buy the shares of other corporations. Until 1971, if one company borrowed, say, $1 billion to buy out another company – whether a competitor or any other kind of firm – it could not deduct the money it paid in interest. Under the new rules, it could. For a corporation borrowing $1 billion at 10 per cent, the charge would be $100 million a year. At a corporate tax-rate of 50 per cent (it has since gone down), the company would pass on $50 million of its costs to the general taxpayer.

We brought in this legislation because the Americans were doing it, as Finance Minister Edgar J. Benson made clear at the time. "The deduction for interest provides a substantial incentive for Canadian corporations to invest in other corporations and permits them to compete on an even footing with foreign corporations. Assuming a tax rate of 50 per cent, the cost of borrowing money for 1971 share purchases will be cut in half."[8] Cut in half for the company, that is; the other half is simply added to the deficit. The more firms you bought out, the less tax you paid; keep on buying, and you will never pay corporate taxes again. And the really neat thing is that you can use this gift from your poorer, tax-paying neighbours, to wipe out your trade rivals by absorbing them. In your spare time, you can make speeches about the glories of competition. In the wink of an eye, historically speaking, we had created in the modern corporation a creature that had been removed entirely from any meaningful control, and could pass on to the taxpayer much of the burden of any mistakes it made by trying to grab everything in sight.

These advantages flow to every kind of corporation. Olympia & York, though, is a particular kind of corporation. It is private. None of the shares were bought and sold on a stock market, or even "over the counter." A corporation's shares embody the company, because each share has one vote, normally, on matters of policy, such as the election of the board of directors and the appointment of senior management. The shares are issued from the company treasury, and registered in the name of the person who buys them. Anyone who owns 50 per cent plus one share can make any decision he or she likes concerning the company, because he or she has control at the annual meeting, when the votes are counted and the current management is renewed or fired. Indeed, anyone who holds a substantial block of the shares of a company, say more than 10 per cent, can and will ask for representation on the board.

When shares are sold to the general public, in return for the money this brings into the company treasury, control goes out the window. If more than half the shares representing the common stock of the company are sold into the stock market, then control has passed from the original shareholders to the public at large. This doesn't matter if, as is usual, the shares are sold to thousands of people in small amounts. Enough of them have to gang up together to force the company to pay more than lip service to the shareholders. It does matter if a large enough block of shares can be put together to swing a majority vote at a shareholders' meeting and depose the current management. So, although "going public" brings a great advantage to the public company, in increased capital, it also brings with it a modicum of danger.

In turn, once a company has gone public, it must provide a certain amount of information to the shareholders and the public at large. As a general rule, the level of information is determined by the stock exchanges on which the company shares are traded and by the rules of the relevant stock commissions; the Ontario Securities Commission, say, or the Securities and Exchange Commission in the case of companies whose shares are sold in the United States. Generally, you can find out more about a company whose shares are traded on the New York Stock Exchange than on any Canadian exchange, because the NYSE has stricter disclosure rules, a matter of deep regret to many of its listed companies.

The Reichmanns, like the Eatons, never went public. They used their own money, or the banks', or they borrowed by issuing bonds – debt instruments constituting a loan against the company – rather than equity instruments, which carry ownership. This meant that they never, until their filing for bankruptcy protection, had to divulge to the great unwashed any information they didn't care to divulge. Moreover, they didn't have to listen to a lot of unsolicited advice from shareholders who thought they might do things in some other way. There were no "outside directors" on the O&Y company boards, either to tell the brothers what to do, or to warn them that what they were doing might lead to trouble. As we know, Samuel Reichmann was the chairman of the board until his death in 1975, then Renée, then Albert. The board members were family members or senior employees of the company, and, indeed, the shares were all held in the names of the family or of foundations set up by family members. The shareholders are listed in Appendix II.

They were never in danger of being taken over by another company, the favourite sport in today's stock markets, and looted for the cash in the till, for the simple reason that their shares were not for sale. They didn't have to worry that Carl Icahn or the Belzberg brothers, or any other takeover artist, would swoop down on their stock, gain control, use the cash flow to pay off the debt incurred in buying the company, and then break it up to cash in the assets. They could, and would, do this to other companies, as we shall see, but it could not be done to them.

It was the particular kind of incorporation they had followed that gave the Reichmann brothers such an advantage when they began to use the money, power, and prestige that began to come their way after the New York triumph. They could and did consult others, but they could make up their own minds to act, and act quickly, on any proposition laid before them. The banks, who were providing the money in most instances, had to be persuaded that it would be repaid, but, with the Reichmanns' track record, this was never a problem. The banks were eager, overeager, to advance funds, largely on the say-so of the company itself that the money would be repaid, with interest.

In one case, says a lawyer who acted for a bank dealing with Olympia & York, the only information the company provided was in a three-ring notebook which was actually taped to a desk in an office at Olympia & York. The bank's accountants could look at the pages and make notes, but could not copy them. The loan went through. This eyebrow-raising incident wasn't even all that unusual, in the heady days of the 1970s and 1980s. In their account of the Brascan empire, Patricia Best and Ann Shortell recount the occasion when Michael Cornelisson, a Bronfman executive, approached Citibank Canada for a loan on behalf of Trizec Corporation. He came with a "blue book" on the company's finances. Charles Young, then the president of Citibank, told him, "Mike, I don't even want to read it. That book looks so beautiful, I just want to lend you some more money." [9]

With all the capital now available to them in the late 1970s, [10] the Reichmanns began to look around for someplace to put it, someplace where they could use leverage. They quickly learned, as everyone does who looks at these matters, that you get more lift for your dollar if, instead of actually going out and building things, you just buy another company that builds things. Or drills things. Or buys and sells things. They flirted with buying Daon Development, a Vancouver company that had, like themselves, several projects under way in the United States. But it appeared that, while they could buy up enough Daon stocks on the public market to gain control, Jack Poole, who had created the company, would put up a fight. The Reichmanns had, so far, made a public point of the fact that they would never take over someone else's company in a hostile way. It's just not the way they did things. Actually, this need not have been merely a matter of being too darn nice for such a roughhouse; takeover battles can be very nasty, and lead to lawsuits in which a lot of information is divulged to the public. It went against everything the Reichmanns had been doing since the beginning.

Then they had a look at Block Brothers, at that time British Columbia's largest real-estate firm. Here there was no objection, so they bought into the public company in 1978, and soon owned 80 per cent of its shares. Then they took its shares off the market by buying the other 20 per cent back from its owners. The jargon is, "they took it private." That was all right, and it made O&Y some money (as a private company, Block Brothers no longer had to report its profits, so there was no telling how much this was), but it didn't begin to sate the Reichmanns.

So they went over to England, and ran smack, dab into another Canadian real-estate empire, owned by the Bronfman brothers.

Trizec, the company formed by William Zeckendorf when he was still struggling to stay afloat was, you may recall from Chapter Two, owned in part by two British companies, one of which had a real-estate arm called English Property Corporation, which had developments under way in Britain, Belgium, and France. With the collapse of Webb & Knapp, English Property had effective control of Trizec, which owned, among other Canadian properties, Place Ville Marie in Montreal and Yorkdale Shopping Centre in Toronto.

In March 1976, Trizec, in turn, ran into money troubles; in fact, it could not meet the payroll.[11] So English Property sold the 51.5 per cent of Trizec shares it then held – the rest was held by individual shareholders in the publicly traded firm – to Edper, the Toronto conglomerate put together by Edward and Peter Bronfman, nephews of the sometime bootlegger Sam Bronfman, the founder of Seagram Company Limited. The Bronfmans rolled Trizec into a holding company called

Carena Properties Limited, which was actually held by another hold-ing company, Carena Bancorp (the name came from Canadian Arena Company; the brothers owned the Montreal Forum at one time). The Bronfmans gave English Property $52 million in cash and 49.99 per cent of Carena, the holding company. This was leverage with a ven-geance; Trizec, although short of ready money, held properties worth about $900 million, and Edper had obtained 50.01 per cent of the hold-ing company that owned control of it for just over one-seventeenth of that.[12] The cash part of this transaction came, mostly, from the recent sale of the Montreal Canadiens and the Montreal Forum.

As part of this arrangement, the two companies, Edper and English Property, signed a "standstill agreement." Under this agreement, nei-ther firm would attempt to increase its holding in Trizec, a publicly traded company, before July 1, 1979. That was because nearly 49 per cent of the shares of Trizec were not owned by Carena. Better avoid unpleasantness.

The Bronfmans brought in an accountant, Jack Cockwell, to res-tructure the finances of Trizec, and he did – so successfully that Patricia Best and Ann Shortell call him a "genius," and who are we to argue? One thing the genius did not foresee was that somebody else might buy English Property. The Reichmanns did.

In January 1979, when English Property shares began to fall in the midst of a recession, Olympia & York began to accumulate stock, and within a month they were in a position to make a public offer to take over the British company. The Edper group said "Yikes!" or whatever it is financial geniuses say when they discover that they have safely bolted the front door, but left the back one open. If the Reichmanns got English Property they would own a substantial share of Trizec, and after the Bronfmans and their hired help had gone to all that work and expense to fix it up. Trizec was now worth about $1 billion, and the Reichmanns could pick up the company that owned half the holding company that owned half of it, if you follow me, for the price of the English Property shares on the London market, not much more than $100 million. This was almost as lavish a bit of leverage as the

Bronfmans had used in the first place to get Trizec. These things are easier to follow on the knee-bone-connected-to-the-thigh-bone principle. So, to reiterate, Edper owned 80 per cent of a company called Carena Bancorp, formed with the Bank of Nova Scotia. Carena Bancorp owned 50.01 per cent of Carena Properties, and English Property owned the other 49.99 per cent. But then, Carena Properties owned 51.5 per cent of Trizec. Ergo, whoever owned English Property had, through English Property's 49.9-per-cent holding of Carena, a substantial hold on Trizec.

The Reichmanns made a public offer for the remaining shares of English Property on Wednesday, February 21, 1979. The price was 50 pence a share, and the shares were then trading at around 37 pence. The Bronfmans put out a press release of their own, describing Olympia & York's actions as "unfriendly," and stating that they "would regard the company as an uninvited and unfriendly partner in Trizec."[13] Two "unfriendlys" equals "I hate you." Apparently, the Reichmanns' insistence that they did not want to be involved in an unfriendly takeover did not survive the rigours of an English winter. The *Globe and Mail* quoted an unnamed analyst as saying that "there is going to be one terrible fight."

For a while it looked that way. A Dutch company made a counter-offer, and Eagle Star Insurance, which still owned 21 per cent of English Property, offered to buy all the rest, then changed its mind and sold its 21 per cent to the Reichmanns, instead. On Friday, two days after the original offer, they upped their bid for the shares to 54 pence, which the management of English Property said they would accept. That wasn't the end of it, though, because English Property didn't control enough shares to deliver the company to the Reichmanns. The Dutch then raised the ante, over the weekend, to 56 pence, and formed an alliance with Edper to keep the company out of O&Y hands.

On Monday, February 26, the Reichmanns upped the ante once more, to 60 pence. It is in the speed of this sort of turnaround that the firm's narrow command structure proved valuable; there was no need to consult a board, to say nothing of shareholders, before making an offer that would raise the price of the takeover, already at $157 million Canadian, by several million dollars. Paul Reichmann went public for the first time to say that he and his brothers were not after Trizec at all, but English Property. The Bronfmans didn't believe him for a minute. Why should they? After all, when Edper had taken over Trizec, they had given a very similar assurance, and then had proceeded to clean the place out from top to bottom. They naturally expected O&Y to return the favour. A senior Edper executive then announced that if O&Y got hold of English Property, "They would consistently be in a conflict of interest position between Trizec and their private property holdings."[14]

Conflict of interest is always an interesting concept. Trizec was already in bed with another large Canadian real-estate company, Bramalea Limited, which it would eventually take over entirely. Apparently, this did not present a conflict, but the O&Y move would. Paul Reichmann replied smoothly that "reasonable people can find a way to insulate transactions if there is a possible conflict of interest," but no one paid the slightest heed.

To try to reassure the Bronfmans, and end the bidding war, Paul Reichmann noted that he thought Trizec was a well-managed company, and had no intention of changing its management structure. Since O&Y would be entitled to four members on the board of Trizec, this was an important statement, but it only got Edper more excited than ever. Yeah, yeah, that's what they always say before they dump you. Harold Milavsky, the president of Trizec, had been given his job when Edper got control; if they lost, he could lose it. He was not about to take that chance.

In March, Milavsky led a team from Edper over to London to join in mortal stock combat. The three key members of this team were Milavsky, Jack Cockwell, and Trevor Eyton, a lawyer who would soon go to work directly for Edper. These three were sitting in the lobby of their London hotel when Paul Reichmann walked in. They approached him, shook hands, and sat down in the lobby to talk things out. The Edper group finally got it into their heads that O&Y did not want Trizec, and really wasn't planning to take it over and shake it up. It had just been shaken up. Olympia & York wanted to invest, that was all.

From that chance meeting came two more formal meetings in Montreal, and a deal under which Trizec agreed to stop opposing the o&y bid for English Property and the Reichmanns agreed not to mess with Trizec.

Everybody agreed that everything was wonderful, including all the financial writers from that day to this who have written about this momentous hotel meeting. As an example of how well the Reichmanns kept to their promise to avoid conflicts of interest, Patricia Best and Ann Shortell record the following: "When both [i.e., Trizec and Olympia & York] were qualified to tender for the Canadian Broadcasting Company's new Toronto headquarters in 1987, Olympia & York withdrew after the Reichmanns discovered that Trizec was planning a bid." [15]

Good news for o&y and Trizec, of course, but why anyone else should have been pleased because two of Canada's largest development companies declined to compete on a major project is beyond me. The joining of these two firms did what it always does: produced a lot of hot air about the wonders of competition, while carefully avoiding it in practice. The cbc complex was put up by Cadillac Fairview, by this time owned by a syndicate of thirty pension funds and jmb Realty Corporation of Chicago, o&y's partners in a number of New York properties.

The English Property deal moved o&y onto a new plane; it was now in the international big leagues, both as a property developer and as a market player. It also brought the Reichmanns into contact with Edper just when that empire was, largely through the machinations of Jack Cockwell and Trevor Eyton, about to take off. Not long after the truce was declared, Edper launched an assault on Brascan Limited, the former Brazilian Traction, Light and Power Company Limited, which had once almost run Brazil. In due and inevitable course, Brascan had been driven out of the South American nation by an increasingly nationalist government. The company sold its Brazilian assets to the government for $447 million,[16] which came clanging into the Canadian company's treasury in April 1979. A company with that much cash on hand is a natural prey for takeover artists, for the simple and obvious reason that you can buy the company's shares for far less than the cash on hand, pay for the takeover, and wind up with both the firm and whatever money is left.

To make itself less attractive to this process, Brascan, under the direction of its fiery and autocratic president, Jake Moore, set out to buy F. W. Woolworth, the giant U.S. retailer, which had $6 billion in annual sales, but which was losing money. This strategy is known as "the poison pill"; a company about to be swallowed swells itself up with debt, to make the swallowing more difficult. Edper decided to attempt the feat, anyway, and launched an attack, buying Brascan shares in private and, in public, denouncing the attempt by Brascan to take over Woolworth. The result was a long, protracted, and very expensive battle, which made a lot of lawyers rich, and ended, in May 1979, with Edper getting control of Brascan, and Jake Moore losing his job to Trevor Eyton.

One of the architects of this takeover was Jimmy Connacher, a hyperactive Bay Street investment dealer, whose firm, Gordon Capital, has been involved in many of the most controversial stock deals of recent Canadian history (he was, for example, in the midst of the Sinclair Stevens scandals that would rock Ottawa in 1985).[17] Through the Edper connection, Connacher became an important advisor, and stock-accumulator, for the Reichmanns. He was not, like many stockbrokers, content to play the role of middleman, but would often go out and accumulate blocks of stocks in companies he thought someone else might want to take over, and offer them for sale to the highest bidder. He was sometimes known as "the Piranha," sometimes as "the Barracuda,"[18] and he was connected with many of the deals put together by both the Bronfmans and the Reichmanns in the 1980s. If he seems like unlikely company for the diffident, courteous, and self-effacing Reichmanns, well, politics is not the only game that makes strange bedfellows.

The Reichmanns were no longer tile-makers, nor developers. They were becoming yet another multinational corporation in the company-buying business, using leverage not merely to multiply the value of real estate, but also to gain control of other corporations in the paper-making, energy, and even financial fields.

In ten short years, from the founding of Olympia & York Developments Limited in 1969 to the English Property takeover in 1979, the "shy gentlemen," as one of the British newspapers called them, had built a major financial conglomerate. But it was still, in essence, a small family firm, run by three men. Certainly, they were smart, but is anybody *that* smart?

CHAPTER SIX

A Marriage Made in Bay Street

One thing attained with difficulty is far better than a hundred things procured with ease.
— The Talmud

$

The joining of Edper and Olympia & York was like the mating of giant octopi, massive, complicated, and accompanied by a good deal of thrashing around. It was, on the face of it, a strange joining, despite superficial resemblances between the two groups. Both were the creations of brothers, and both sets of brothers were Jewish and ambitious. They were, in addition, of the same generation. Edward Bronfman was born in 1927, two years before Albert Reichmann, and his brother Peter was born in 1929, the same year as Albert and two years before Paul.

But the Bronfmans were born and brought up in upper-class Montreal, surrounded by all the advantages of affluence. They were the sons of Allan Bronfman, younger brother to the redoubtable Sam, who treated his sibling as something between a partner and a step-and-fetch-it in the family firm, Seagram Company Limited. Edward and Peter were pampered and protected, whisked off from the Westmount mansion, next door to Sam's, to American preparatory schools. When they came back home, it was to find increasing tension and rancour in the bosom of the family, which had none of the serenity, tradition, or hierarchical sense of the Reichmanns. When you said the Bronfmans were Jewish, you were describing a cultural inheritance, not an all-embracing religious philosophy.

The family battles grew out of Sam's determination that his children, Edgar and Charles, the same ages as Edward and Peter, would inherit Seagram's. He went about it in a straightforward way. A private company, SECO Investments, held all the shares in the huge conglomerate, and CEMP, a trust fund Sam had set up for his own children, held two-thirds of the shares in SECO. Allan's shares were in a trust he had set up for *his* children, called Edper, for Edward and Peter. Sam used CEMP's majority to pass a resolution barring Edward and Peter from Seagram's, and that was that.[1]

Allan's boys, with a few dozen millions, were thrust out onto the street. They hired themselves the best advice they could buy, and went into the stock business, buying companies, and did very well indeed. They moved from Montreal to Toronto, shed wives, married again. Peter has been married three times, Edward twice. Edward was hurtled into newspaper headlines in 1983 when, in the middle of the night, his live-in girlfriend, Delores Ann Sherkin, fell backwards to her death out of the window of their Toronto townhouse.[2] He is the quieter of the two, soft-spoken where Peter is loud and frequently profane. Patricia Best and Ann Shortell, in their book on the brothers, quote an unnamed business acquaintance as remarking, "I always thought of Edward as a no-brainer, but he's not that dumb."[3] This is known as a back-handed compliment. Because of the pain associated with their own succession problem, the brothers made an arrangement by which Peter's sons would take over their joint effort,[4] and, in 1989, Edward bowed out and Peter took the conglomerate public, although there is still a majority of private firms within the corporate shell.

Peter is also the more active and aggressive of the two, a Yale graduate who "took the easiest courses I could," but who works hard and takes great pride in the masses of money and companies that Edper has gathered up over the years. Not so unusual, for billionaires, the Bronfman brothers, but entirely different in background and personal relationships from the Reichmanns. Most importantly, perhaps, the Bronfmans' empire is one that others built for them, by and large. The one irreplaceable figure in Edper is Jack Cockwell, not a Bronfman. The Reichmanns, in contrast, built their own empire.

Oceans of ink and tons of paper have been devoted to explaining what a brilliant marriage the Edper–O&Y union was, with the Reichmanns providing real-estate expertise and the Bronfman hired hands providing management and financial skills to the companies they swallowed. Wrong though it may seem to dispute this conventional wisdom, already enshrined in a score of books and a thousand magazine articles, two mild caveats may be entered.

In the first place, the financial success of giant corporations in the real-estate business in expansionary times is not a complete surprise. Edper and O&Y owned Trizec and, in 1986, Edper would complete a takeover of Bramalea Limited, while O&Y owned a series of companies – it tended to set up new firms for each major project – in the realty industry. When real-estate prices were shooting up, as they did with only minor dips during the late 1970s and the early and mid 1980s, it was not supremely difficult for people with a lot of money to make more, and for people with the nerve to use leverage to the limit to make very much more.

Most of these purchases were done on a principle enunciated by Wimpy, Popeye's sidekick in the comic strip: "I will gladly pay you Tuesday for a hamburger today." Developers borrowed money, bought property, watched it increase in value, sold for a profit, borrowed against the rise in profit, and did it again, in ever-increasing amounts. The real skill came in knowing where to buy, and how much to pay, but not many people lost money in the real-estate business while the markets were rocketing upwards.

In the second place, there was, until after the English Property deal, an essential difference between the way Brascan, the major operating arm of the Edper empire, and Olympia & York did business. The pattern established by Brascan was to find a company which was either cash rich – the case with Brascan itself when Edper grabbed it – or undervalued, to buy control, and then to move in and "slim it down." Also known as firing people. Under the remorselessly driving Jack Cockwell, managers at the middle and upper levels were worked harder, longer, or thrown out on the street. It wasn't very nice, but it was efficient, and Brascan made a lot of money doing it. It is part of the pervasive corporate theology of our time, under which people who have worked for a company for a score or more of years can be trashed to give the balance sheet a temporarily better look, and to goose the stock to help pay the costs of the takeover that led to the firings.

It didn't much matter what kind of company was subjected to this sort of treatment. Brascan took over Noranda Mines Limited, the John Labatt Corporation, MacMillan Bloedel Limited, the paper giant, Canada Wire and Cable, and dozens of others in the energy, manufacturing, life insurance, resource, and financial sectors. By and large, the pattern followed was the same: the stocks were purchased, heads rolled, profits fattened, and the process was repeated elsewhere.

This is the pattern of giant corporations all over the world who specialize in grabbing things rather than doing things, and why it should bring down hosannas is a question for a psychologist, not a journalist. "Big" equals good, "bigger," best. I can't see it myself, but it is the wisdom of our age. It seems to me, and to a few misguided zealots like E. F. "Small Is Beautiful" Schumacher, that giantism is not only a problem for society as a whole, but is bound to be, in the end, a problem for the giant itself. As I write this in mid-1993, the Edper group is in deep trouble, the result of over-expansion, heavy debtloads, and a certain amount of confusion brought on by the group's unaccountable shyness in revealing pertinent information in a timely way. There are thirty-five public companies and a hundred private ones in the group, and it has assets of $100 billion.[5] Because so many of the companies are private, no one knows what the liabilities are. We do know, though, that the stocks of many of the public companies have dropped like a stone, some, like Bramalea, which had to apply for bankruptcy protection in November 1992, by as much as 93 per cent in the past year. Since late 1989, the average price of the group's public stocks has declined by 52 per cent.[6] At the same time, Edper is coming under increasing attack for its lack of candour, to put it at its mildest, in its dealings. Two of the group's main assets, John Labatt Corporation and MacMillan Bloedel, have been sold to staunch the bleeding, along with its trust company, Royal Trustco Limited. Two major debt-rating agencies have downgraded key companies in the group, including Hees International Bancorp Incorporated, one of the major holding companies, Brascan Limited, the major operating arm, Trilon Financial, and Trizec.[7] Dividends are drying up, and it is now being suggested that what Edper needs to pull it out of a tailspin is a massive economic recovery across the board. So do we all.

Another important difference between the two marriage partners was that the Edper group usually financed its takeovers by what is called "topdown financing." A holding company would buy the shares of Company A, and Company A would use this money to buy the shares of other companies in the group. Brascan's investment in Noranda was used by Noranda to buy the stocks or bonds of other companies. It was another way of using leverage, and, right up until the moment when the whole thing began to come apart, it was held to be a technique that would make Edper "recession-proof," because it was not so dependent on bank loans as, say, O&Y. The company was actually "praying for a recession," so that it could show everyone else how clever it was.[8] But the recession, when it came, came close to bringing down the entire empire, although, of course, like O&Y, it is too big actually to fail. Let us just say that its future is clouded.

Is it possible, just possible, that the magic behind huge corporations with money to risk is a general growth in the surrounding economy, not inherent genius? And that the level of detectable genius within these monsters tends to plummet when bad times intrude? The question is relevant to our inquiry into Olympia & York because, before its mating with Edper, O&Y behaved in quite a different way. Up to this time, it contented itself with its expertise in one specialty; two, if you count Olympia Floor & Wall Tile, but that played little part in the expansion of the empire. It developed. It found likely real-estate prospects, built magnificent buildings, and then either sold them for a profit or ran them, very well, for a profit.

But when it tasted blood in the English Property chase, O&Y evolved into quite a different company. Its strength had come from doing what it knew best, building on a knowledge acquired over the years. Edper's strength came, if you like, in not knowing anything except how to take over, rework, and exploit other companies. The Reichmanns tried it both ways; they continued to build and develop, and, at the same time, they got into the takeover game. But they had no burgeoning bureaucracy, with shoals of managers and quires of committees, and legions of financial experts backed by battalions of directors, both inside and outside, like Edper. Instead, they had Albert and Ralph and Paul. "There was never anyone," says a man who worked with them, "who could say to Paul Reichmann, 'Don't do that. It's foolish.'"

A number of explanations have been given for the way the Reichmanns plunged into so many projects at once. Andrew Sarlos, who knows the Reichmanns well, contends that they were building an empire that could be left to their children – there are fourteen children among the three brothers – but which the next generation would not have to manage. "The whole diversification program was to pass on to the next generation properties that could be professionally managed. They didn't expect them [the children] to do it themselves."[9]

This is, in fact, what the Edper empire seems to be about, a flotilla of corporations, all run by experts, pouring cash into the coffers. The difficulty with this approach for the Reichmanns, Sarlos says, was "the one-man-show" syndrome. "There is a very dangerous phenomenon that if you have been successful, you don't have to listen to anyone. People didn't want to give them advice because they wouldn't listen to it, partly because they didn't want opposition."

Besides, why should they listen, when everything was going so well? Peter Foster argues that "their real estate was so successful, generating so much cash, that they were now almost *forced* [his emphasis] to diversify."[10] The alternative, of course, would have been to use the cash to pay down the debts that were accumulating, but only an unimaginative churl would have done that.

In 1979 they bought into an oil-and-gas company called Canada Northwest Land Limited, which had wells in Spain and North America and was doing exploratory work in Australia. The next year, they bought control of Brinco Limited, which had started out as a company formed by William Mulholland, before he became president of the Bank of Montreal, to develop the Churchill Falls hydro project in Labrador. When Newfoundland took over the project, Brinco, for something to do, merged with an oil company and gas company and became Brinco Oil & Gas. It was controlled by Rio Tinto, a British company, while two Japanese firms and an American one owned substantial shares. There was a certain amount of disquietude over its foreign ownership on the part of Canada's Foreign Investment Review Agency (later dismantled by the Mulroney government) and, after a long period of negotiations, Olympia & York bought control for $95 million. The deal was completed in November 1980, by which time the Reichmanns were in the middle of another deal, in quite a different sphere. They collided with Robert Campeau and plunged into the Royal Trust affair.

On the morning of August 27, 1980, Kenneth White, the chairman and chief executive officer of Royal Trustco, the holding company for the largest trust company, and largest real-estate brokerage firm, in Canada, was having a quiet breakfast on the lawn of his estate at Bromont, southeast of Montreal, when he was rudely interrupted by the arrival of a taxi, which discharged an excitable, arm-waving man. Robert Campeau had come to call. Actually, he had been trying to arrange a meeting with White for four days, but the crusty former army officer kept putting him off, so Campeau hired a helicopter to fly him to Sherbrooke, then took a taxi to Bromont.

Campeau, the son of a blacksmith from Sudbury, Ontario, had made his first modest profit building a house in Ottawa for $5,000 with his cousin Tony, and selling it for $7,500. It seemed a better way to make money than sweeping floors for Inco, back in Sudbury, for fifty cents an hour. Ambitious and brash, he was soon building and selling more houses, then whole subdivisions. He struck on the then-novel idea of building office space for government departments, financed with the leases from the departments themselves, and remade the Ottawa skyline. The Ottawa zoning by-laws that established restrictions so that no building could exceed the Peace Tower in height gave him little pause; he got friendly Ottawa councillors to push through variations. John Rothchild, an American who has written one of the many books about Campeau,[11] uses a nice phrase about this aspect of his rise: Campeau "pygmatized the national government."

He expanded into the United States, building condominiums, office towers, and shopping centres. He built the Harbour Castle Hotel and a cluster of condominiums on the Toronto waterfront, and arranged for a guard of honour from the Royal Regiment for the official opening. He took the salute himself, standing at attention in front of the hotel. Then he bought a house on the Bridle Path, the ritziest area in the north end of Toronto, and had an official opening there, too, with singer Paul Anka flown in by helicopter to do the honours.

By mid-1980, he was wealthy, ambitious, and brash. One of his less-endearing traits was to make long speeches boosting himself and knocking governments, any government, for rolling up debts – which seemed a bit much, considering how much money his companies had swallowed and how much debt he was carrying. The business establishment viewed him with equal amounts of admiration and alarm.

On the one hand, he had made all that money. On the other, he was a ranter, a show-off, a loudmouth. Just not quite the thing. But there was, after all, all that money . . .

Campeau told Ken White that he had decided to take over Royal Trustco, would be making his formal bid that very afternoon, and expected White's co-operation and support. The offer was for $413 million, and the money would be provided by the Bank of Nova Scotia. White was astounded, and outraged. According to Campeau's recollection of their conversation, White said, "I really don't like you, Campeau, and I don't like Paul Desmarais and I don't like Conrad Black and I don't like Edgar Bronsman (sic). I don't like all these guys making bids for public corporations and I wish to Hell you would stay where you are and don't bother us."[12] The "us" in this quote is not specified; presumably it meant "The Right Sort," of whom Campeau was not one.

Gripping Campeau by the arm, White escorted him back to his taxi, and bade him farewell with the words, "Pull the bid! Pull that damn bid!"[13] It dawned on Campeau that this was not going to be one of those friendly takeovers you read about.

White quickly gathered a team of the right sort to pull together enough stock in the company to keep it out of Campeau's reach. Banks, insurance companies, industrial companies, even pension funds were called on to sop up shares, and no less than three law firms were retained and told to stand by, with writs at the ready. The main defence would be mounted by Austin Taylor, then chairman of McLeod Young Weir, the prestigious Bay Street investment house, who proceeded to call everybody he or anyone on the Royal Trustco board knew who might make a friendly stock purchase. The Reichmanns were approached by Howard Beck, one of the lawyers acting with Taylor, who knew Paul Reichmann and had handled his legal affairs for years.

Would Olympia & York take a block of Royal Trustco stock? Would they ever; in fact, the Reichmanns offered to buy 50 per cent. This was not exactly what White had in mind for what he referred to as "my company," and the offer was refused. Paul Reichmann came back with an offer to buy 9 per cent, in return for positions on the board, and that was accepted. They paid about $33 million. By this time it was clear that Campeau could not get control, and he had no interest in any company he couldn't run. Accordingly, he sold out the shares he had accumulated, for a profit of $2 million, to O&Y.

The Reichmanns wound up with 23.9 per cent of a company they knew very little about, in a business with which they were not familiar, so Paul Reichmann went round to his good friends at Brascan. The upshot was that Brascan bought 17 per cent of Royal Trustco, later raising their hold to 20 per cent, and the Reichmanns asked the Edper resident geniuses to look after both blocks of shares. They were happy to oblige. The Toronto-Dominion Bank also asked Brascan to handle its Royal Trust shares, about 10 per cent of the company, so the Edper group wound up firmly in control.

The Ontario Securities Commission looked into the Royal Trust affair and produced a report that slapped the wrists of Ken White and Royal Trustco for putting their own interests ahead of the interests of the shareholders at large. The idea is that the chaps in charge should have encouraged the bidding of rival factions so that small shareholders would get the best possible price for their stock, instead of freezing the puck the way they did. It is one of the pleasant myths of the stock business: that the managements of corporations think first of the little shareholder, always, and only afterwards, if ever, of their own hides. Every now and then, there is a show-trial to prove the truth of this fable, and this was such an occasion. The Reichmanns were exempted from any criticism by the OSC. They had nothing to do with the way the matter was arranged, they had merely stepped in to make an intelligent investment. Later, in 1983, they swapped their Royal Trustco holdings for $40 million in cash and shares in Trilon Financial Corporation, another Edper-controlled financial holding company in which they already had an interest.

Ken White was gone by then, of course. Brascan issued the usual statement saying that he was going of his own volition. Trevor Eyton replaced him temporarily, until Brascan could restructure the company and install Hartland Molson McDougall in his place.

When all the dust and writs and charges and countercharges had settled, Brascan was calling all the shots at Royal Trustco, with the Reichmanns on the board as substantial minority owners. In the end, Royal Trustco became one of the companies whose dismal performance dragged down the Edper group. In 1991 it lost $850 million, and teetered on the verge of bankruptcy. In March 1993 the saleable assets were dealt off to the Royal Bank for $1.6 billion. These included Royal Trust and its 146 branches. The holding company was left holding $4.3 billion in loans of uncertain value.[14]

However, whatever the future held, the Reichmanns had been accepted as part of the solid Canadian business establishment. And Ken White, who had fought off Robert Campeau, wound up being bounced by one of those "Bronsmans."

Nobody said life was fair.

CHAPTER SEVEN

Building a Palace on a
Mountain of Muck

They are not the landlords of little old ladies. They are the landlords to business, and, as long as you know what you're doing, that is a very good thing to be.

    – William Moore, A. E. LePage, 1979 [1]

$

While the Royal Trust affair was still working its way into the history books, the Reichmanns had launched two new, massive ventures in real estate. The first was an ambitious plan to redevelop a twenty-five-acre patch of downtown San Francisco, to be called Yerba Buena Gardens. In 1980 O&Y won the right to build the project, in the middle of San Francisco's financial district, against such other Canadian bidders as Robert Campeau and Cadillac Fairview Corporation. [2] It would cost $1.8 billion, and O&Y would pay the San Francisco Redevelopment Agency, which owned the land, $68 million in land rent, which would be used to put cultural amenities, including theatres, art galleries, museums, and gardens, into the area.

This was still very much on the drawing boards when they plunged into another project, just as big, back in their old haunt of Manhattan, where they had triumphed before and were about to triumph – at least for a time – again. They would build this triumph, literally, on a pile of muck along the Hudson River, in the area of Battery Park City. The Battery, on the tip of Manhattan, was named for the guns that used to stand guard there. In 1968 Governor Nelson Rockefeller came up with a plan to revitalize the decaying waterfront and redevelop the area west of the World Trade Center, while, at the same time, saving millions of dollars by getting rid of the debris excavated for the buildings. The state, which owns landfill sites as part of its riparian rights, formed the Battery Park City Authority. This authority would provide housing for the homeless of New York,[3] ho, ho.

We are talking about a lot of debris. The World Trade Center consists of six buildings, topped by two monster towers, each 110 storeys high, containing 28 million square feet of office space. New York's tallest buildings, at 1,350 feet, and among her ugliest. It took seven years to build the complex, beginning in 1966.[4] The excavation produced one million cubic yards of earth, rocks, garbage, and treated sewage. (Among this, the workmen turned up a bronze breech-loading swivel deck gun, bearing the mark of the Dutch East India Company. It was probably from the *Tyger*, a Dutch ship burned in the harbour in 1613. The gun went into a museum, the rest of the *Tyger* is still somewhere at the bottom of the river.)[5] This mountain of muck was dumped into the Hudson River, and formed a landfill site of twenty-five acres, which was grafted onto Battery Park City.

When it is finished, this project, which covers 92 acres in all, including the dumped debris, will house 25,000 people in 14,000 rental and co-operative apartments, although how many of them will be from the city's current 90,000 homeless is a matter for conjecture. When Brendan Gill went to visit the project in 1990, for a *New Yorker* article that was generally favourable, especially towards the design aspects of Battery Park, he noted that "the cheapest rental apartments, in what passes for the older section of Battery Park City (constructed in the early eighties), cost around eight hundred and fifty dollars a month, while the most expensive cost over three thousand."[6] The world was entering into its love affair with "market forces" in the later 1970s, and market forces were calling forth luxury housing and office centres, not roofs for the rubes.

In 1979 the authority was absorbed into the New York State Urban Development Corporation, whose responsibility was to promote development, especially commercial development. Construction bids were invited, and the corporation had a set of guidelines for the Battery Park area drawn up, the purpose of which was to generate as much commercial revenue as possible so that $200 million in bonds, which had been issued by the authority, could be paid off before they went rancid. In the fall of 1980, Paul Reichmann went to see Richard Kahan, the chief executive of the Urban Development Corporation, bearing, as Peter Foster tells it, a single sheet of blue paper containing the repayment schedule for the bonds, issued when the bonds were first sold.[7] He offered to guarantee the bond repayments in return for the right to develop the World Financial Center, a $2-billion centrepiece for Battery Park City.

Among the other promises he made in subsequent meetings with the Urban Development Corporation, Paul Reichmann said he would finish the project in five years, faster than any of the other eleven bidders for the work, and that he would pay $50 million in ground rent when the buildings were scheduled to be finished, not when they actually were, so that, if there were a delay, the money would still be forthcoming.

By the time Olympia & York was awarded the contract, in the midst of a severe recession (though shorter-lived than the 1989-plus model), the company was building another $750 million worth of office towers in other U.S. cities through its American subsidiary, Olympia & York (U.S.), as well as the Yerba Buena project in San Francisco.

They had also run into the first blast of bad publicity the company had earned in New York when they served notice that they intended to evict the downtown branch of the Whitney Museum, then located in O&Y's 55 Water Street building, because the museum couldn't pay its rent of $90,000 a year. Before O&Y had taken the building over, the museum had been paying a token $1 a year in rent. In July 1980, the *New York Times* ran a rather mild editorial saying the landlord should have explored other ways to solve the problem than by an eviction,[8] but O&Y replied that the $90,000 rent was not full market value anyway. It was pretty close, though; the museum had premises that took up 5,000 square feet; $90,000 represented a charge of $18 a square foot – not much of a bargain when similar space was going for between $20 and $25 a square foot.[9] The museum was left in place until the lease ran out in September, then it moved. The incident made Olympia & York look pretty chintzy, and made the company, if anything, even less anxious than ever to have its affairs discussed in public.

The two men the Reichmanns sent down to make sure there were no bad vibes from the grand new project down at the tip of Manhattan – although always, of course, the brothers remained in charge of both large plans and small details – were Ron Soskolne and Michael Dennis, the young turks from the City of Toronto with whom they had first clashed, then worked, when planning First Canadian Place. Soskolne had left his job as chief city planner in 1978, and had gone to work for O&Y in Boston, where he oversaw the development of Exchange Place. Dennis had left the city payroll after pushing through the St. Lawrence Market development, and also went to work for O&Y, who assigned him to New York. Another of the key figures on this project was Edward Minskoff, the broker who had brought them the Uris Package for their first Manhattan merry-go-round. Old home week. Soskolne was responsible for working smoothly with city and state authorities, Dennis and Minskoff with rounding up clients for the buildings-to-be.

With its customary confidence, O&Y pledged to start the project in 1981 and complete it in 1985. The starting date was met, but a number of problems, chiefly with some of the venal construction unions of New York, pushed the finish back by two years.

There are four office towers in the complex, all designed by Cesar Pelli, the Argentine-born dean of architecture at Yale. They surround a glass-vaulted Winter Garden, complete with sixteen, forty-five-foot-tall palm trees from the Mojave Desert in California (they were kept inside for four years to accustom them to conditions in their future home before being freighted to New York), and a four-acre plaza.

Sometime when you are in New York and have run out of things to do – taking in a show, riding the subway, getting mugged – catch the IRT No. 9 train downtown and go for a walk around the World Financial Center. It is worth examining, not only for itself, but for the contrast between this complex and the World Trade Center across the way.

The Trade Center is big, humoungous, in fact, but when you have said that, you have said it all. Slab-sided, monolithic, the towers of steel and glass contain ninety-nine elevators each, and each tower represents a land area of just over one hundred acres of space. Oh, yes, and there are 21,800 windows in each tower – none of which can be opened – and enough aluminium to build 9,000 houses. The Financial Center is clad in attractive reddish marble. Every day, the 50,000 people who work in the World Trade Center generate 50 tons of garbage, use 2.25 million gallons of water, and produce roughly the same amount of raw sewage. The dizzying height draws visitors, at $4.50 each, to an observation platform on the 107th floor of Two World Trade Center, the southernmost of the two towers; it also draws nuts and publicity-seekers to the outside of the tower. In 1974 a French aerialist with a crossbow shot a rope between the two towers and walked across. A year later an unemployed construction worker from Queen's parachuted from the top. Two years after that, a mountaineer named George Willig scaled Two World Trade Center, using a special harness he had designed to fit the window-washing rig on the building's outside. He was charged, when he got to the top, with "wrongfully scaling and climbing the South Tower of the World Trade Center." He paid a fine of $1.10, a penny for each floor, and promised not to do it again. [10]

Gimmicky, that's the word I'm looking for. The World Trade Center is a huge, ugly office complex with a lot of gimmicks attached, chiefly its very size. Inside, it looks like any other office building, except that there is so much more of it.

The World Financial Center is huge, too, in fact, with eight million square feet of office, retail, and commercial space. It is almost as large as the Trade Center. But it somehow doesn't seem as huge and impersonal. For one thing, the buildings are strung along and near the river, and penetrated by green space. For another, the Winter Garden, as large as the main terminal in Grand Central Station, is breathtaking, and the Plaza is correctly described in a guidebook as "a stellar example of public space design."[11] Excellent small touches – very good doorways, lots of public washrooms (rare across the street), and a feeling of openness – pervade the buildings.

The erection and furbishing of this complex did not go smoothly; there were strikes, and threatened strikes, and, New York being New York, a few death threats sent to John Norris, the O&Y construction chief for the project.[12] There was also quite a lot of creative accounting on the worksite, and a subsequent inquiry into the construction industry revealed that one union representative pulled in an annual salary of $570,000 through, among other wonders, working twenty-six hours a day. Still, O&Y were expert builders, and all of the tricks and shortcuts refined at First Canadian Place and a dozen other jobs were put to work. Then there were all the compound bureaucratic complications that attend any massive undertaking, plus some that were induced by the Reichmanns themselves. Since they would not allow work on the site on the Jewish Sabbath, some of the unions that were involved demanded, and got, holiday pay. But the work was done, and the general consensus of informed opinion was that it was magnificently done.

The question of whether it ought to have been done at all was not one that concerned the Reichmanns. They are not in the business of making political or social decisions; they stick up buildings. Still, it must have crossed somebody's mind, sometime, that, having already shoved a city-sized complex down at the tip of Manhattan in the form of the World Trade Center, there might be better things to do with the city's, and the state's, time, effort, and money – for none of these giants is ever built without tax breaks, transportation subsidies, and other goodies – than shoving in another one beside it.

What New York needed, and still needs, is less congestion, not greater congestion; it needs more housing, schools, transportation, hospitals, and other social amenities, and fewer towers. However, you can't make money out of social amenities, and there is a theory, not yet in human history substantiated by provable fact, that the spending of a couple of billions here and there will somehow trickle down to the folks who sleep on gratings and live on the garbage chucked out at the back of the nice restaurants in places like this.

These matters were of no concern to the Reichmanns, probably never crossed their minds, but they must have begun to wonder, when they went after the large, long-term leases that you need to make a project like this work, whether the New York market had not, after all, become sated in the line of office space for the time being.

Michael Dennis and Edward Minskoff spent weary hours trudging from one potential client to another, all over New York, trying to line up lessees with, at first, very little success. They were reduced, in the end, to offering substantial inducements to lure in the customers. In the case of American Express, they actually bought the Amex building for $240 million, and moved the company into the largest of the four World Financial Center towers, with a thirty-five-year lease worth, over that period, $2.4 billion. When this deal was announced, in March 1982, before the shovels had even gone to work on the building, it was hailed as "the largest real estate transaction in history."[13] Other potential lessees were given their moving costs, or O&Y would offer to pay for all the fittings that specialized firms required. As much as 50 per cent of the Center was filled with the aid of various inducements, which included buying whole buildings, or taking over long-term leases, to persuade prestige firms to pack up and move.[14] The same techniques would be applied, less successfully, at Canary Wharf a decade later.

The Reichmanns had "created an address," but at a cost. Once the project was firmly anchored in this way, they could, and did, charge much higher rents for the remaining space, filling in with doctors, dentists, and lawyers, who would meet the rent-roll by charging exorbitant prices to their neighbours. Wall Street's version of Marxism; from each according to his ability to pay, to each according to the landlord's need.

Putting together the financing had presented problems, too. Not that the Reichmanns had had any trouble with the banks, far from it, but they wanted to get the best deal they could get and, at the time, interest rates were high and rising. Paul Reichmann had made a deal with Teachers Assurance and Annuity Association of America to borrow $250 million U.S. for one of the World Financial Center towers. Part of this unusual arrangement was a sharing of some of the profits from the tower with the association. The contract had been agreed upon, but not implemented, when he found another, cheaper, source of money and broke off the deal. The association launched a lawsuit for $120 million, the amount it calculated it had lost because of the abrogation of the contract, and the case dragged on for years. It would blow up, as we shall see, at the worst possible time. [15]

But that was far in the future. Gradually, the major leases were set, the buildings were under way, the money was rounded up and put to work, and the press notices seemed to agree that the remarkable Reichmanns had once more pulled off a triumph in New York City.

Time to plunge again.

CHAPTER EIGHT

The Acquisitors

The Holy One – blessed be He! – often brings afflictions on the right-
eous though they have not sinned, in order that they may learn to keep
aloof from the allurements of the world and eschew temptation to sin.
From this is it plain that afflictions are good for man.
  – The Talmud

$

One day Ken Field was feeling particularly disgruntled about his job.
As president of Bramalea Limited, the Brascan subsidiary, he felt that
the Edper group, to whom it belonged, were mismanaging things. (He
was obviously right; Bramalea would file for bankruptcy protection in
1992, and its shares would hit a low of 28 cents.) [1] He went to call on his
old friend Albert Reichmann at First Canadian Place. Albert had been
put on the board of Bramalea, and Field found him intelligent,
humorous, and much more approachable than the redoubtable Paul.
He told Albert about his problems, but the older man just kept saying,
"We don't want you to go." Field said he was determined; he was leaving Bramalea.

Not long after, on a Sunday afternoon, Field was just about to take his girlfriend and his children out on his boat when Albert called him at home. "Come and see me right away," he said.

Field recalls, "I told him I was taking the family out on my boat, and he wanted to know where the boat was. I said, 'If you look out your window, you can see it.' And he said, 'So you couldn't drop in on a friend on your way past?'

"I said, 'Do I have to put on a suit?' And he said, 'I am wearing a suit.'"

So Field, grumbling, dressed up in a suit, took the family down to the waterfront, and then came back up to call on Albert. "He said, 'Ken, I thought you were a smart boy, and here you are quitting, just because you get mad.' I said that wasn't it; he would remember from board meetings that changes had been promised at Bramalea, and they were never made. I told him that I was writing a book, had been making notes for a long time. I had the file with me. 'Read this,' I said. 'Then we'll talk.'"

Field came back several hours later and found Albert no longer in a suit; shockingly, he was in shirtsleeves, with the collar open. "He said, 'You gave me quite a day. I spent the whole afternoon reading your book.' I asked him how he liked it, and he said, 'I liked the parts about me.' I really admired him, and it showed. Then he said that, having read the book, he could see that I had to leave Bramalea, but I would be bored. Olympia & York would find something for me to do."[2]

A few days later Paul Reichmann phoned, and the two men talked about projects Field could take on for the Reichmanns, but no definite offer was forthcoming. Paul hung up after saying, "I'll be in touch in six months."

Field left Bramalea, set up his own investment firm, and forgot about the O&Y offer. Months later, on a holiday trip to the U.S. southwest, he went out to lunch at a country club, where his brother is a member, in Palm Springs, California. During lunch there was a page, announcing a telephone call for a "Mr. Field," but Ken paid no attention – who knew he was even in California? – until the message specified, "Mr. Field of Toronto." He scrambled for the telephone, but it was too late; the party who was calling had hung up. The bewildered Field immediately got through to his office, back in Toronto, and his secretary told him that Paul Reichmann was trying to get hold of him. Curious and excited, Field phoned O&Y, but by this time it was 4:15 on a Friday in Toronto, and Paul had left to observe the Sabbath.

Over the weekend Field kept wondering what it was about. Why would Paul Reichmann be tracking him down in California? Finally, he decided that Reichmann must be offering him something in the area. Probably Yerba Buena, the huge San Francisco development O&Y was working on. That must be it.

First thing Monday morning he telephoned Toronto, and was put straight through to Paul Reichmann, but all that came across the three thousand miles of telephone wire was chat about miscellaneous business.

"Finally, I said, 'Well, what were you calling about?'" Field recalls. "And he said, 'I had a note in my book to call you in six months. It is now six months.'"

Reichmann's secretary had been given the job of sleuthing after Field; she it was who found out from his brother where he was having lunch. The two men did, in the end, discuss a project. Olympia & York was busy taking over the U.S. railway giant Sante Fe Pacific, and they thought that might be something Field could help with.

"Paul said he would send me something to read, and I said okay.

"I took the family up to Vail, Colorado, and we went skiing. One day when we got back to the chalet, there was a note from Federal Express, they had something for me. I phoned Federal Express and told them I would be out skiing again the next day, but, whatever it was, they could just slip it under the door.

"The Federal Express guy says, 'Under the door? There's four boxes of the stuff here!'"

Soft steamrollers, that's the Reichmanns. Utterly absorbed by what he himself was doing, Paul Reichmann could not see anything unusual in shipping four boxes of documents across the continent to a man on holidays, who didn't want to plough through anything more challenging than a foot of snow.

It was this singleness of purpose that the Reichmanns turned on other corporations once they had contracted the conglomerate bug from the Edper group. In 1978 Andrew Sarlos, the Bay Street guru and Reichmann ally, and Maurice Strong, who is today the chairman of Ontario Hydro, launched an assault on the world's largest newsprint-producer, Abitibi. This was a combination power-and-paper company, which had been founded in 1912 by a former railway ticket-agent named Frank H. Anson, on the Abitibi River, at Iroquois Falls, Ontario. In 1974 it had been combined with The Price Company Limited, an even-older firm started by British investors in the early-nineteenth century to secure a supply of timber for masts for the British navy.[3] The takeover, which cost $130 million, was no sooner completed, than paper markets collapsed, and a crippling strike hit the firm. It took four years for markets to recover, and the vulnerable company was ripe for a takeover in turn. Consolidated-Bathurst, which had bid against Abitibi for Price, and still owned a block of Price stock, bought 10 per cent of the shares of Abitibi (which became Abitibi-Price Inc. in 1979). The scent of blood in the water, as always, brought others.

Sarlos and Strong, with backing from Peter Bronfman and Paul Nathanson, heir to the Famous Players movie fortune, gobbled up $31 million worth of Abitibi-Price shares in a five-day sweep in the spring of 1981.[4] But their attempt to muscle their way onto the board on the basis of shares they had themselves, and a block of shares other investors allowed them to vote for them, was coldly rebuffed by Abitibi-Price management. They sold their shares, for a profit, to West Fraser Timber, a West Coast company. In the meantime, Sarlos had interested the Reichmanns in the company and, in the following months, they accumulated about 10 per cent of the paper giant's shares. This brought in yet another firm, Federal Commerce & Navigation Limited, a Montreal shipping company, and soon a full-scale bidding war was raging for control. Federal offered $27.50 a share; the Reichmanns upped that to $28.50. That was bettered by a joint offer for 8.5 million shares – about half the stock outstanding – from a group led by Thomson Newspapers, whose chairman, Ken Thomson, was a member of the Abitibi-Price board, and Nu-West, a Calgary-based petroleum company.

The Reichmanns topped the offer by another dollar, raising it to $32, and offered to buy whatever amount they could at that price. Within days they had accumulated 92 per cent of the company, paying $670 million, then one of the largest takeovers in Canadian history. The bulk of the financing was arranged through the Canadian Imperial Bank of Commerce, with whom the Reichmanns were becoming major customers and commercial allies.

The brothers had never, apparently, intended to swallow the whole thing; it was just something that happened, as it often does, when the bidding war began. There is at least as much machismo as financial sense in these matters. The fact that $32 a share was too much to pay, which is why all the other holders of blocks of stock tendered theirs at that price, got lost in the thrill of the chase.

However, once the Reichmanns had Abitibi-Price, they did not perform a Brascan, bringing in head-office experts (they didn't have any) to run the show, trim it down, and make it more profitable. They even persuaded Ken Thomson and a key advisor, lawyer John Tory, to stay on the board. They were just in for purposes of investment, they said, not for the pleasures of bossing another business. They contented themselves with the knowledge that they now owned one of the world's largest commercial real-estate empires, and the largest newsprint operation anywhere. Abitibi-Price would later turn out to be a disaster, but at the moment, as newsprint prices surged ahead nicely, it looked like another brilliant Reichmann coup, their second in an area completely foreign to them.

The Abitibi-Price takeover was announced on March 6, 1981. A month later the Reichmanns were back, with their wallets out, to pick up 20 per cent of MacMillan Bloedel Limited, the West Coast forest conglomerate, for $214 million. This was another Edper–O&Y production, which was set in train when Brascan arranged to buy 7.9 million shares of the giant, widely held resource company, Noranda Mines Limited, from Conrad Black. This rang alarm bells in Noranda's executive suite, then controlled by Alf Powis, chairman and chief executive officer. Brascan, which was run from Commerce Court, three floors above Noranda's forty-fifth-floor offices, now owned 16.3 per cent of Noranda, enough to make it a major force in the company. Powis dismissed, as the applesauce it was, the assurances of Brascan's Trevor Eyton that his group was not trying to change the policies or management of Noranda; they just wanted to help with the decision-making, to look after their block of shares.[5]

To defend itself, Noranda tried to flood the basement. The company issued 14 million more shares, which had been previously authorized, but never issued, priced at $19. These were snapped up by three of its own subsidiaries. Since there were now more shares out than previously, the effect of this was to dilute Brascan's holdings to 14 per cent. That was the first step.

Then, in May 1981, Noranda laid out $629 million to buy 50 per cent of MacMillan Bloedel. This was the poison-pill tactic we have come to know and love (see Chapter Five); it would make Noranda that much harder to swallow, because it was swollen by another company almost as large as itself. Unfazed, Brascan lined up an ally to help with the swallowing, the cash-rich Caisse de dépôt et placement du Québec, which already owned about 18 million Noranda shares. The two formed a new company, Brascade Resources Incorporated, to hold their joint shares. With 21.5 per cent of Noranda's shares, this company was now the largest single shareholder.

Noranda gave up, and the Edper group got four seats on the Noranda board. It was in the middle of this struggle, in April 1981, that the Reichmanns bought into MacMillan Bloedel, and became enmeshed in the Noranda takeover of that company. Then they traded their 20 per cent of MacBlo into the Noranda bid by Edper, and wound up with a stake in Noranda and about 10 per cent of MacMillan Bloedel. Another link with Edper, and another load of debt.

The Noranda investment was a disaster for Edper, and not much better for the Reichmanns. In 1982 the company lost $82.9 million, and the share price dropped to $11.375 from a high of $40.[6] Never mind, the main thing in these acquisitions is to keep on buying.

So the Reichmanns did, gulping down one million shares, or 7 per cent, of Bow Valley Industries, a Calgary-based petroleum firm, in two bites. This was another company in which Bronfmans had a substantial holding. Not the Edper Bronfmans, this time; the holding was with the CEMP Investments empire of Sam's children. On this occasion the Reichmanns made some money, by selling out, in mid-1982, to Jimmy Connacher, the Bay Street operator at the head of Gordon Capital, who was their ally in many of these operations. Connacher paid the Reichmanns $29.5 million for one million shares, for an after-tax profit to them of $14.5 million. But they turned rancid on him. Peter Foster wrote, "Gordon was only able to start selling off the block at $22 on the way down, and Connacher took a million-dollar bath. But Connacher never whined. They were all big men, playing in a big man's world. Paul Reichmann liked that in a man."[7]

I told you this was all a game of machismo. A broker's gotta do what a broker's gotta do.

The reason the Reichmanns were selling off their Bow Valley shares, besides the fact that they would make a nice profit on them, was probably because they needed the money. That, in turn, was partly because of some problems in their real-estate holdings, which we'll come to in a minute, and partly because they had begun to buy shares in Hiram Walker Resources Limited.

This giant, venerable firm had actually begun as a small grocery business, in 1856, in a small town outside Detroit, Michigan.[8] Hiram Walker sold bulk, unbranded whisky in his store, and the whisky, and the grain from which it was made, became a larger and larger part of his business. In the late 1850s there was a threat that the United States might establish Prohibition, and Walker bought 468 acres of land just over the border, around Windsor, Ontario, and began to grow grain and make and sell whisky there. He built the town of Walkerville for his workers, which still exists, although absorbed into the larger city. It was a company town, with schools, a music hall, a church, modest houses for the employees, and mansions for the executives. The fire department and police force were hand-picked by Walker himself. The *Detroit Journal,* in an article published in 1890, pronounced Walkerville as "The Queerest Place in All Christendom," and attacked the founder as being "as much a dictator as the Russian czar."[9]

The unbranded booze became Walker Club whisky, and when the Americans passed a law requiring the country of origin to be shown on liquor labels, it became Canadian Club. The company was bought by the Hatch family of Toronto when Prohibition was, in fact, introduced in the United States in 1919, and it gradually expanded to become one of the largest distillers in the world. In the late 1970s, Hiram Walker began to run into slow sales in the whisky business, not helped by a report in *Time* magazine that a number of distilleries, including Hiram Walker, had reduced the percentage of alcohol in their whisky, without telling anyone. Pressure from HCI Holdings Limited, a conglomerate that owned a lot of Hiram Walker stock, persuaded the company directors in 1979 that they ought to diversify.

So they merged with Home Oil Company Limited and Consumers' Gas Company Limited and became a conglomerate themselves. Home Oil was the creation of the bouncy, hard-drinking Bobby Brown of Calgary, which, after making a lot of money gambling on oil deposits, lost a lot by investing in lands near the giant oil strike in Prudhoe Bay, Alaska, in 1968. Home Oil had failed to make a strike, and the company's shares had fallen sharply, although it still had other valuable oil properties in the United States, the North Sea, Indonesia, and Australia. When Brown announced that he was selling his company, the Canadian government made it clear that the sale to a foreign firm would not win the necessary regulatory approval. We used to worry about the fact that most of our resources belonged to outsiders.

So, Brown sold to Consumers' Gas. The alternative was to be bought into PetroCan, which he considered to be a fate worse than death. The result was a new company, Hiram Walker/Consumers Home Limited, one of the uglier names in corporate history, which became Hiram Walker Resources Limited in June 1981.

It immediately fell on hard times, in part because of a very bad deal to which Home Oil had committed before the merger: the purchase of a U.S. company, Davis Oil, for $759 million. It turned out that the seller, Marvin Davis, had been mistaken when he talked about all the oil and gas there was on the 767,000 acres of leases involved, and Home Oil had never done an independent survey. Oh, dear. Then there was a dip in oil prices, causing the Hiram shares to drop quite sharply. The Reichmanns, among others, thought the new resource giant was undervalued, and began to buy shares, investing $130 million for 3.8 million shares in three days at the end of July 1981. They then owned just under 6 per cent of the company.

Over the next few months they assembled about 10 per cent, and then Paul Reichmann took an elevator down to talk with William Wilder, the deputy chairman of Hiram Walker, which had corporate head offices in First Canadian Place. Reichmann told Wilder, who told his boss, Clifford Hatch, the company chairman, that it would be nice if he and his brother Albert were given seats on the board of Hiram Walker. Hatch told Wilder, who told Reichmann, No sir, and we don't mean maybe. Paul Reichmann was reportedly enraged by this rejection, but there wasn't much he could do about it at the time. He had other problems.

The Olympia & York conglomerate was now working on huge complexes in New York and San Francisco, along with a score of other projects in Canada and the United States. In addition, it had its English Property–Trizec empire to look after, and now its substantial investments in resources. It had spent more than a billion dollars on Brinco, Abitibi-Price, MacMillan Bloedel, and Hiram Walker, to say nothing of its stake in Royal Trustco. And none of them, to tell you the truth, was doing all that well. On paper, O&Y's shares in these companies were down by about $300 million, [10] and the country was in the middle of a recession, which started in 1980 and didn't do anything for the rents.

Nobody beyond the family circle knew that anything was going wrong, of course. That was the beauty of being a private company. Outsiders could work out that the public companies were hurting, but no one knew whether O&Y itself was winning, losing, or breaking even. When Paul Reichmann gave one of his rare interviews to *Fortune* magazine in the spring of 1982, [11] he allowed himself to estimate, and the magazine accepted, that "O&Y's assets, carried at cost, are valued on the books at U.S. $7 billion." That is, the amount paid for the assets was $7 billion; their actual market value at that time, what with rising prices, *Fortune* calculated, was $12 billion. Olympia & York was worth $5 billion net. A lot of money.

Of course that didn't pay the bills, and, if *Fortune* had it right, a dubious proposition, there was still, however you cut it, that $7 billion in debt to be serviced; so the $5 billion in net value didn't help a whole lot, unless and until the Reichmanns started to sell some of the assets.

When Reichmann spoke to *Fortune*, his company was already putting out the word that some of the Uris buildings were for sale. In due course, two of the smallest ones, at 850 Third Avenue and 10 East 53rd Street, went for $225 million U.S., or about 70 per cent of what the Reichmanns had paid for the entire collection in 1977. At about the same time, 245 Park Avenue, where the company had its American headquarters, was remortgaged, bringing in another $308 million U.S. The pressure was off, at least temporarily, and there was some cash in the till.

Paul Reichmann was going to go back to those guys at Hiram Walker, and tell them where they got off.

CHAPTER NINE

Gulf Wars

My brother and I goofed somewhere along the line. A misunderstanding developed.

– Paul Reichmann, April 10, 1986 [1]

$

With a jingle back in their jeans, and a fire in their eyes, the Reichmanns went to work, over the next three years, to make themselves into a really BIG conglomerate. They succeeded, probably beyond their wildest dreams, and then must have wound up contemplating the adage that you should never pray for what you want, because you might get it.

What they did, in effect, was to use one of their subsidiaries, Abitibi-Price, to take over Gulf Canada Limited, the nation's second-largest integrated oil company, and then use Gulf Canada to grab off Hiram Walker Resources. And it all went terribly wrong, and brought them, for the first time, a measure of that direct, blunt public criticism that is so good for us all but which is much more blessed to give than to receive.

In October 1983 Paul Reichmann flew to Pittsburgh to discuss with the top executives of Gulf Corporation the possibility of buying their Canadian subsidiary, Gulf Canada Limited. He was there on the suggestion of Jimmy Connacher, who had told Gulf that the time had come for it to find some way to make itself into a Canadian company, and was promoting Olympia & York as the way to do it. He had good reason for making the suggestion. The federal government had announced a National Energy Program on October 28, 1980, which was based, as it turned out, on a number of totally false assumptions, such as an oil price of $77 a barrel in Canadian funds by mid-1986.[2] Nevertheless, the NEP aimed at a goal many Canadians sympathized with: to return Canadian resources to Canadian hands. In 1979, 82 per cent of all Canadian petroleum moved to our markets through foreign firms, and we had just seen, in the twelve-fold jump in gasoline prices at the pump, what that foreign dependence, joined to a touching willingness to believe whatever the oil companies told us, could cost us. Accordingly, the government would make it harder for foreign companies to buy Canadian oil firms, and, through a series of grants, tax breaks, and other subventions, subsidize Canadian ownership. Although the program was later dismantled by the Mulroney government, at the time it seemed to pose a real danger to foreign-owned firms in the Canadian oil patch, and sent waves of alarm and despondency through the boardrooms.

Suddenly, there were advantages to being a Canadian, rather than an American, Dutch, or British oil company in Canada, and that naturally turned the thoughts of Gulf executives to Canadianizing their operations up north. But, when Paul Reichmann came calling, they were not ready to sell. They didn't find his (undisclosed) price offer high enough. Instead, they plunged into a number of projects in Canada, such as an ambitious drilling program in the Beaufort Sea – which cost nearly $700 million, but not to worry, the federal government picked up 80 per cent of the tab – and a piece of the action in the Hibernia oilfields off the coast of Newfoundland. Neither of these was returning any money, nor probably ever would, but that didn't matter so much because, suddenly, the whole Gulf empire was being gobbled up by Chevron, a subsidiary of Standard Oil of California.

The way to get a handle on the philosophy of all these corporate swallowings is to think of one of those cartoons in which a whole series of fish, each larger than the one before it, are gobbling each other. Except that, in the corporate world, it is often the small fish who does the swallowing, or, in many cases, the large fish, lunging away from a smaller predator, scoots right into the mouth of another larger fish, and gets swallowed anyway. That is what happened to Gulf. It was being pursued by T. Boone Pickens, the takeover king, who had made a fortune by "greenmail," which I have described elsewhere as "the technique by which someone suitably unsuitable grabs enough of the stock of a target company to threaten control, and has to be bought off by the current management, who repurchase the stock from the raider at a premium. Give me your wallet or I'll buy your house."[3]

When Pickens rides into town, strumming his portfolio and fingering his junk bonds, strong men tremble. The Gulf management panicked. In a defensive campaign of monumental ineptitude, even for a huge corporation with squads of lawyers on hand to give it bad advice, Gulf managed to convince most of the stock market that it had no idea what it was about. Among other gaucheries, it sicced private detectives onto Pickens, to see if it could find something juicy enough in his past to wreck his present. This stunt, which had backfired on GM when the auto giant tried it on Ralph Nader, backfired on Gulf, too. There were proxy fights, and press releases, the live ammunition of these affairs hurtling over the trenches, and, through it all, Pickens and a group of allied investors, which included the Belzberg brothers of Vancouver, continued to pick up Gulf stock.

The blood in the water brought, once more, circling predators, which included the Atlantic Richfield Company, another oil giant which had to be taken more seriously than T. Boone and his gang. In March 1984, Gulf bolted into the maw of Chevron. It was the "white knight" that would ride to the rescue of the besieged company. The difference between succumbing to a white knight and being grabbed by a hostile knight is roughly the difference between seduction and rape. The price paid by Chevron for each share of Gulf U.S. stock was $80 U.S., a total of $13.2 billion, the world's largest takeover to that time. T. Boone and friends had paid less than $50 each for their shares, and made $760 million U.S. in the takeover,[4] which shows us all the value of hard, honest work. It always intrigues me, when I hear the cries from our financial leaders about the need to raise productivity, slash costs, and curb waste, to note that a little thing like throwing $760 million to T. Boone Pickens excites no comment whatever, although the money, in terms of its productivity, might just as well have been poured out of a boot. A very large boot. The takeover battle did not do a single thing for the oil business, except to create a crater of debt, but this, we are to believe, is just a way station on the road to the lean, mean corporation of the global village.

Now we had a problem. Two problems. The first was that Chevron was badly strapped for cash, having just laid out $13.2 billion, most of it borrowed, to complete the takeover. It needed to sell something, like, for example, a subsidiary. That played into the second problem. Chevron already owned a Canadian subsidiary of Standard Oil, called Chevron Canada, but it also had inherited just over 60 per cent of Gulf Canada, a company worth about $5 billion. It could roll Gulf Canada into Chevron Canada, or it could sell it for cash. However, the Canadian government would have to approve either transaction, and the likelihood of that happening, without a long struggle, could be summed up in two words: fat chance. But there were the Reichmanns, waiting in the wings, having left their card at the stage door several times in the last few months. Negotiations began.

In February 1985, the federal government finally pronounced on the Chevron takeover of Gulf Canada. The acquisition would be approved only if the subsidiary was first offered "for sale to Canadian controlled purchasers." This limitation would be lifted on April 30, but, until then, only Canadians need apply. Chevron could only own

Gulf if it agreed to sell it. There appeared to be only one buyer who qualified, and had shown any interest, and that was Olympia & York.

Olympia & York offered $2.8 billion for 60.2 per cent of Gulf Canada – all the Chevron shares – on March 19, 1985,[5] and Chevron accepted, on the basis of a condition that would not come to light for several months. For the deal to work, the Canadian government would first have to approve a tax dodge that went by the name of "the Little Egypt Bump."

The Little Egypt Bump arose from an attempt by the Canadian government's tax experts to right a wrong, back in 1971. It had to do with the wind-up of partnerships. The tax rules, at that time, said that, where a partnership was discontinued by one partner selling out to another, or to a new partner, there would be a capital gain, and thus a tax, on the increase in assets within the partnership, while it existed. This could lead to double taxation in the case where new partners were brought into a partnership which was wound up in the same taxation year. The old partners would pay a tax based on the capital gain from selling to the new partners, then everybody would pay a second time on the increase in the assets within the partnership between the time of the new formation and its wind-up.

Revenue Canada folks, who don't worry about the double taxation you and I pay in dozens of ways because of the operation of the GST, worry about things like this, especially when all the corporate lawyers who spend their lives defending the rich from the possibility of paying fair taxes raise their eyebrows. So, in 1971, regulations called "partnership step-up rules" went out to the far corners of the country. It was decreed that, in the case of a partnership bringing in new partners and then being wound up, the assets would be written up to the first sale price. This would eliminate the double taxation, because now the assets were valued at the sale price, once, but not twice; for the other disposition of these assets, there was no capital gain, and thus no tax.

Faster than you can say manoeuvre, this had been turned into a tax dodge. All you had to do was set up a partnership, have the assets transferred into the partnership, give them a very high price, and then wind up the partnership. You would now have, instead of a capital gain, a giant loss, which could be written off against future earnings.

This manoeuvre came to be called "the Little Egypt Bump," after a famous belly-dancer in Chicago in the 1930s, who was also attractive, round, and profitable; this name had more of a ring to it than "partnership step-up rules." The Little Egypt Bump had enormous potential in the oil and gas industries, among others, because it was the normal practice to carry assets on the books of such companies at the value at which they were purchased, not at market value. This is one of the ways companies get to be takeover targets, when someone notices that the assets are worth much more than they appear to be worth on the books. Oil in the ground, which was purchased for $2 a barrel in 1972, before the huge escalations of the next eight years, was worth, by 1985, ten or twelve times that much, but was carried on most company books at the old figure. If you could translate that difference into a tax break, it could mean hundreds of millions of dollars. You could, and it did.

Petro-Canada used the dodge to escape taxes in 1981, when it took over the Canadian assets of Petrofina, a Belgian company. The auditor-general of the time, Ken Dye, severely criticized the practice, but nothing was done to stop it happening again. There is no record, and no way of finding out, how many times it was used after that, or how much it cost, until the loophole was closed after the Gulf Canada deal came to light.

On July 19, 1985, behind a veil of secrecy, the federal government produced the necessary ruling. Little Egypt could bump. The deal could then go ahead, and it did, on August 2, 1985. The agreement called for O&Y to pay $2.8 billion for Chevron's 60.2 per cent of Gulf Canada. As soon as this went through, Gulf Canada rolled its assets into a partnership with Norcen Energy Resources, then part of the Black Group, owned by Conrad Black and his brother Montague, longtime Reichmann allies. Then the partnership was wound up, and the assets were redistributed between the partners. Now Gulf owned the same resources, but they had been written up for the partnership, and the company could write off the difference between the two figures against future earnings.

On August 17, 1985, fifteen days after the deal was signed, the *Globe and Mail* carried a major article by Christopher Waddell, outlining the complex tax arrangements, and that afternoon, John Turner, the Liberal leader of the time, claimed in the House of Commons that the taxpayer was giving O&Y, all in all, a billion-dollar tax break through the Little Egypt Bump. Paul Reichmann broke silence long enough to deny that; the break would be worth $500 million over five years, "with another $50 to $60 million saving after that time."[6] Well, thank God for that; I thought we were talking about real money.

There was another wrinkle to all this. Marshall A. Cohen, who was the deputy minister of finance when the Little Egypt Bump was approved, had been approached by Paul Reichmann early in 1985 about joining O&Y, for whom he had done some legal work before moving to Ottawa. He did not make any immediate decision, but, in October, he did go to work for the company, as president of Olympia & York Enterprises, a new holding company for O&Y's public investments. Cohen had been deputy minister of finance, not national revenue, but that didn't keep opposition members from raising the issue in Parliament, when the announcement of his O&Y job was made. Some details of the arrangements leaked out, and Prime Minister Brian Mulroney was forced to deal with the subject, evasively, at a press conference. It emerged that, soon after the O&Y approach, Cohen had consulted a lawyer to make sure that he would not find himself in a conflict of interest under the then-existing guidelines for such matters. Furthermore, he had informed both the minister of finance and the prime minister of the fact that he was considering a job offer from a firm about to benefit from a tax ruling to the tune of several hundred million dollars. He then excluded himself from any discussions on the matter, including, on one occasion, leaving a meeting to visit the washroom when the Little Egypt Bump came up for discussion.

He was busy in any event, he said later, working on the federal budget, which came down in March. Both the minister of finance, his boss, and the assistant deputy minister, his aide, had been involved in the ruling.[7] The offer of a job was made in February 1985 and the ruling was brought down on July 18, by which time Cohen had already accepted the O&Y offer. But the announcement that he was going to work for the company did not become public until October, when he began work there, and the date of the ruling was never made public. It appeared that there was something amiss. This caused Liberal leader John Turner to ask, on October 22, 1985:

> Mr. Speaker, my question is directed to the Minister of Finance. At his latest press conference the Prime Minister stated flatly that, in negotiating the tax ruling in favour of the purchase of Gulf Canada, it was handled completely by bureaucrats in the Department of National Revenue. However, the former Deputy Minister of Finance stated categorically that both the Minister of Finance and his Assistant Deputy Minister in charge of tax policy were intimately involved in the deal.
>
> What was the role of the Minister of Finance in negotiating the purchase of Gulf Canada? What was the role of his Assistant Deputy Minister in charge of tax policy?[8]

Michael Wilson, then finance minister, simply ducked, by replying, "Mr. Speaker, my role is to act as Minister of Finance."

This unhelpful response brought more questions, which made it clear that Cohen had been placed in an impossible position, which he could have avoided only by either quitting and joining O&Y, or turning down their offer. Turner asked:

> Why, in these circumstances, did the Minister of Finance keep Mr. Cohen as his Deputy Minister?

And:

If Mr. Cohen felt it sufficiently vital and if the Minister of Finance felt it sufficiently vital to exclude Mr. Cohen from any negotiations relating to the Gulf Canada purchase, why was Mr. Cohen left in charge of a budget which was bound to affect all major companies in Canada, including Olympia & York?[9]

Once he had been approached by O&Y, Cohen cut himself out of the discussion of what amounted to a tax expenditure of, using Paul Reichmann's figures, somewhere over $500 million, although he was, at the time, one of the key people in government dealing with the budget. He couldn't win; outsiders, and not just opposition MPS, were bound to see something wrong in the whole process, but there is no sign that the Reichmanns ever got the point. Their position was, and remains, that "the federal government did not give any 'tax break' in respect of the takeover of Gulf by Olympia & York. Rather, Revenue Canada through its advance ruling process issued a ruling confirming the application of existing provisions of the *Income Tax Act* to the facts of the acquisition." Perfectly true. Just as the law in its impartial majesty prohibited both rich and poor from loitering in public toilets, it allowed both billionaires and bums to deduct a few hundred millions from their taxable incomes, in the right circumstances. Marshall Cohen got drawn into the argument along the way, as was bound to be the case.

Cohen worked for O&Y for three years, before going to Molson Industries as president and chief executive officer of the Molson Companies, the job he holds today.

The whole affair left a bad taste in the mouth, and it didn't do much for the pocketbook, either. Not even the Reichmann pocketbook. In 1986 the price of oil, instead of soaring to $77 a barrel, which would have made the NEP look good, to say nothing of boosting the profits, and share prices, of Gulf Canada, drooped to $14.[10] Gulf shares sank accordingly. The takeover had been structured on an assumption of wellhead prices of $33.75 in 1985 and $35 in 1986; the minimum, Paul

Reichmann later told Dunnery Best of the *Financial Post*, was an $18 price. These were nice, conservative assumptions, but wrong.[11] Not to worry, the next stage in the drama was already under way.

On March 19, 1986, Albert Reichmann woke Bud Downing, the chairman of Hiram Walker Resources, from a dreamless sleep in a hotel room in California, where he was on holiday. It was eight o'clock in Toronto when Albert put in the call, but only five a.m. on the West Coast. Downing was not much mollified by what Albert had to tell him. The Gulf board of directors had decided to make an offer for the shares of his company that very morning. Between the last pass O&Y had made at Hiram Walker in 1981, and this one, Hiram Walker Resources had become even larger by merging with Interprovincial Pipeline Incorporated, controlled by Imperial Oil, Canada's largest independent petroleum company, through a share swap. Also between that pass and this one, Hiram Walker had changed its mind and invited the Reichmanns onto its board, but they rejected the overture. Now Gulf was offering $32 a share for 26 million common shares of Walker, then trading for $28, and $28.62 for a class of preferred convertible shares (which were non-voting shares that could be turned into voting shares), then trading for just under $26. The offer didn't cover all the Walker shares; Gulf only wanted 38 per cent of the voting shares, and it would only buy Canadian stock. With what O&Y already owned, this block would give the group 49 per cent, or effective control, of Walker. It would cost $1.2 billion.

Downing hustled back home to mount a defence that involved, among other people, Jimmy Connacher, as a paid adviser to Interprovincial Pipeline.

On March 26, the Hiram Walker board rejected the Gulf offer. At almost the same time, the company launched a lawsuit in the United States, claiming that the offer discriminated against U.S. holders of the stock, because only Canadian shares were being accepted. The press release announcing this action claimed that Gulf was making "a coercive attempt to pressure shareholders into a hasty decision."

The great gainers in these takeover wars are always the green-mailers, because they know prices will be shoved up relentlessly when the two sides bid against each other. Ivan Boesky, who was not yet in jail, rode in with a bunch of cronies and bought a block of Hiram Walker shares, which he later sold back for a nice profit.

But that wasn't a defence. The main defence that Hiram Walker and its advisers came up with was to create a new company, called Fingas, which would make a counter-bid for the Walker shares. Fingas would be jointly owned by Walker and the British conglomerate Allied-Lyons plc the mammoth British firm that owned thousands of pubs in Britain, hundreds of liquor stores, and such food brands as Baskin-Robbins ice cream and Tetley Tea. It was itself under threat of takeover by Elders IXL Limited, an Australian holding company. There was also a Canadian operation, including a liquor and wine company jointly owned by Allied and Corby's, which was in turn controlled by Walker. Sir Derrick Holden-Brown, the Allied-Lyons chief executive officer, denied that the purpose of the Fingas deal was to make his company too big for Elders, which was much smaller than Allied-Lyons, to swallow. That would have been the effect, though.

The idea was that Walker and Allied would put up the money – or, rather, the loans – to take the Walker shares into Fingas, and then Fingas would sell the liquor part of the Walker empire to Allied for $2.6 billion. This is the money that would pay for a share offer of $40 to beat back the Reichmanns. It was another of those wonderful pay-you-Tuesday-for-a-hamburger-today schemes that financial wizards create, and there is no point in complaining that all these gimmicks are stupid and wasteful, because they pour millions into the pockets of the boys and girls who dream them up.

Adding to the fun was the fact that Allied-Lyons had offices in First Canadian Place, on the sixth floor, while Interprovincial, which so far was a Walker ally, was up on the thirty-seventh, five floors above the Reichmanns. Walker was across the street.

On Easter Monday, March 31, Gulf, little knowing of the Fingas construction, announced that its $32 bid would apply to all shares –

thus knocking that U.S. lawsuit on the head – and that it had now lined up Interprovincial on its side. The bait had been that Home Oil, the Gulf subsidiary, would be dealt off to Interprovincial, and that Interprovincial would tender its shares, about 22 per cent of Walker, to Gulf. Before Interprovincial's board voted on this arrangement, Hiram Walker members of the board were ordered to leave. They left.

By now, the Walker board was convinced that the real purpose of the takeover bid was to break up the company and sell off its pieces. They, at least, were only selling off a little less than half the company – the liquor business. The same day, the Fingas construction was announced across the street, which rather wrecked the effect of the horn-tooting from Gulf. Fingas had topped their bid by $8, for 50 million Walker shares.

Everybody now moved over to the courts. On April 2, Olympia & York applied for an injunction to block the sale of Walker's liquor division to Allied, which it contended could not be allowed until the Walker shareholders had been consulted, and another injunction to set aside the Fingas offer, on the grounds that it was a sham. Which, of course, it was – although not a sham, a cynic might have noted, in any different league than, say, the Little Egypt Bump. Interprovincial wanted an injunction to block the Fingas deal until the Walker shareholders, which included themselves, could be consulted on the matter.

Part of the Reichmann case was an affidavit from Mickey Cohen, to which was appended a letter from Edgar Bronfman, the chairman of Seagram's, to Bud Downing, the Walker chief, in which Bronfman expressed a "strong interest" in buying the liquor business. Downing, Edgar Bronfman wrote, had refused to give Seagram's any information about the liquor division. This letter was introduced to suggest that Walker management and Allied, in selling the liquor business to Allied, were acting on their own behalf, instead of, heaven forfend, on behalf of the shareholders, because they wouldn't look at an offer from Seagram's. What it suggested rather more strongly was that, because the letter could only have come from the Bronfmans to O&Y, there was some kind of deal being cooked up with Seagram's.

On April 4, while these injunctions were being mulled over by Mr. Justice Robert Montgomery, Gulf upped its bid for Walker to $35 a share, conditional on the Fingas deal being blocked. The press release announcing this had barely cooled when, on April 9, Mr. Justice Montgomery came down with his ruling, rejecting all the injunction bids and putting the thing in a nutshell: "This is a battle over money. Gulf and IPL want the company and its assets at the cheapest possible price." He said that the Walker directors had acted at all times in the interest of their shareholders, but that "Neither Olympia & York nor IPL can represent [these] shareholders. They are antagonistic to and totally opposed to the interests of the other shareholders."[12]

He compared O&Y and IPL to "Goliath" and said that "an earlier Goliath was dispatched with a sling shot. Fingas is neither a sham nor a puppet as suggested by the applicants." Of course not, it was a slingshot. It would soon lose its sling.

The Reichmanns were still reeling from this abrupt and brutal public thrashing when they got some more bad news. TransCanada PipeLines, controlled by Bell Canada Enterprises, waded in with an unofficial offer of $36.50 for all the Walker shares. It would finance the deal in part by spinning off the liquor business to Allied-Lyons. The Walker board accepted this offer, even though it was never made firm, and unstrung its slingshot. The Fingas construction was dropped, and, instead, the board took two steps to protect itself. The first was to file – with the Securities and Exchange Commission in Washington, which likes to know about these things – a series of golden handshakes for the top eight executives of the firm: three years' severance pay, and other benefits. The second was to approve the sale of the liquor business to Allied, come what may. If the unstoppable Reichmanns got Walker, they would only get half of it, anyway. Neither of these moves was announced.

Paul Reichmann then gave an interview to the *Globe and Mail*, a snippet of which is quoted at the top of this chapter. "Had we known it [the takeover] would be unfriendly, we would not have gone near it," he said. "It's not our style."[13] There was a certain amount of flummery in this; there was nothing friendly about the Abitibi-Price takeover. But Reichmann made a more valid point when he said that he had not cleared up the misunderstanding about O&Y's intentions. "They thought we were going to dismember the company. Our purpose was the opposite. We wanted to diversify. We goofed because we didn't get the message across clearly enough until they were too deep into another route."

Later that same day, Gulf increased its bid to $38, although there was no indication that it had suddenly become a friendly takeover. The going was now getting too rich for other bidders, and TransCanada PipeLines pulled back. That was the end of the battle for Walker; their only hope had been that TransCanada would up its bid.

When the Walker board finally decided to accept the Gulf offer, the Reichmanns had caused Gulf Canada to pay $3 billion for 69 per cent of Hiram Walker Resources, half of which was on its way to Allied-Lyons. (So they would get 50 per cent of their money back.) Paul Reichmann said, in another *Globe* interview, that it was the liquor business, in large measure, that he was after, and that, had he known it was unobtainable, he might have pulled back.[14] The purpose of the takeover, he said, had been to diversify, and what they were left with was another oil and gas business, part of which, Home Oil, would shortly be dealt off to IPL in return for IPL's Walker shares and a package of cash and debentures.

Just the same, Paul Reichmann wasn't through. Mickey Cohen was installed as president of Hiram Walker, in place of Bud Downing, and eight of the Walker board were replaced with Gulf nominees. The devastating Montgomery decision was under appeal and another suit was launched to attempt to block the sale of the liquor business to Allied. That sale would have to be approved, in any event, by Investment Canada, the Tories' replacement for the Foreign Investment Review Agency. Maybe this thing could be turned around after all, if the Walkerville folks could be brought on side to lend support to the Ottawa lobbying effort to kill the Allied sale.

The Walker management, and the unions, wanted the sale to Allied-Lyons to go through; it was widely believed locally, that, if O & Y succeeded in killing the Allied deal, the takeover would end with Walker's liquor division going to the hated rival, Seagram's, and many of the locals going out on their ears.

To counter this hostility, Paul Reichmann called Bill Shields, the business editor of the *Windsor Star,* and asked him to send one of his reporters, Brian Bannon, to Toronto, for an exclusive interview. Since it was a Sunday, he would send the company jet down to pick the reporter up.[15] As it happened, the reporter couldn't get free until Monday, but he did get his exclusive, which the paper ran under a giant page-one headline that read, "REICHMANN VOWS NOT TO SELL WALKER DISTILLERY; 'JOBS SAFE.'"[16] Reichmann told Bannon that selling off the liquor division was never part of his plans for Walker, and that, while he had spoken to Edgar Bronfman, it was not to try to strike a deal so that Seagram's could take over that division; it was just a matter of information, to let him know that "the bid was for the purpose of diversification." The interview also indicated that Reichmann had a very limited understanding of how the liquor division worked. He said, in part, "Gulf and myself as the controlling shareholder of Gulf are making statements that the operations of Hiram Walker will not be affected in the Windsor area, nor will they be in British Columbia." In point of fact, a good deal of the work in Windsor had to do with overseeing the overseas and U.S. parts of the empire; if these were to be sold – and there was no reassurance on this point – Windsor jobs would have to be sacrificed. Reichmann just made things worse.

The union at Walkerville, which had always got along well with management, sailed into the fray with a Windsor press conference, hammering the Reichmanns and all their works. This helped to set the stage for a visit, on April 30, from Sir Derrick Holden-Brown, the Allied-Lyons boss, who guaranteed the Windsor workforce their jobs, something Paul Reichmann would never do; his reference to the jobs being safe merely indicated that he didn't plan to sell the liquor business. Holden-Brown was hailed as a saviour, and the Windsor city council fired off a note of support to Investment Canada.

By this time, the Reichmanns had hired a PR firm, which persuaded them that the only thing to do was for Paul Reichmann to go down to Windsor and hold a press conference, to turn public opinion around down there. He had never held a press conference before, and he shouldn't have held this one. It took place in the Canadian Club room of Hiram Walker's Windsor plant on the morning of May 27, 1986. Reichmann raised as many questions as he answered, when he spoke of the years of litigation that lay ahead with Allied-Lyons, which could only make the community, and indeed the entire industry, nervous. There were no assurances about jobs. Reichmann went back to Toronto, leaving behind a thoughtful silence.

On June 2, Sir Derrick was back in Canada, to announce a $9-billion lawsuit against Gulf Canada, Paul and Albert Reichmann, and a number of their executives, including Mickey Cohen, for interfering with the sale of the Walker liquor division to Allied.

That suit would never come to court. On July 9, the Ontario Supreme Court upheld the decisions by Mr. Justice Montgomery; two days later, Investment Canada gave its blessing. Now that it had won its point, Allied-Lyons, still battling with Elders IXL, and very much strapped for cash, made a deal with the Reichmanns under which the sale went through, and Allied immediately sold 49 per cent of Hiram Walker-Gooderham & Worts, the liquor division, back to Gulf, for $800 million.[17] The battle was over.

The Reichmanns had brought off their triple play, but Olympia & York had been subjected to its first extensive spate of bad publicity, and its executive vice-president, Paul Reichmann, had taken his first canter out into the fields of public exposure and come back covered in bruises.

By now, the Reichmanns' acquisitions had set them back more than $7 billion, even if O&Y was able to cut the bill down by selling off some of the parts along the way. Time to round up some more money.

CHAPTER TEN

The Campeau Capers

Men make mistakes not because they think they know when they do
not know, but because they think others do not know.
– Sholom Aleichem, 1920

$

In 1984, the Reichmanns were still in the throes of putting together the
World Financial Center in New York, and, throughout the Abitibi-
Gulf-Walker imbroglio, were patting bits of the empire back into place
every time the damn things threatened to come unstuck. What with
labour troubles, and leasing troubles, and money troubles, the New
York City project was a constant worry. However, the $250 million U.S.
loan from the Teachers Association in connection with the World
Finance Center had been signed, although not yet implemented; and
the fact of the signing was enough to help attract other lenders. There
was more good news: in August 1984, O&Y was able to announce that
Merrill Lynch & Company, the giant stockbroker, had agreed to lease
two of the four towers at the World Financial Center, which the stockbroker would, in part, own. As well, O&Y's U.S. arm would buy the

building Merrill Lynch currently occupied, at One Liberty Plaza, just up the street. The leasing program was given a boost, but it was hard to see how O&Y could make much money if it had to buy an old building every time it wanted to move customers into one of its new ones.

At the same time, the Reichmanns plunged into a complicated arrangement with Chicago-based JMB Realty Corp., which was expanding like a balloon by using a new and fancy way to own real-estate ventures. The company was named for three partners, Robert Judelson, Judd Malkin, and Neil Bluhm, who had grown up together in the west end of Chicago and attended the same high school.[1] Bluhm and Malkin became roommates at the University of Chicago, where they both took accounting degrees; Judelson became a real-estate broker. In 1969 they formed a partnership and, using seed money from the Continental Bank, went into real-estate syndication. Instead of turning to the banks for most of the money needed for a new project, the developer would sell off a large number of small packages of the equity in each deal to a syndicate of small and medium-sized investors. It was another variation on the magic elixir of finance, leverage. The developer needed very little money of his own, while he and the investors would both benefit from the rising value of the real estate. For the investor there were high returns, as long as real-estate prices kept rising, and a limited risk, because no investor could be held responsible for more than the equity he had put into the partnership in the first place.

Once a syndicated project was well launched, it could be leveraged in turn, using some of the assumed profits to finance a spate of new developments. If developers could actually teach buildings to breed, we would be saved a lot of trouble.

The tax laws smiled on these schemes by allowing high interest deductions and high depreciation to each of the partners in the syndicate, a fact that drew in a lot of rich Americans anxious to find investments where they could hide income. Syndication projects sprang up all over the United States, but the difference between JMB and most other syndications was that they invested mainly in high-quality projects, on the theory that, when an inevitable recession hit, these would be more likely to survive. They were right, and prospered accordingly through the 1970s and 1980s, when others stumbled.

Judelson dropped out in 1973, but JMB kept on growing, especially after a change in the law allowed pension funds, with their enormous resources, to join such schemes. In 1979 a separate company, JMB Developments, was formed to handle the partnership's own real-estate deals, as opposed to the syndicates it was managing for others. This company bought up successful developers and paid them to continue their work, while sopping up the profits. In 1983 JMB made a deal with Federated Stores, the retail chain, to form a company specializing in the ownership and running of department stores and shopping malls.[2]

A year later, O&Y formed a joint venture with JMB to buy three more skyscrapers in New York, for $1.4 billion. Fully a fifth of one of these buildings, at 2 Broadway, was occupied by Drexel Burnham Lambert, Inc.,[3] the stockbroker whose head of mergers and acquisitions, Michael Milken, was making millions and earning plaudits for his imaginative use of junk bonds. Boy, that looked good. Two more buildings were added to the package later, with O&Y serving as the managing partner for all five. The two buildings that O&Y had sold out of the Uris Package were more than replaced; the Reichmanns were now the largest private owners of office space in New York, outstripping the Rockefellers. Their eleven buildings contained 24 million square feet, 8 per cent of all the office space in the city.

Still, there was this constant need for money. Some more came in from the largest mortgage ever at that time, a $970 million U.S. whopper raised in March 1984, mostly through savings and loan associations, those galleons of gullibility that had been floated out onto the financial world by the deregulatory delirium of the Reagan administration. The S&Ls took mortgages on three O&Y buildings, at 2 Broadway, 1290 Avenue of the Americas, and the Atrium on Park Avenue, just beside the O&Y head-office building. The money did not come cheaply; the fifteen-year deal was based on mortgage bond rates that floated 1.75 per cent above the rates being paid on U.S. Treasury bills, which were adjusted every month. Under this deal, O&Y could pay as much as 17 per cent per annum for the loans.[4]

Expensive or not, the money was in place, the World Financial Center was moving towards its projected official opening in October 1985,[5] and the Reichmanns could turn their attention, for the rest of 1985 and 1986, to their dubious battle with the Abitibi-Price, then Gulf, then Hiram Walker takeovers. Those matters more or less in hand, they moved forward again, in June 1987, with a complicated, and brilliant, restructuring of the Gulf empire that caused more money to come shoaling out of the ground.

Gulf Canada shares were trading sluggishly at the time, in part because it was such an awkward lump of a thing. Olympia & York now owned 78.6 per cent of Gulf, which was an oil company, but also a holding company, since it in turn owned shares in Hiram Walker. In turn, again, Gulf was actually owned by Abitibi-Price. There might be, and there were, a lot of assets in the package, but stock-market investors tended to be wary of the shares, because it was so hard to evaluate them. If you wanted to invest in an oil company, you would do that, rather than invest in a company that happened to hold an oil company, among other things. This wariness directly affected O&Y's ability to use the potential leverage in the shares. If the stocks outside the company's own control were trading sluggishly, they were worth less; if they were worth less, so were the stocks O&Y held, because it is the day-to-day trading that sets their prices. If you wanted to use shares as collateral for bank loans, you needed to see them trading at a higher level.

Olympia & York accomplished this by breaking Gulf into three parts. Caesar, you will recall, did the same thing with Gaul. One company, Gulf Canada Resources Limited, was a pure oil and gas company. It was a new venture, and issued shares to provide financing. Abitibi-Price was cut out on its own, and a new company, GW Utilities Limited, was set up to hold the various bits and pieces gathered up in the Hiram Walker takeover.

The market responded by stampeding for the shares in Gulf Canada Resources. While 23 million shares were offered, investment firms handling the issue received orders for more than 45 million.[6] The brisk demand drove up the price, not only of the Gulf shares, but of the publicly traded shares in Abitibi-Price and Hiram Walker, as well. Gilt by association. Over a period of two months, Gulf shares went from $15 to $30, and the other companies fared almost as well.

Meanwhile, back at Hiram Walker, a new deal was distilling. The Reichmanns, letting bygones be bygones, swapped their stake in the liquor division of that company, which they had bought from Allied-Lyons in September 1986 for $800 million, back to Allied-Lyons. In return they got Allied shares worth $1.3 billion, earning themselves a nice profit, and became the largest single shareholder in that conglomerate, with about 10 per cent. *Maclean's* magazine trilled, "And, according to industry analysts in Toronto, the arrangement could produce a profit of up to $500 million for the media-shy Reichmanns."[7] Actually, you didn't need to be an industry analyst to work out that if you traded something you bought for $800 million for shares worth $1.3 billion, $500 million was the number to look at, but we'll let it pass. The phrase about the "media-shy Reichmanns" had nothing to do with the profit; it had just become obligatory to throw in some such phrase every time the brothers were mentioned. Paul Reichmann, for one, hadn't been particularly media-shy during the Gulf wars, he had just tried to get the stories written his way, which is not quite the same thing.

While all of these positive developments were going on, and, as we will learn in the next chapter, an exciting new project was being hatched in England, a small cloud was forming on the horizon, which would one day become a thunderstorm. Its name was Robert Campeau.

The Reichmanns had already encountered this energetic and erratic developer during the fuss over Royal Trustco, back in 1980. He had gone on to greater things, and now ran an empire comparable to the Reichmanns'. Not that he was much like the Reichmanns. Indeed, it is hard to exaggerate the differences in style between the Reichmanns and Campeau, even if *Fortune* magazine chose to quote an unnamed Toronto security analyst as saying that "their thinking on real estate is similar."[8] So it was, come to think of it; that thinking was based on the notion, which is perfectly sound, that over the long run, real estate will always appreciate in value. The corollary – so let's borrow some money and go out and buy some more because we can always pay for the debt off the increase in value – hasn't proven quite so sound.

Campeau was flamboyant, outgoing, boastful, and noisy. His home life, too, was eventful. He had had two children by his mistress, Ilse Luebbert, before he was divorced by his wife, Clauda Leroux. He had one family, Clauda's, in Ottawa, and another, Ilse's, in Montreal, and commuted. He and Clauda had one daughter and two adopted sons. When Clauda filed for divorce in 1969, Campeau went back to her, temporarily, and when he suffered a breakdown, she took him to a Montreal psychiatrist, Alan Mann, whom he later put on the board of Campeau Corporation. During a trip to Florida with Clauda, Campeau flew to New York, to spend a weekend with Ilse.[9] Then the divorce went through, he married Ilse, and when Clauda developed breast cancer and died, in 1979, his three oldest children were deeply upset because their father would not visit her in her final months.[10] There was also a messy lawsuit with his eldest son, Jacques.

Erratic he might be, but nobody ever said Campeau was stupid, or that he lacked nerve. He built an empire with annual revenues of $8.7 billion,[11] based on housing schemes, office towers, condominiums, and shopping malls all over North America. Then he decided to take his genius into the retailing business. In the spring of 1986, Thomas Randall, the chief executive officer of a small investment firm in New York, whom Campeau had asked to "look around" for potential investment vehicles for his growing pile of cash, mentioned a retail chain called Allied Stores to the Canadian entrepreneur, who had never heard of it.

It included, Randall told him, Brooks Brothers, AnnTaylor, Jordan Marsh, Bon Marché, Sterns, Garfinkel's, and Bonwit Teller – 670 stores

This is the only picture of Samuel Reichmann I have ever seen. It is on the carte d'identité issued to him in Tangier in 1946, when he was forty-eight.

Two views of the first great triumph of Olympia & York, the First Canadian Place complex in Toronto. In the photograph at right, you can see how the Bank of Montreal tower was designed with notches to provide more corner offices, and thus more high-rent space. The photograph below shows the Stock Exchange and Exchange Tower, next door. *(Photos by Joan Stewart)*

Whatever you say of the Reichmanns, they build magnificent buildings. Above, we are looking through the vaulting Winter Garden in New York's World Financial Center. At right, we are looking down on the complex from its taller, ugly neighbour, the World Trade Center. *(Photos by Walter Stewart)*

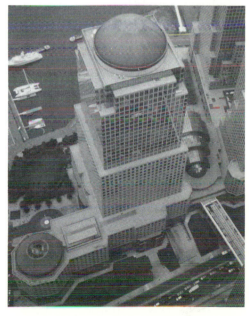

G. Ware Travelstead, the tall, tanned Texan in the middle, wears the satis-
fied smile of one who has just managed to unload Canary Wharf, and all
its troubles, onto Olympia & York. The others are, from left: Christopher
Benson, who was chairman of the London Docklands Development
Corporation when this picture was taken in July 1987; Michael Dennis of
O&Y; Jeffrey Parker of First Boston Inc., one of the finance partners; and
Reg Wood, then chief executive of the LDDC. *(Photo by the Docklands Forum)*

The new Canary Wharf rose from the ruins of the old. A fifty-storey
tower would replace this old warehouse. *(Photo by the Docklands Forum)*

Peter Wade, dressed as an undertaker, prepares to march in protest on
Canary Wharf. The not-too-subtle point was that the Travelstead scheme
would kill the community. *(Photo by the Docklands Forum)*

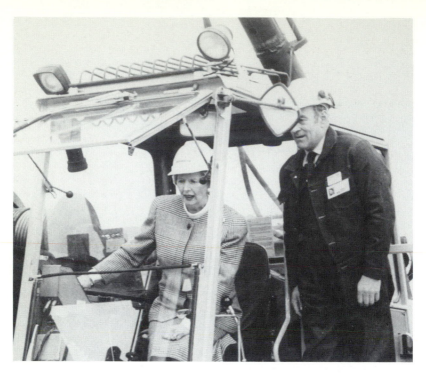

With characteristic aplomb, Prime Minister Margaret Thatcher prepares to drive the first, ceremonial, pile for the Canary Wharf development after the Reichmanns took it over. Her support proved crucial to getting the project going. (*Photo by the Docklands Forum*)

Lovely, isn't it? Empty, isn't it? We are looking towards Canada Tower from one of the many parks the developers provided for public use. This photograph was taken at noon, and there is no public in sight. (*Photo by Joan Stewart*)

One Canada Square is the giant tower, while the lower building is part of Cabot Square, which straddles the station. The vaulted structure on the left is the Canary Wharf station of the "Dear Little Railway," with a train peeping out. (*Photo by Joan Stewart*)

One of the rare photographs of Reichmann brothers Albert (left) and Paul (right) as they emerge after a meeting with their bankers in April 1992. They appear pleased; the bankers were not.(*Photo by Jeff Wasserman,* Financial Post)

in all. Campeau had heard of Brooks Brothers. The upshot was that Campeau wound up buying Allied Stores, for $3.7 billion U.S., almost every penny of it borrowed, after a bitter takeover battle which had the usual effect of such slugfests. That is, it doubled the value of the shares, but dumped the cost of the takeover onto the balance sheet of the targeted company, which went from easy affluence to a staggering debtload.

There were the usual machinations, with bids and counter-bids, and Allied Stores lined up the usual white knight; in this case, an octogenarian billionaire from Ohio named Edward DeBartolo, who was a long-time friend of Allied's chief executive, Thomas Macioce. He ended up as an ally of Campeau – the trouble with these white knights is that you never know which way their lances are going to point.

Campeau won Allied Stores with what is known as a "street sweep." The idea was to accumulate enough shares to control the company, and he had offered $66 a share for 40 million shares, 80 per cent of the total outstanding. He had picked up 2.1 million shares, 4 per cent of the company, over a period of months, from purchases made through various brokers, at an average price of $46.61 U.S. per share, [12] but once the word got out, share prices jumped, which is why he had to offer $66. Allied formally refused his $66-a-share offer and decided to sell to its white knight, DeBartolo, for $67 instead. Campeau, on the advice of First Boston, whose mergers and acquisitions department was masterminding the deal, dropped his formal offer. Everybody over at Allied Stores heaved a sigh of relief. Then, within half an hour, Campeau bought a block of 25.7 million shares, accumulated from the street by an investment dealer named Boyd Jeffries. On October 24, 1986, he had majority control of Allied. Provided, of course, that he could pay for the shares by the end of the year, when his tenders would expire.

Two New York banks, Citibank and First Boston, were advancing the cash to make the takeover work, and they required Campeau to put up $300 million U.S. in equity, just as you or I would be required to put up the down payment before the bank gave us a mortgage. He got $150 million of this by flying back to Canada and getting Citibank Canada to lend it to him, on the basis of his Canadian real-estate holdings. The American head office was not too pleased when this deal came down for signature, but felt it had to let it go through. [13]

So far, so good. But Campeau still had to come up with another $150 million, and the deadline at which the money was to change hands was fast approaching. Kim Fennebresque, a young lawyer with First Boston, came up with the idea of getting the Reichmanns interested. At a meeting in Toronto, Paul Reichmann politely declined. He didn't know anything about retailing, and would not invest in something he knew nothing about. [14] (He had already invested in a trust company, and in oil and paper, about which he had no great knowledge, but no one who wanted to keep on his right side would point that out.)

The man who finally did put up the missing $150 million was Edward DeBartolo. Not personally; he arranged for Citibank to lend it to Campeau on his backing, in a complicated arrangement that had Campeau Corporation buying a bundle of shopping centres from DeBartolo in return. Citibank had demanded equity from Campeau, then loaned him the money to cover its demand. The Allied Stores financing was finally in place on December 30, hours away from the deal's expiration, and Campeau bought the remaining shares from Allied itself for $69. The total bill came to $3.6 billion U.S., or well over $4 billion in Canadian funds. There was another $800 million U.S. in debt within Allied, which Campeau assumed, taking his total over $5 billion in Canadian funds. [15]

Campeau's success astounded New York, a town that had never heard of the man until he came crashing through the ceiling with his pockets stuffed with IOUs and junk bonds, which were what were used, in the main, to finance the takeover. There was money for everyone. The banks got about $200 million for their part in the fray, and another $50 million or so went to finders' fees, other bankers' fees, brokers' fees, junk-bond fees, disbursement fees, legal fees, and golden parachutes for the Allied Stores bigshots who wound up on the street. The company president got a going-away present of between $15 and

$20 million U.S. Four hundred of his employees got pink slips.[16] Have to cut costs somewhere, you know.

Campeau made a victory tour of the divisions of his new retail empire, and then went back to Canada to borrow more millions from the National Bank of Canada, so he could buy shares in his own company, which, he noted, was obviously about to take off. He already owned 76 per cent of the company; National loaned him $150 million – secured, in the main, by the shares themselves – to buy 13 million shares at just over $11.50 each.

Then he went to Toronto to talk to his financial advisers about a new plan. He would take a position in the shares of Federated Stores, a company about twice the size of Allied, which owned such well-known emporiums as Bloomingdale's, Abraham & Straus, Burdines, and Goldsmith's.

He was going to have to have some more cash, so he made another deal with the Reichmanns, selling them a half-interest in his latest Toronto building triumph, Scotia Plaza, for $50 million U.S. In addition, O&Y took over half the $440 million in mortgages against the building.

In early October, 1987, Campeau began buying Federated shares through a dummy corporation, Perez Capital, at $45 U.S. a share. When the stock-market crash of October 19 wiped about a trillion dollars off the value of companies trading on the world's major markets, Federated shares sank to $34. Campeau resolved that – at these bargain prices, he couldn't pass up the chance to take it over, lock, stock, and barrel. In January 1988, the board of Campeau Corporation, without a dissenting vote, approved Project Rose, the quaint name coined for the capture of one of the largest retailing chains in the world. On January 25, Campeau made a formal offer of $47 a share for all 90 million shares of Federated Stores, a total cost of $4.23 billion U.S. He would borrow that, too.

In New York the first reaction to Campeau's new onslaught was incredulity. Already up to his thighs in debt, where would he get the money? That was easy; Brooks Brothers, which was one of the most attractive parts of the Allied Stores holdings, would be sold. He had vowed, and the holders of the Allied bonds were relieved when he vowed, that he would never sell Brooks Brothers. Words, words. When the deed was done, and Brooks Brothers was sold for $750 million U.S., $550 million went to retire Allied debts; only $200 million was available to Campeau, but, for the moment, what counted was that the Canadian invader appeared to have at least some financing. [17]

The Federated board was expected to turn Campeau down flat, and it did, on February 5. Six days later Campeau increased the price to $61 a share, and announced that he would soon have more financing in place from Edward DeBartolo, his recent ally in the Allied operation, and from the now-famous Reichmann brothers of Toronto and New York.

Once more Campeau had flown to Canada to ask the Reichmanns to inject money into his operation by buying shares of Campeau Corporation. Once more they declined, and for the same reason: they did not know retailing. However, they did know real estate, and Campeau had nearly $3 billion worth of real estate in Canada, including such gems as Scotia Plaza, just east of First Canadian Place on King Street, of which they had just purchased half. He had also recently won the astounding victory of the Allied takeover, and was to be taken much more seriously than before. They made a deal, although it was not formalized until March 21, 1988.

On that day, Olympia & York Developments Limited entered into an agreement with Campeau Corporation to purchase a convertible debenture for $260 million U.S. This was a loan, paying interest of 7 per cent per annum, but with the feature that the bonds could be converted into shares at any time on or before March 31, 1994, at a conversion price of $26 U.S. per share. [18] If the Federated gamble worked, they could convert their shares; at $26 they would own ten million voting shares of Campeau Corporation, 25 per cent of what would then be a very profitable company. If it didn't, well, there was all that Canadian property to back the loan.

The Federated takeover proved even more complex, and irrational, than the Allied one. There is a rivetting description of all the infighting in John Rothchild's book *Going for Broke*, but, for our purposes, it is enough to know that Campeau wound up making a deal in March 1988 with R. H. Macy & Co. Inc., the white knight Federated had called in to help, for a joint purchase of the Federated chains. Macy's bought three of the Federated divisions, Bullock's, Bullock's/Wilshire, and I. Magnin, from Campeau for $1.1 billion. Fat lot of good it did Macy's, they had to seek bankruptcy protection not long after. [19]

With this resale in hand, Campeau paid $73.50 U.S. a share for Federated, instead of the $33 at which it had been trading six months earlier. The total cost of the deal was $6.61 billion, and Campeau was now in debt to the tune of $13.4 billion U.S. [20]

There was the usual division of spoils when the din died. For the executives of Federated, $28 million in golden parachutes, and, for thousands of Federated employees over the next few months, pink slips. By June of the next year, 3,400 employees had been fired. The interest on the borrowed money had to be paid, after all. The fees for the two lead banks, Citibank and First Boston, were another $200 million U.S., which, as John Rothchild points out, was "more in fees and charges than the entire Federated, with all its stores nationwide, earned in a year." [21]

Campeau threw himself a huge victory party, renting the Temple of Tandoor at the Metropolitan Museum for the purpose; but few outside his own circle wanted to come, and eventually the staff at First Boston, for whom he had rung up another banner year, made up most of the guests. Campeau made his usual long-winded speech of self-congratulation. It might have been an occasion for celebration for Campeau, but it was a dumb takeover, at a dumb price, at the wrong time. Within weeks it was clear to anyone who hadn't yet grasped the point that Federated could never generate enough cash to pay off the loans incurred in its own acquisition, and Campeau began to dismantle the newly bought chain to cover some of the costs of its purchase. He sold the Filenes and Foley's divisions to the May Company for $1.5 billion U.S., to cut debt. Then he withdrew cash from AnnTaylor, another of the (hitherto) successful chains in the Allied Stores empire, for the money to pay off $500 million he had borrowed from two Canadian banks. But in the end he didn't get $500 million, only $407 million, by dumping AnnTaylor. Then he sold Gold Circle, MainStreet and The Children's Place, three other successful Federated chains, for another $562 million U.S. It was still not enough.

But this was not something the Reichmanns had to worry about, was it? They, after all, were not that involved; they had bought half of Campeau's Scotia Plaza, and loaned him $260 million, which was covered tenfold by his Canadian assets. But that was the limit of their connection with the man. Wasn't it?

Despite some subterranean rumblings, their own empire seemed eminently secure. They had gobbled up more companies, buying 19 per cent of Sante Fe Southern Pacific Corporation, the railway company, and 15 per cent of Sante Fe Energy Resources, which had real-estate, energy, and forestry interests.[22] Their shares in Abitibi-Price were not doing well, but Gulf was all right, and the Walker shares they had converted to Allied-Lyons looked solid, too.

If Campeau had problems, they could afford to consider them with a certain detachment and even disdain. They were sitting on top of the world.

It seemed only right that they should fall off.

PART III

The Road to Canary Wharf

The Central London communications infrastructure is old, tired, overcrowded and near to collapse. The point has been reached where one relatively minor incident, traffic accident or inconsiderate parking causes complete chaos and gridlock, compounded by the hordes of sightseers, tour buses and weight of business traffic. The fares policy on public transport and lack of discipline on the roads is bound to culminate in disaster. In short, Central London is, for business purposes, moribund.

– Confidential Memo, Peter Corfield to senior executives at Ogilvy-Mather advertising, entitled "Why Canary Wharf?" February 13, 1990

CHAPTER ELEVEN

Down in the Docklands

It was the haunt of river pirates, revenue officers, scuffle hunters, mudlarks and night plunderers.

– Colm Kenigan, 1982 [1]

$

One morning in the summer of 1985, Archibald Cox, the chairman of Morgan Stanley International, a subsidiary of the giant investment banking firm, and Michael von Clemm of Crédit Suisse First Boston, a joint venture between Swiss and American merchant banks, took a taxi out to the Isle of Dogs, in London's east end, for a look around. They were fed up with the prices their companies had to pay for office space in the City, the financial centre of London, fed up with the buildings, designed for an earlier age, fed up with the British assumption that nothing could be, or should be, improved, and that the City would naturally evolve into the financial centre of the emerging European Community. What was particularly infuriating was that the City, which has its own local government, had regulations framed so as to prevent any large new building projects within the Square Mile of the financial district, the area centred on Threadneedle Street and the Bank of England. The lads in the bowler hats wanted to keep office space short and prices high; at this time they were running as much as £35 a square foot for annual rent.

Merchant banks need huge open spaces for their trading floors; they also need buildings especially constructed for modern communications. The distance between floors has to be much greater than that in standard-built buildings, for one thing, or there is no room for all the conduits required for the impressive electronics that are part of modern banking. Von Clemm thought he might have found the answer, and had brought Cox out to have a look at it.

It wasn't much, an unimposing peninsula thrust into the Thames three miles east of the City: acres and acres of desolate quayside, abandoned railway sidings, mudflats, decaying buildings, dank canals, and dreary homes, relieved, here and there, by bright new office buildings rising above the mire on pilings of subsidies and tax breaks offered by the government's whizzy new authority, the London Docklands Development Corporation. There was also a small scattering of elegant waterside homes, in which none of the locals would ever be able to afford to live. Over everything lay the exotic, uneven history of the Isle of Dogs.

This area used to be called Stebunheath Marsh, or Stepney Marsh, back in the fourteenth century, because at high tide it was often flooded by the Thames. An embankment was built which gradually encircled the marsh and, by the 1600s, the area was drained so that it could be used for pasture. Windmills were built along the western embankment, facing the river's Limehouse Reach, mostly for pumping water, and cattle and sheep were brought to the rich marsh grasses for fattening, on their way to the markets in London. Today this part of the island is called Millwall. Until early in the nineteenth century, the place must have looked like a bit of Holland that had somehow floated across the Channel; flat, windswept lands carved up by drainage ditches. Except that, unlike Holland, there were almost no people here, only cattle and sheep, with perhaps a sprinkling of ghosts at night. Then the docks came.

From the days of Elizabeth I, when British merchants began to follow British adventurers (often they were the same) to the far corners of the earth, ships poured their cargoes into the London area. A Royal Commission was established in 1560, to select and establish licensed wharves, where all goods entering the port of London could be landed. The Queen wanted the incoming stuff to go somewhere she could collect her duties. Twenty "legal quays" were created between the Tower of London and the site of Tower Bridge, with customs officers appointed for each, to collect the money.[2] These quays came to be the place where four out of every five tons of imports to England were landed,[3] and by the late seventeen-hundreds, the congestion in what was called the "London Pool" was appalling. Queues of ships stretched along the river, moving up towards the legal quays a few yards each day; sometimes it took as long as six weeks to find an open wharf. Accordingly, Parliament passed The West India Dock Act of 1799, a bill permitting construction of docks on the Isle of Dogs.

The new docks were given a monopoly on the trade from the West Indies, running for twenty-one years, after which other docks began to sprout nearby, and facilities for handling cargoes from areas other than the West Indies were built by other companies. Docks especially built for the handling of one particular cargo became more common as the nineteenth century wound on, docks such as Tobacco Dock, the Mahogany Sheds, and Rum Quay. Rum Quay ran right down the middle of the north end of the Isle of Dogs. High walls were built around the docks in an effort, if not to stop the thievery attendant on all such enterprises, at least to make it more difficult. Armed guards patrolled around the prison-like warehouses that sprang up beside the wharves.

Industry moved in, rope, iron, and chain-cable firms, corn millers and match manufacturers, bringing the belching chimneys, grimy factories, and the hard working conditions common in that time. Some of the workers who came in to fill the jobs in the docks and factories or to service those who did – coopers, lock-keepers, clerks, carters, stable boys, smiths, porters, stevedores, laundresses, street-sellers, shirt-makers, and nurses – came from Poplar, Limehouse, or other parts of nearby London. Others came from as far away as Scotland, Wales, and Italy.[4]

When a recession struck in 1866, and a number of large firms went bankrupt, wages were cut savagely, workers were laid off, and contemporary newspapers reported widespread destitution – even starvation.[5] This was always a tough area; Charles Dickens wrote of the opium dens in nearby Limehouse, and Jack the Ripper stalked the streets nearby. His 1888 murders were within a long knife-throw of the West India Docks.[6]

In the 1870s, as local industry recovered from the recession, the workforce began to respond to its harsh conditions by forming unions, which were savagely put down, until in 1888 a strike of hundreds of exploited women in the match factories (they were called "match-girls," though many were long past girlhood), and a dockers' strike the following year, brought on a wave of public revulsion, and some modest reforms. Militant unionism and political activism, especially among the dockworkers, became an ingrained tradition.

But the competition between these docks and the great docks built nearby in the Victorian era, which could handle the massive new steam freighters, kept wages abysmally low, and the population that gradually swelled the nearby towns and hamlets was, by and large, poor, ignorant, and desperate, even after the private dock companies were nationalized as part of the formation of the Port of London Authority in 1909.[7]

Eve Hostettler, a local historian, paints a grim portrait of life in the area during the first half of this century.

> Life depended on wages, charity or poor relief. Wages varied according to skill, personal fitness and the state of the economy. Living standards on the Island varied, too. Some people could afford to dress up in best clothes, have photographs taken, buy a

piano to put in the parlour and go on a holiday to Yarmouth. At the same time a man could die of starvation in Samuda Street, and when school photographs were taken, children who had no boots or shoes to wear had to sit at the back of the class so that their bare feet would be hidden from the camera.[8]

During the Second World War, the dock areas, and indeed the whole east end of London, where much of the city's industry was centred, were pounded, night after night, in bombing raids. Whole streets of houses, and a third of the factories, were destroyed. Hundreds were killed, thousands more left the area, never to return, and the island's population dropped from about thirty thousand to eight thousand.

Then came a brief, blissful period of prosperity and rejuvenation, as the docks were rebuilt and began to hum with activity once again. By the early 1960s, sixty-five-million tonnes of cargo were moving through the area annually, wages were up, and unemployment down, not just here, but in the vast complex of docks stretching five miles upstream to London Bridge. The old Rum Quay was refurbished to handle tomatoes from the Canary Islands and was renamed Canary Wharf. It did well, too.

But the pendulum swung again. By the late 1960s, competition from European ports, combined with poor labour relations and a lack of space for modern shipping and cargo-handling techniques along the warehouse-crowded river, doomed the entire Port of London. Containerization had revolutionized shipping, and required containerization ports built for the purpose, of which there were none on the Isle of Dogs. Trucks to and from the Continent were rolling on and off ferries at Channel-side, cutting into business even more. The area was becoming "dedockized," a word that would soon be accepted into the *Oxford English Dictionary*. At the same time, factories shut their doors, one by one, and the great, swinging cranes stopped, fell silent, and then vanished from the skyline. The wharves sank back into despair, the workers crept away to look for work elsewhere, or went on the dole. The last to close were the Royal Docks, in 1981. Only the dock at Tilbury, twenty-six miles downstream from Tower Bridge, remained in operation. Employment in the Port of London fell from 50,000 in 1960 to 3,000 in 1985; in the Docklands area alone, 18,000 jobs vanished, and unemployment stood at 24 per cent in 1986.[9]

It was only after the region began to sink into its slough of despond that it acquired the name "the Docklands." A political catch-phrase. Peter Walker, then secretary of state for the environment, flew over in a helicopter one day in 1971, and pronounced that the section, ten square miles on both banks of the Thames, from Tower Bridge downstream to the Royal Docks, just east of the Isle of Dogs, would be called "the London Docklands."[10]

In 1974 the local governments, led by the five boroughs in the immediate area – Tower Hamlets, Lewisham, Greenwich, Leatham, and Southwark – formed an association, the Docklands Joint Committee, the DJC, to do something about their collective plight. This committee had councillors from each of the boroughs, and representatives of the Greater London Council, or GLC, the body that had overriding planning authority in the region. Within two years – at lightning speed, by the usual pace of such things – the DJC produced the Docklands Strategic Plan, addressed to the GLC, an ambitious, expensive, multi-purpose plan for the entire area, with an emphasis on housing, retraining, and education.

Ben Kochan, a long, lanky, bearded former journalist who now works with the Docklands Forum, one of the local lobby groups that supported the plan, says, "We would use the land that was becoming vacant to address the local needs of people living in and around the area. Not," he adds, "the needs of developers."[11] The docks were to be filled in, where that had not already been done, and used for housing estates and parks. The area was to be consolidated and improved, not drastically altered, and the money would come from government, not venture capital.[12]

The key principle of the plan was put this way:

To use the opportunity provided by large areas of London's Dockland becoming available for development to redress the housing, social, environmental, employment/economic and communications deficiencies of the Docklands area and the parent boroughs and thereby to provide the freedom for similar improvements throughout East and Inner London."[13]

East London had always been ill-served by the extensive city underground. While you could get to the West End from the City in minutes, there was no tube link to this area at all. To remedy this, the Docklands Joint Committee favoured a plan then being promoted by London Transport to extend a tube line already under construction. It was called the "Fleet Line," because it would run from the West End to Fleet Street, across the river and east. In all, it would cross and recross the Thames five times, so the name would later be changed to the "River Line."[14] We will meet it again.

It was not, perhaps, the best time to advance a project that would cost the central government, as well as the GLC, an indefinite, but large, sum of money over a period of years. Nonetheless, the committee began to implement the plan, reclaiming land, building social housing, planning new schools. But money was tight, and, by 1979, not much progress had been made when the roof, a.k.a. Maggie Thatcher, fell in. Within a very short time there would be an entirely new approach, a free-enterprise approach, an approach that would generate jobs, clear away the tangles of red tape, unleash the powers of the private purse, to make this area not only the pride of London but the financial centre of the world.

Or not, as the case might be.

CHAPTER TWELVE

Trickling Down on the Isle of Dogs

The Isle of Dogs is a pertinent lesson in the key factors which under-mined urbanism in the Thatcher years: the dominance of the car, the moral imperatives of corporate interest over private ones, and the trend towards large scale, single land use development. With no civic vision other than to regenerate, the LDDC had produced a new office city for London where in the early nineties 50 per cent of the property lay empty, only 10 per cent of the jobs created had gone to local people, and investment in roads had exceeded that in housing and environ-ment put together.

  – Dr. Brian Edwards, 1992 [1]

$

Peter Wade wants to make one thing clear. "You're not going to get any company line from me." The formal requests for interviews with Olympia & York staff in London have all been duly noted, and filed for future reference – sometime, perhaps, in the next century. When I ask for Wade by name, the PR lady for O&Y tells me shortly, "He doesn't work here any more." But Ben Kochan, the young political activist with the Docklands Forum, has his home telephone number, and Wade is at home. Wade used to be in the councils of righteousness, Kochan tells me, or, to put it another way, he was once the sharpest thorn in Canary Wharf's side. Then he went to work for Olympia & York, as the head of their Community Affairs Department. Now they have fired him. He should be worth talking to. Wade snorts when I tell him on the phone that I understand he doesn't work for O&Y any more. "Fat lot they know," he says. "I was laid off like everybody else, but then the phone calls started to come in, and they've brought me back again, part-time." He tells me to come to see him at his office in Canary Wharf the next day.

I feel it necessary to warn him that, if his employers knew about this interview, Olympia & York would probably forbid it.

"Then we won't tell them, will we?" he suggests.

The next day I run the gauntlet of receptionists and security guards and find, when the elevator door slides smoothly open on the thirtieth floor of One Canada Tower, a shirtsleeved, thick-set man of fifty, who shakes hands, looks me up and down, grunts, and says, "Follow me." We trudge along eerily silent corridors, past the scale models of O&Y developments (Toronto's Queen's Quay, New York's World Financial Center, London's Canary Wharf), between abandoned offices, where empty chairs and desks stare out through the floor-to-ceiling windows, along hallways where hastily packed cartons bear mute testimony to the sudden emptying of the building, and finally to Wade's office, a bright, cluttered, medium-sized office overlooking the mostly completed first stage of the project. I turn on my tape recorder. I tell him I guess he is probably, what with one thing and another, pretty cheesed off with the Reichmann brothers.

"Wonderful men," he replies.

As he begins to talk, swinging back and forth in his chair, picking up and laying down a pencil, looking out the window and then back again, jumping up to find documents to lay before me, I begin to understand. To comprehend the passion of a plain, sturdy man like Wade – "I was born here, lived here all me life" – for such exotic birds as the Reichmanns, you need to know something of the background of this place, and of the Reichmanns' predecessor here, Gouch Ware Travelstead, formerly of Texas.

The election of the Thatcher government ended the Joint Committee's Docklands Strategic Plan as effectively as if it had been towed out into the river and sunk. England had moved into a new world, where public enterprise was out and private enterprise in, and spending money on sluggards and layabouts who not only weren't holding down jobs, but also tended to vote Labour, was not to be countenanced.

"Her new environment secretary, Michael Heseltine," writes John M. Hall,[2] "also took the synoptic, bird's-eye view. He also viewed the tripartite DJC as a hindrance to the regeneration (new word) of the area. From now on, the private sector would lead and fund, outweighing public investment by a ratio of 5:1. We were now in the era of 'demand-led planning,' or, to use a once-popular lyric: Que sera, sera — whatever will be, will be."

The overriding needs of the area, then as now, were low-cost housing and jobs. So what would demand-led planning provide? Office complexes and small factories, with a dash of expensive waterside mansions, of course. They pay.

In 1980 Michael Heseltine's Department of the Environment, which, in Britain, includes urban development, created the London Docklands Development Corporation, which came into being on July 2, 1981. All of the planning authority once held by the local councils was immediately vested instead in the LDDC. (The Greater London Council would be disbanded in 1985, leaving the thirty-two London boroughs to get on with it by themselves.) But the LDDC was not, in any normal sense, a community-planning authority. It was, instead, a developer's handmaiden, charged with a duty to "regenerate" – the phrase was never defined – the entire Docklands area, as quickly as possible, as economically as possible, and as privately as possible. The LDDC had only to clear the way. It was given the power to assemble land by expropriation, and a budget that would come directly from the Department of the Environment, or DOE, with very little scrutiny from anyone outside, and none at all from the five boroughs whose lives it would change so drastically.

The LDDC was only one, although by far the largest, of eleven Urban Development Corporations established in England, Scotland, and Wales, with the deliberate intent of bypassing the local councils, a regrettable number of whom were dominated by Labour, and making life easier for private enterprise, while regenerating the inner cities of Britain.[3]

The way the enabling legislation put it, "regeneration" would be achieved by "bringing land and buildings into effective use, encouraging the development of existing and new industry and commerce, creating an attractive environment and ensuring that housing and social facilities are available to encourage people to live and work in the area."[4]

While housing was mentioned, it was the last of the duties assigned to the LDDC, and there were no provisions to plan for it. Indeed, there was to be no planning in any real sense; that would come from the private sector, and the jobs and homes would trickle down from the prosperity that was bound to flow from the freeing of enterprise. (Despite the rhetoric about the private sector leading and funding, however, the poor old thing would be burdened down with a few billion pounds of public money to see it on its way.) Jobs would ooze out of the ground. "The creation of new jobs or the maintenance of existing jobs will flow naturally from much that the corporations are doing to secure regeneration."[5] And again, "If you regenerate the land automatically it will solve the problems of employment. The purpose of what [Urban Development Corporations] are to do is to create the physical environment where employers indeed want to come in due course to provide employment."[6] Have faith, brother, and all else will follow.

The creation of "the physical environment" was to be achieved in the usual free-enterprise way, with government handouts. The act created creatures called "Enterprise Zones," areas selected by the Department of the Environment to massage things along. The very first of these zones was a five-hundred-acre swath at the north end of the Isle of Dogs, including Canary Wharf. The goodies included cheap land – the LDDC would assemble the package, then sell it to the developer – a ten-year exemption from all taxes on commercial and industrial property within the zone – including corporation taxes – depreciation allowances of 100 per cent on capital expenditures for industrial and commercial buildings, faster and more simplified Customs procedures to import materials, exemption from industrial training levies, the waiving of most planning permissions – including environmental ones – and speedier administration of whatever rules remained in force.[7]

One thing the government would not, dammit, not, provide, was the transport infrastructure. Let the developers who would benefit pay the shot. It was the Thatcher way. For now. The Enterprise Zones would not last forever; they had a ten-year term, so that those created in 1982, like the one around Canary Wharf, would expire in 1992. And there would be no new ones. After an independent review of their operations in 1987, which concluded that they were, in effect, a licence to print money, the secretary of state for the environment announced in September 1987 that they would be discontinued "save in exceptional circumstances."[8]

It's interesting that the loud protests we hear about government interference so seldom cover the business of handing out billions to private corporations; at the Docklands they were to get the stuff in sackfuls. But that didn't matter, did it? Because the money would trickle down and fertilize housing and jobs as it landed.

Just to end the suspense, you may want to know how the trickling down worked out. Not too well. Between 1981, when the act was passed, and 1990, according to a written answer given to Parliament on August 5, 1991, a total of 41,421 jobs were attracted to the Docklands area. This is the figure used by government and the London

Docklands Development Corporation, to show that their policies have "created" 41,000 jobs. The answer goes on to note, however, that 24,862 jobs were transferred from other places to the Docklands, and 20,532 others were lost. In all, there was a net loss of more than 4,000 jobs, and the best jobs were going to people who had been brought into the area, not the locals. There were, for example, several hundred printers and journalists brought in from Fleet Street, to work at the *Telegraph* and the *Financial Times*, among others, as part of a process of the widespread shedding of labour by the newspapers, as they moved the papers to modern, more-productive printing plants.

In London, I was given a copy of a document called, intriguingly, "Bull Points," prepared for the environment secretary to use in answering questions about the Docklands. Sure enough, it has a paragraph that reads, "Transformed the local economy: new diversified economic base, with new forms of employment. About 1,500 companies moved in and 41,000 jobs attracted or created (March '91.)" An LDDC pamphlet entitled "A Decade of Achievement," uses the same figure. Both were prepared after the parliamentary answer showing a net job loss was tabled. In July 1981, there were 36,805 unemployed in the Docklands; in April 1991, 62,293. [9]

The automatic generation of housing didn't work much better. The LDDC had no specific house-building function, and indeed, it denied at first that it had any responsibility even towards the people made homeless by its expropriations. Let the boroughs look after them, although the boroughs were given no money with which to perform this task. The number of families defined as "homeless" in the Docklands rose by 284 per cent between 1981 and 1991; this was a much greater percentage than in London as a whole, where the increase was 66 per cent. (In 1989 there were 33,375 households in the Greater London Area officially designated as "homeless"; 39.7 per cent of all public-sector housing was designated as "unfit" or in need of major renovation; 24.3 per cent of private housing stock fell into the same category, while the waiting list for public housing hit 222,458 in

1990.)[10] The "demand-led" building was, predictably, speculative building of homes far beyond the reach of the residents. As Nicholas Breach, author of *East End & Docklands*, writes:

> We are given acres of high-priced identikit estates, lacking the remotest spirit of community, and aimed exclusively at the upwardly mobile (during those halcyon days when it seemed that property would appreciate forever it was the declared intention of many to take a quick profit and get back to Chelsea or Fulham as soon as possible). The interests of the original residents, in the enterprise zone especially, have been neglected, often scandalously; viable local businesses have been and still are being displaced, and housing prices are hopeless. For local people employment opportunities within the zone are pathetically few, no more than ten per cent of the whole. They are victims of the draconian powers vested in the London Docklands Development Corporation: and it is private gain, not public good, that has dictated policy.[11]

Housing and jobs remain the crying needs in London generally, and in the Docklands in particular, and the billions spent there have only resulted in a worsening situation.

Of course, that is not how it was seen at the time. At the time, the experiment with this region was, as Eric Sorenson, the current chief executive officer of the LDDC told me in an interview, "the showcase for Thatcherism." Turning the private sector loose would show what wonders could be worked without any heavy-handed bureaucrats sticking their long noses in.

If you want to put up a fish-and-chip stand in London today, you have to apply for a planning permit, and allow twenty-eight days for public comment. When a ten-million-square-foot, $8-billion complex was approved for Canary Wharf, there was no permit, no delay, and no public input. Worked well, didn't it?

When the LDDC was set in motion, developers must have thought they had died and gone to heaven. Instead of red tape, tax breaks;

instead of nosy questions about the environment, subsidies; instead of demands for low-cost housing as part of the project, grants in aid.

To make sure everything went smoothly, the LDDC was given an appointed board of thirteen members, responsible to the Department of the Environment, but with no local accountability whatever. The board members have always been almost entirely chosen from the world of property development and construction, and the chairman has always been a developer. Board meetings are always closed. Dr. Brian Edwards, senior lecturer in urban design at the University of Strathclyde, notes, "The main benefit of a property-dominated LDDC board has been to attract many of the big commercial developers to the area, and to put little in their way when grand schemes were being hatched."[12]

Indeed, that was the whole point. Gareth Bendon, chief of the LDDC's executive office, told me, "We were set up to provide a single-minded, fast-track organization, with powers to assemble land, through powers of compulsory acquisition, and to exercise government's control powers."[13]

The LDDC had a government's muscle, and bankbook, without the need to report to, or even pay the slightest heed to, the local communities in which it operated.

It was the opportunity opened by the Enterprise Zone concept that drew Michael von Clemm and Archibald Cox down to the Isle of Dogs. Between them they could see a need for anywhere from 150,000 to 300,000 square feet of office space for their companies over the next few years, and, at the rate of £35 a square foot that landlords were now asking in London, that came to a pretty penny – £4.5 million a year. They'd be better off to come out here, take advantage of all the tax breaks, and stick up their own building. They would be doing exactly what earlier merchants had done, moving east from the crowded London Pool to the open spaces farther along the Thames. The same open spaces.

It was not that simple, of course; nothing ever is. But the two banks,

Morgan Stanley and Crédit Suisse First Boston, formed a syndicate, and brought in colourful Texas developer G. Ware Travelstead, who had already done some work for Morgan Stanley, to draw up a plan. And that's how Canary Wharf was reborn. (Although G. Ware doesn't rate a mention in the O&Y material on Canary Wharf; you are invited to conclude, if you like, that the Reichmanns thought the whole thing up themselves.)

Travelstead, a large, handsome, loud-spoken man, came through the area like a Texas tornado, spouting facts and figures and irritating many of the locals intensely. He produced a master plan calling for ten million square feet of buildings, with (to quote from his original specs):

- A minimum of 8.8 million square feet of offices and state-of-the-art financial trading floors.
- Two hotels, with some 800 rooms and associated conference and banqueting facilities.
- A minimum of 0.5 million square feet of shops of all kinds and other support amenities, such as pubs, restaurants, and bank and building-society branches. [14]

Nothing in there about parks, but there would be parking "for up to 11,000 cars." This would be contained in a series of multi-level car parks slung over the tracks of a railway line to serve the project, called the Docklands Light Railway, and the buildings would go on up from there. The effect would be that of a "city above the city," looking down on London. The plan would include twenty-four buildings in all, dominated by three huge office towers, taller than anything in Europe, a Canary Concourse with a glass roof, and a Founders' Court, "a hard paved area featuring an oval basin with a fountain." The project would be built in two stages, with the opening stage costing £1.5 billion, and the whole thing costing £3 billion, and taking seven to ten years to build. Construction would begin in February 1986. It would be developed by the Canary Wharf Development Company, which was made up of First Boston International, a subsidiary of First Boston, and the

Travelstead group, along with Crédit Suisse, which had been First Boston's partner in this venture from the start.

The LDDC loved it; the locals, who immediately dubbed it "Wall Street on the Water," hated it. There was no provision that they could see to guarantee any jobs for them, and attempts to approach Travelstead or his minions were generally rebuffed, sometimes, but not always, politely. When the local community associations demanded a public inquiry before the plan was implemented, Travelstead threatened to kill the project, and that was the end of that. [15] The local complaints were ignored.

The Canary Wharf project was on a scale quite unlike anything that had yet been established, or even contemplated, for the Docklands. The original expectation had been that somewhere between four to eight million square feet of office space would be summoned into existence over the years on the Isle of Dogs. [16] This one project would stuff in more than that in one lump. So far, there had been a series of small-scale developments, some of them attractive, some ugly. Stephanie Williams, author of *Architecture Guide to the Docklands*, described them as "a series of absurdly coloured and unrelated sheds and simple buildings." [17] There was no infrastructure, either in place or on the drawing boards, no public transport, roads, housing, or schools for anything remotely like this. It takes, as one of the key government planners who worked on Canary Wharf told me, "about ten to thirteen years to prepare for a project like this. But no one seemed to be concerned about that."

Huge problems loomed in the minds of everyone who thought about it for a moment, including the local councils. The main problem had to do with transport. A project like this would have fifty thousand, eventually one hundred thousand, people working in it. How were they going to get there? And go home?

At this time the roads were a mess, bus service was uncertain, taxis were few and far between. The LDDC had been instrumental in getting an elevated light railway started, but the Docklands Light Railway would not be complete until August 1987, and would have an initial capacity, on the rare occasions when it was running well, of 1,500 passengers an hour. If you had to get a workforce of, say, 50,000 to and from the site every day, and it took 33 hours to transport them, one way, you had a problem.

The most outspoken opponent of Canary Wharf when it was unveiled was Peter Wade, then chairman of the Association of Island Communities, the largest community organization in the country. He had grown up on the Isle of Dogs, the son of dock-workers, left school at the age of fifteen, and went to work on the tugs. "I'd been identified as dock fodder at the age of thirteen. That was all right by me; very nearly two hundred years my family goes back on the river." When containerization hit, and he could see the writing on the wall, he went back to school, at the age of thirty-two. "Did my youth and community diploma, and then worked for the London Education authority for fourteen years," while, on the side, continuing to run tugs. One of his projects was a tug called the *Christopher W.*, named for a grandson who had died. It was devoted to providing training cruises, and, incidentally, courses in sociability, to youngsters from the Isle of Dogs. Wade had been elected chairman of the association in 1980, and was immediately flung into battle against the LDDC.

Wade, a cheerful man with an accent that announces his background beyond mistaking, remembers that "we had been used to working with the Greater London Council, and here was this quango [quasi-non-governmental organization] coming in with private powers, taking them away from the locally elected body."[18]

After the bill setting up the LDDC had gone through the House of Commons in 1980, Wade spent fifty days in the House of Lords, petitioning, in vain, for a change in the law that allowed elected councillors to be bypassed by government appointees. Over the next five years he led protests – once, dressed as an undertaker, in a "Funeral for Democracy" march across the Isle of Dogs – and did everything he could to slow down, derail, or otherwise impede the LDDC.

"We weren't against regeneration. We're not Luddites, you know. We were against the make-up of the LDDC, and I was fighting for the principle that you couldn't simply set aside locally elected people and still retain a democracy. I still believe that."

He also wanted a guarantee of jobs for locals. "We were getting the tea-ladies' jobs and the receptionist jobs, and all the good-paying jobs were going to trained people the various developers brought in from all over the place." The association was also pressing for money to be put into the communities, for schools, housing, and other amenities.

When G. Ware Travelstead bobbed up, with his massive plans, Peter Wade and some of his colleagues went to call on the Texan. "It was obvious that the local community was not a high priority. In fact, G. Ware's favourite saying was, 'We're not here to pour money into black holes.'"

Wade left the meeting, and went home to formulate his plans. The official sod-turning for Canary Wharf took place on a sunny day in early July 1986, and the honours were performed by Sir Robin Leigh-Pemberton, governor of the Bank of England, before an appreciative international audience of bankers, realtors, and, it was hoped, potential tenants. Attendance was by invitation, with few press cards issued (Peter Wade had one), and steps were taken to ensure that no ruffians turned up waving the distressingly common placards that read, "Kill the Canary, Save the Island." The main security step was to block off the only entry to the island at six p.m. on the night before the ceremony. G. Ware Travelstead was well satisfied that all would go well on the morrow. But little did he know, as they say in suspense novels, that it was too late.

"I had a tug refit operation on the wharf itself," Wade recalls with glee, "so they couldn't keep me out. The night before, we brought in two hundred people, and a whole bunch of beehives and herds of sheep and goats from the community farm at Mudchute. They just got the ceremony under way when out we come." Must have been quite a sight, when about two hundred thousand honey bees and a gang of sheep and goats joined the celebration.

"The Japanese bankers were petrified, because when they have demonstrations back home, generally somebody ends up getting killed. All we had was a bunch of people running around slapping their necks." And the livestock was munching the mums around the podium.

However, as it turned out, stinging bees and foraging sheep were not G. Ware Travelstead's big problem. It was money. The City had begun to move and stir itself, and to mount a campaign against the whole idea of a project outside the Square Mile around Threadneedle Street, where the dollars and pounds congregate. In March 1986, the planning restrictions were varied to allow construction of an additional twenty million square feet of office space in the City.[19] As the jackhammers began to bang out their profitable tune, some of the bankers in the Travelstead syndicate were getting nervous, and demanding more and more reassurances from Travelstead and his group.

What was required was what is always required in these cases: the announcement of a series of large, long-term leases, and, in the teeth of the increasing hostility of the City, Travelstead just couldn't come up with them. He did have a number of American clients ready to offer, but no major leases had been signed, and the British banks, which would have to be among his major tenants, were shuffling their feet and looking the other way. First Boston and Morgan Stanley both backed out of the development company, although both would become tenants in the new project. No public reason was ever given for this, but it wasn't hard to find; the change of regulations in the City meant there might not be a shortage of space after all, and the £25-per-square-foot leases that Travelstead's dream was based on were fading fast. Another critical factor was the 1986 resignation from First Boston of Michael von Clemm, who had had more to do with the original idea than anyone else.[20]

For more than a year after the official sod-turning, the Travelstead group struggled on, and then it came bang up against an immovable deadline. The Master Building Agreement, the document implementing the original plan, signed with the LDDC, required the developer to come up with £68 million on July 18, 1987. The money was to be paid over to the LDDC, which had taken over, and was vastly expanding the capacity of, the Docklands Light Railway. The day before the cheque was due, G. Ware was gone. He had sold out, for an undisclosed price, which was believed to cover only the money he had already spent – about £80 million[21] – to a group hardly anybody in the Docklands had ever heard of, the Reichmann brothers of Toronto.

Peter Wade, although he didn't know it yet, was going to love them.

CHAPTER THIRTEEN

The Manufacture of a Live Grenade

Canary Wharf is like a live grenade. If the Docklands was a stock that started out with a value of 100, it has fallen to about six.
— Ira Luskin, July, 1990 [1]

$

There was nothing mysterious about the way in which the Reichmanns moved in to pluck the torch from G. Ware Travelstead's failing grasp. Charles Young, the president of Citibank Canada, which was on the thirtieth floor of First Canadian Place, had invited Paul Reichmann onto his board. Not long afterwards Young was transferred to London, and became an enthusiast for Canary Wharf, which he mentioned to Reichmann a number of times. Then Travelstead approached Michael Dennis, when the money was getting short, looking for partners, and negotiations between the Travelstead group and O&Y went on from September 1986 to February 1987, when O&Y called them off, mostly in a disagreement over control of the project. When it became clear that Travelstead would not be able to raise the money for the development,

O&Y stepped back in.[2] To round it off, Young was hired to help with the project in London.

Now we would see a development by people who knew what they were doing. The Reichmanns had a number of advantages over the Travelstead group, including membership in a mutual admiration society with British prime minister, Margaret Thatcher. They spoke the same language. Not Hungarian, of course: free enterprise. They agreed that private entrepreneurs could always do the job better than government, they agreed that regulations should be waived to let the entrepreneurs get on with the job, and they agreed that these large projects should pay for themselves, with no mollycoddling. Except, of course, for a billion pounds here and there for infrastructure. We must have infrastructure. Then there were the tax breaks. The Canary Wharf phoenix, as it rose from the ashes of the Travelstead attempt, would cost £4 billion by the estimates then being used; the Reichmanns would get a tax benefit, since they were building in an Enterprise Zone, of £1.33 billion.[3] What could be freer than that?

In the end, Canary Wharf turned out to be a massive miscalculation for the Reichmanns, just as it had been for the Travelstead group. Both were victims of what the farming business calls "the hog cycle." You notice that the price of hogs is going up, so you buy some piglets and start producing hogs. So does everyone else who has noticed the same cycle. By the time you get the damn things to market, the price has dropped again. You take a beating, and get out of hogs. The price goes up. The City's decision to meet the challenge posed by Canary Wharf by removing the building restrictions on office space turned loose a whole herd of hogs; by the time the first phase of the project was done, vacancies in the City were running at 10 per cent of the space available, and leasing rates were down.

That was before the recession hit.

Olympia & York had thought the whole thing through, of course. They always do. They knew that there would be a business slump sometime during the building phase; in fact, Charles Young, in his new capacity as president of Olympia & York UK, the company set up in Britain to do the work, calculated on "at least one or two recessions" before the entire, ten-year development came to its glorious fruition.[4] But Paul Reichmann, the company strategist, calculated that he had so many built-in advantages that the scheme could not fail. They started with, and depended on, the Thatcher link. Sigh.

In the first place, he knew the infrastructure would be harried into place by a bureaucracy that had been given its marching orders. He was right, too, as long as Thatcher was in office. ("We were not to raise objections," as one senior civil servant in the Department of Transport put it to me. "We were to get on with it.")

In the second place, long-term leases with government departments would provide a basic underpinning for Canary Wharf. Civil servants, crawling around cluttered cubbyholes in Westminster, would be shifted, whether they liked it or not, to magnificent new, open, airy offices in Docklands. It was not to be.

In the third place, O&Y was now so large, so financially sound, that it would not have to depend solely on financial institutions to advance the money, step by grudging step. They would finance it themselves, without prearranged banking, and without partners. "We will fund it ourselves. We can complete it on our own strength," Paul Reichmann told journalists at a press conference in London in 1987.[5] This was unheard of, and mightily impressed all the *cognoscenti*. It was also disastrously wrong.

In the fourth place, O&Y could build better, faster, and cheaper than anyone else, because of their long-standing expertise. Michael Dennis, who had done so well in New York, was brought over as the company's point man in London.

In the fifth place, there were all those tax breaks, which would allow the developer to depreciate not only the building costs, but also "the costs of site preparation, service roads and car-parking,"[6] for work done within the Enterprise Zone – and that meant more than three-quarters of the area enclosed by Canary Wharf. Because of the secrecy surrounding the Master Building Agreement, it is not possible to work out exactly what this has meant, but one academic study puts it at £1,303,500 in tax savings, and comments, "To put this level of subsidy into perspective, this represents one-third of all expenditure by the Department of Employment for 1990/91."[7]

Then there was the price of land. The LDDC press release covering this subject said that "the price paid for the 20 acres of LDDC-owned land on Canary Wharf equates to £1 million per acre, of which £8 million is payable in cash and £12 million is represented by the developers' commitments to various on-site works of public benefit. . . . The land price taken together with all other aspects of the agreement yields a value at least equivalent to the market value of LDDC's land holding as at April 1987."

Just kidding, folks, just one of those little jokes we press-release writers like to play. The phrase "on-site works of public benefit" referred to the parks, internal roads, and riverside walkways O&Y was going to have to build anyway. So O&Y was allowed £12 million for doing what it had to do, and for expenses it was going to be able to write off on taxes, anyway. Then there was the area of twenty-six acres built on pilings over water. The Travelstead master building plan called for a payment of £10,000 per acre to the LDDC for this. Since the O&Y agreement was never released, we can only guess what, if anything, the developer did finally pay. The land "giveaway" was criticized by the National Audit Office in May 1988, in a report which brushed aside the fanciful notion that O&Y was paying £1 million per acre, knocked off the £12 million and came up with the real price: £400,000 per acre. Land prices at the time for that area were "above £1 million an acre," (in fact, a site on North Quay, just above Canary Wharf, sold for £5 million an acre in 1988), and, the Audit Office report noted, "Subsequently, the DOE took action designed to prevent the LDDC from entering into any similar option agreements without their knowledge."[8] However you cut it, Paul Reichmann knew he was going to get land cheap.

Finally, O&Y would solve the infrastructure problem, and the way they went about this is the key to understanding one of the major problems posed by Thatcherite, or Reaganite, or Reichmannite, economics. They would demand-lead the planning process. We will come back to this, to see how the concept worked. In the meantime, we have to build the project.

The plan that was presented to a bedazzled business audience, when Prime Minister Thatcher (who else?), wearing a hardhat and a smile, got the thing going officially by taking the first whack with a pile-driver on May 11, 1988, was much bigger, and much better, than the Travelstead version. There would be forty buildings in all, erected in three stages, over seven to ten years, in what was to be the Canary Wharf District. This would lap over onto Heron Quays and Port East, and create "a major business district in Central London within ten minutes of the City."[9] (This was developer geography; to make this "Central London," you had to shove the entire city eastward by about two miles.)

Canary Wharf itself would contain ten million square feet of office space, 500,000 feet of retail, restaurant, and leisure space, another 425,000 square feet of residential space, and 6,500 car-parking spaces; but they would not be stacked over the railway line as Travelstead had envisioned; they would be stuck underground, where they belonged.

Phase One, which is now complete (without any residential space at all), consists of nine buildings. The centrepiece of this phase is One Canada Square, which replaced the three towers Travelstead had in mind. (He would not have been able to build his, anyway; at 850 feet, they would have interfered with access to the new London City Airport, a commuter airport just east of Canary Wharf.) One Canada Square is an allowable fifty feet shorter, an eight-hundred-foot, fifty-storey tower, the highest in the United Kingdom. It was designed by Cesar Pelli, the man who had worked so brilliantly on the World Financial Center, in the form of an obelisk, with a semi-matte stainless steel skin that makes it glow like a beacon at sunrise and sunset. It is topped by a pyramid roof lit from within; "A symbol," as the O&Y

brochures put it, "of the growth and vitality of Docklands, and Olympia & York's confidence in the future of London." Or, a symbol of a hell of a pile of debt.

Around the base of this tower runs an "Edwardian banking mall," a railway station, covered by a glazed arch, for the Docklands Light Railway, and two modern office blocks. Across from the railway station, around Cabot Square, are clustered five more buildings, with a lovely fountain in the centre.

The development covers seventy-one acres, including twenty-six acres supported on pilings over the water, with twenty-five acres, more than one-third of the area, devoted to parks, open space, and riverside promenades.

No formal planning permission was required, and there was no study of the impact of the project on its surroundings, but Olympia & York did issue a comprehensive set of plans and views, which Dr. Brian Edwards, the design expert we met in the last chapter, summarizes simply, saying, "These are of breathtaking beauty."[10] Prince Charles did not agree. When he had a look at the place, he said that it "will cast its shadow over generations of Londoners who have suffered enough from towers of architectural arrogance."[11] These are, of course, matters of opinion; in my view, Dr. Edwards is right, and the prince wrong. If you are going to build something like this, this is the way to build it.

It soon became clear that a difference in design concepts was not the only thing that separated the O&Y approach from the Travelstead approach. Peter Wade, the arch opponent of Canary Wharf, became the best witness to the change.

"O&Y came along and nobody had ever heard of them. I called for a meeting with them and Charles Young, the senior English director, attended. We had a lot to say about what the company should be doing for the community, and a couple of weeks later they approached me and told me to put my money where my mouth was. They offered me a job. I would have nothing to do with that; turned the whole thing over to the Association of Island Communities. We needed to know more about the company. We had made a lot of contacts with the national and international media, so we sniffed out a man from the *Wall Street Journal*; they were tenants in the World Financial Center in New York, and they gave us a glowing testimonial. On that basis, I agreed to come and work for O&Y for six months.

"I made no bones about it; I told O&Y, 'I'm here to get everything I can out of you for this community.'"

Not surprisingly, the day the announcement was made that Wade had joined the enemy, painted slogans appeared on the walls of his house. More surprisingly, the same unprintable insults were daubed on stones around the grave of his grandson, Christopher Wade, for whom his tugboat is named.

"A number of people, and particularly the political activists, groups like Docklands Forum, screamed 'Poacher turned game-keeper!' That's fine, my shoulders are big enough, but you had to come to terms with the fact that Maggie Thatcher had been here and this thing was going to go ahead. You can stand outside for the duration of the building, but you're getting sod-all from it. So you've got to get inside and screw it."

The traditional way to hire a workforce in the area was for a fore-man to turn up at a local pub. "As soon as the word got out that there was work going, the boys would pour in by the boatload from south-ern Ireland. They would meet in the local, and the foreman would go over, point a finger, and say, 'You, you, and you.' That was the norm, even after we explained to all the developers working around here that we badly needed the work. They said they would try to hire locals 'wherever possible,' but that failed, miserably failed. We had had quite a lot of projects going by this time, at South Quay, and so forth, and we still had an unemployment rate of 26 per cent. I thought O&Y could do something in that way, and they did.

"First, they offered me to go up to Great George Street, in down-town London, where their offices were at that time, and set up a recruiting office there, but I said, 'No sir.' I was given a Portakabin right on the site, that moved with the building. It was always on the public footpath, and anybody who wanted to see me could walk straight off the pavement into my office.

"We set up a recruiting office and a business liaison office to help local contractors get the subcontracts. We would take them through the tendering process; with O&Y this was a very, very tight procedure. You had to go through all sorts of loops and jumps, and for a small business that could be quite intimidating. We sorted them through all that, and we got more than £50 million worth of local contract work on the build.

"On the job side, we got an undertaking that O&Y would provide a minimum of five hundred jobs locally, but one of the problems was that the trained workforce here had been in marine and heavy engineering, with not much in the construction industry. So we joined with the Construction Industry Training Board, the LDDC, and Tower Hamlets to set up a training centre in Eastern New Dock Road. The CITB set the curriculum, and when you were done, you got a national certificate in whatever trade you had taken."

When he realized that Olympia & York meant exactly what they told him about wanting to involve the community, Wade resigned from the Association of Island Communities, and went to work, full-time, for O&Y. Soon the training centre was turning out skilled workers who had only to walk out the door to find a job. The trades were run through the training centre on a time-scale that would produce the workers when they were needed on the project, and so they could get work immediately. "When you begin, you need concrete workers, but not electricians. We worked it so that when you needed electricians, we had a group ready that had just been through a thirty-six-week course."

The government provides an allowance for workers in eligible training courses, such as these, but Olympia & York paid an additional £10 per week to each trainee, as a further incentive.

"In three years we put through just over 400 trainees; 290 came on Canary Wharf, and the rest went elsewhere."

Wade grimaces ruefully, and looks out the window, where a single, still crane looms over a deserted worksite. He spreads out his hands across the top of his desk, and shrugs.

"In a normal economy, that training centre would have been an enormous bonus, but then came the end of Phase One, and we started shedding jobs here, and then the recession. Can we be proud of the fact that we now have four hundred skilled people sitting in doorways on the dole?"

The training scheme cost Olympia & York a little over £30,000,[12] a pittance, but the company did meet the target of providing more than five hundred jobs locally. Far more important, in Wade's mind, was a program the developer would never let him talk about, a community-involvement scheme.

"I am not totally in agreement with their policy, because it does them more harm than good," Wade says, "but somebody ought to know about it.

"Because they are such a private family, they gave away millions with no return to the company. Mr. Paul says, 'To give is to give.' If you are going to take credit for something, get a corporate return, then it's not a gift, because you're looking for a return. . . . I would be sitting at a meeting with British Telecom or British Gas, who also had community programs, never as active as ours, and they would be boasting about what they did, and I would say nothing. You get a bit of a snigger at a meeting like that when you say, 'To give is to give.'"

The O&Y involvement was injected directly into the communities around them, it was private, and it was intended to produce improvements over a long term.

"You'd get a call from a local school that wanted money for a football strip for the school team – £200, £250, something like that. You go down and discuss it with them, and you tell them to ask you instead for £1,500 for a library section, and that's what you would give.

"It was not a question of writing out cheques; it was a question of being involved with what was going on. Lots of times we didn't give money; we'd give the schools equipment, things like that. We were always getting new computers, laser-jet printers, we were always shedding furniture to community centres, seniors' centres. When we finished Phase One, they had furniture flying at them, carpet tiles, all sorts of stuff.

"We had a school that needed to expand, to make major alterations to the existing structure and build an addition. For that you had to have architectural plans to submit to the education authorities. O&Y had an architect in here who had designed schools when she first started out back in Canada, so we seconded her down here for three weeks and she drew up a set of plans that were accepted at once."

In all, Olympia & York contributed £2,633,652.73 [13] by way of training, charitable donations, sponsorship, education, health services, and special projects. One of the few donations that ever made it into the newspapers was one for £350,000 to the Children's Unit at London Hospital. All record of the rest was locked up in Peter Wade's drawer until the whole project came grinding to a halt.

What impressed him about the company was its willingness, even eagerness, to put something back into the community. Ward says, "I had this idea that there ought to be a community tax on development, perhaps 1 per cent of the costs. You would put that into a community trust, and use the interest from that to fund projects. This got a very warm reception from the company, and a very cold shoulder from the LDDC.

"Over there, they have this weird idea that we'll give you a grant for three years, and then you'll be self-sufficient. How can a seniors' centre be self-sufficient? They are closing down community centres all over the Isle of Dogs today because they are 'time-expired' under some grant the LDDC gave them.

"The people from O&Y clearly demonstrated their long-term commitment. The others come in and throw you a few scraps and then piss off somewhere else."

Not everyone agrees with Wade, of course. Ben Kochan of the Docklands Forum dismisses the Reichmanns' generosity with a wave of the hand. "The great philanthropist line is a front," he says. "They bought acquiescence, that's all." Maybe so, but it's a little hard to show that a company that refuses to allow the fact of its donations to be made public is putting up a front, and I have certainly never heard of a developer who went about community involvement in quite the way Olympia & York did on the Isle of Dogs.

Whatever you say about the Reichmanns, Peter Wade has made the case that they are serious, dedicated, scrupulous men. If things went so dreadfully wrong for Olympia & York here at Canary Wharf, and they did, you have to look into the way the project itself was set up.

CHAPTER FOURTEEN

How the Reichmanns Took the Tube

Where you're simply picking off one developer or another and saying, "Hey, give us some money or else," it's not a terribly reliable or reputable way of planning major new infrastructure.

– David Bayliss, London Transport, 1992 [1]

$

The Master Building Agreement for Canary Wharf between O&Y UK and the LDDC was signed on July 17, 1987, a Friday. (Unlike the Travelstead plan, it has never been released, and when Mildred Gordon, MP, put down a written question asking the government for its publication in July 1987, she got a one-word answer: "No.") [2] The Reichmanns missed the ceremony, because they had flown back to Canada for the Sabbath, as they did every week. Just as well; it rained. The groundbreaking, starring Prime Minister Thatcher, took place on May 11, 1988, as we have already seen. Three years later, the main buildings of Phase One were up, including the tower. Not merely up, but finished and, in most cases, ready for occupation.

I have had, and will have, some critical things to say about the Reichmanns and Olympia & York. It is only fair to call to the stand on their behalf Peter Corfield, a senior executive with Ogilvy & Mather, the advertising company, from his office on the tenth floor of No. 10 Cabot Square (most of the buildings and squares at Canary Wharf have names with Canadian associations). Corfield is a solidly built gent, with steel-rimmed glasses and a bright smile, who exudes energy as he explains how he got caught up with Olympia & York, and wound up as one of their circle of supporters in London.[3]

"I'm the group facilities director of Ogilvy & Mather, and we had had space in the City since 1935. We had a long-term lease coming to an end, so I began looking for new space in 1985-86. I did the rounds in the West End of London, and couldn't find anything we could afford, so I came out here, to Docklands. I was singularly unimpressed. The infrastructure was hideous. How were you going to get to work? I wrote it off and went back to looking everywhere else. I even, at one point, looked at the idea of buying a car ferry, refurbishing it, and parking it in the river up by Tower Bridge, but the maintenance would kill you.

"I revisited the Docklands in desperation, really, and got out here in early 1989, just as Olympia & York were hitting their stride. I stood with a very tall New Yorker (Peter Morano, one of the O&Y staff) on a mound of earth, and I always remember he pointed across here – there was a big hole with a few sticks poking out of it – and he says, 'That's the building we're talking about, and I reckon we'll hand that over to you on the first of March, 1991.'

"I thought it was the biggest load of developer-speak I'd ever heard. But there was something about the way they went about it that suggested that, if they said a thing would be done, it would be. I suppose I've met many developers in my time, 120 or more, but of them all I have found Olympia & York to be outstanding in terms of honesty and integrity, of setting their aims and going out and achieving them."

Corfield went to New York for a look at the World Financial Center, and came away impressed not only by that development, but by the thoughtfulness and efficiency of the company. "I phoned up to say I was in town, and next thing you know, there is the Reichmanns' stretch limo pulling up to my hotel to take me on my rounds.

"What was it that attracted me to this development out of all the others that were now sprouting around here? I think the first thing was that it had a sense of scale about it that included people. There were massive buildings, but they kept people to the forefront; there was space to work, to relax.

"We were used to seeing developers who promised the earth and delivered nothing, and here we saw a new city come out of the ground with everything complete down to the last detail, lovely railings around the park, and full-grown trees everywhere.

"But probably the most impressive thing is that you felt they were here to stay. They go in for very-long-range planning; they never saw this as an instant revenue-earner; they were prepared to be patient, and prepared to spend the money to do it right."

Corfield recommended Canary Wharf to his board, and struck a deal to lease 104,000 square feet of space – a full floor at 10 Cabot Square, one of the buildings grouped around a fountain across from the tower – for twenty-five years at £27 a square foot. At the time, leases in the West End of London were £40; he felt he had a good deal.

"On March 1, 1991, they handed me a certificate of readiness. That was less than three years from the time I looked across at that hole in the ground with the sticks poking out of it."

In those three years, O&Y worked their usual miracles, hurling up 4.5 million square feet of office space in the Phase One buildings. One Canada Square, just to touch on that one, soars up from 40,000 cubic metres of concrete poured into a concrete raft in the river bed, on which the whole structure rests. To anchor it all, over 200 six-foot piles were driven 25 metres into the ground, with mufflers fitted around each pile to keep the noise down. The tower itself contains 27,500 tons of steel, and is designed so that, while it is 200 feet taller than the National Westminster Bank building, which you can see out the window, it has only one more storey. That is because the space between floors is generous enough to allow virtually any kind of conduits the lessees may require. The tower also has the same cut-away corners as First Canadian Place, letting in more light, and creating more high-rent offices.

While the building was going ahead, O&Y had been working on their crucial problem of transportation. The government's firm declaration that it would not put money into the roadways leading to the Docklands was slightly modified, to the astonishment of all, once Maggie Thatcher got behind the project and pushed. Faster than you could say bulldozer, the government was committed to expenditures which, through the LDDC, London Transport, and the Department of Transport, will clock in at about £4 billion, or over $8 billion Canadian, for the East London area.[4] These are not, it should be clear, all due to the construction of Canary Wharf, which is only one of the projects in the Docklands. At the same time, as we will see, it was Canary Wharf that galvanized the government into spending funds that would otherwise have gone elsewhere. The LDDC claims that £1.349 billion of public investment has provoked £9 billion of private investment,[5] but that is because it is only counting as "public investment" the money funnelled through itself, leaving out all the expenditures of the departments of Transport and the Environment and of London Transport, as well as all the tax giveaways. It also avoids the fact that more than half the £9 billion figure is attributable to Canary Wharf, and that eight other projects, representing over £1 billion in total, are currently in various forms of receivership.

The LDDC road projects alone have a budget of £850 million so far,[6] led by the Limehouse Link, a 1.8-kilometre-long road sunk into a cut-and-cover tunnel, which opened in May 1993. It joins the Docklands to the City at a cost of £220 million.[7] And there is another cost, not shown in any of the public documents I have seen, but buried in the "Main Bull Points" memo prepared by the Department of the Environment for use by Tory Cabinet members. It reads: "Plus Limehouse Link related rehousing/refurbishment – £105m." Hundreds of houses had to be demolished and families moved for this road, for which the LDDC agreed to pay. That puts the Limehouse Link cost, to date, at £325 million. I say "to date," because it ought to be borne in mind that the original estimate for this project was £40 million.[8] A senior bureaucrat in the Department of Transport told me, in awes-truck tones, that "it cost more than £2,000 an inch." Far too modest. At £325 million, this stretch of highway, which brings central London within minutes of Canary Wharf, cost £4,586.18, or $9,447.54 in Cana-dian funds, per inch,[9] making it the most expensive stretch of road ever to be constructed in the U.K.[10] This link is part of what will become "The Docklands Highway," a series of roads that will make the area easily accessible, not only from downtown London, but from the east as well, on the way to London City Airport, just east of the Dock-lands, and to the Channel.

The LDDC has built the roads within the Docklands itself, but this is not all of it, not by a long chalk. The roads leading in and away are the responsibility of the Department of Transport, which has so far spent about half of a budgeted total of £1.194 billion (call it $2.4 billion Cana-dian) in the area.[11]

Then there is the Docklands Light Railway, which the locals refer to as "the Dear Little Railway," and which we last met struggling along with a capacity of 1,500 passengers an hour. The LDDC, which took over the railway from London Transport, has spent £734 million to upgrade the line, extend it, remodel stations, and purchase new signals and rolling stock. Another £137 million is slated for an extension of the line to Lewisham.[12] Not all of this came from the government. Remember that "private-led" motto? Olympia & York contributed £80 million to link the dear little railway directly to the London tube line at the Bank Street station. In other words, about 9 per cent of the cost came from the private sector.

The result is a railway that can currently carry four thousand pas-sengers an hour, and will soon be able to carry fifteen thousand, and is convenient, comfortable, and swift. Much has been written about the inaccessibility of Canary Wharf, most of it applesauce. On sixteen trips to the wharf, over a period of two weeks, it took me an average of twenty-three minutes on the tube and the dear little railway, going from Russell Square, near the British Museum, to One Canada Square, and vice versa. And it took me seventeen minutes, on average, to get to the City from Canary Wharf. The money has done what it was meant to do; the issue is whether this is an appropriate thing to be doing.

Then there is the Riverbus, owned and operated, at a loss, by Olympia & York and the Peninsular & Oriental Steamship Company (P&O). You can whisk to and from the pier at Charing Cross in about twenty minutes in this, at no cost to the public purse. (At no cost to you, either, if your employer has worked this perk into the leasing agreement with O&Y.)

But the key to the successful development of the complex had to be to get a tube link directly into Canary Wharf, not just a Toonerville Trolley like the DLR. Olympia & York came up with the answer: the private sector would contribute substantially towards the cost, in accordance with Thatcherite economics.

London Transport had been studying the needs of East London, and indeed the entire city, for years. The central government might scorn planning, but London Transport doesn't. As David Bayliss, director of planning, a silver-haired, urbane, and thoughtful man, put it to me, "Nobody knows what London will be like in fifteen to twenty years, but if you have any idea of what you want it to be like, you had better start planning for it now." Heresy, of course.

Olympia & York concluded that the answer to the transportation problem in the Docklands was to extend the Fleet Line, a.k.a. the River Line, whose beginnings we met in Chapter Eleven. In 1977 it had been renamed – again – as the "Jubilee Line" in honour of the twenty-fifth anniversary of Queen Elizabeth's accession to the throne. "In hopes," says Bayliss, "that it might thereby attract some cachet and funding." It did. The line now runs nine miles, from Stanmore in northwest London to Charing Cross station, just off Trafalgar Square. London Transport had prepared a proposal that would extend it by ten miles, across the river to Waterloo, and eastwards through Canary Wharf.

A direct extension of the tube is quite a different matter from transferring from the tube at Bank Street, in the heart of the City, to the DLR. The gains in both capacity and time are enormous. "In the morning peak period it will be able to carry over 100,000 people through Canary Wharf station. As such its capacity will be about three times as great as the DLR even when its expansion is complete."[13] As to speed, "It will be under 20 minutes by train from Canary Wharf to Bond Street," and about five minutes to get to Bank Street from Canary Wharf.[14]

Olympia & York took over this proposal, which had been gathering dust for years. At first they promised to build the line themselves, but, after due consideration, realized that they were builders, not subway operators, and suggested, instead, that they, and others who might benefit from the line, would put up part of the cost. Their contribution, they said, would be £400 million, out of a then-estimated cost of £1 billion.

There was one major problem with this. London Transport had looked at the line, along with two other proposals, in the London Central Rail Study, undertaken by London Transport, British Rail, and the Department of Transport, and had ruled against it. The study concluded that the first job of business should be the other two lines.[15]

Bayliss says, picking his words carefully, "Our priority was to get on with relieving the hard-pressed general rail network through two projects which would have brought considerable relief to the historic west end of the city and the commercial centres. These were the Chelsea–Hackney Line and Crossrail." The Chelsea–Hackney Line was planned from Wimbledon in the southwest, right through Piccadilly Circus and out to the northeast, to relieve some of the great and growing pressure in central London; the east-west Crossrail Line would come in from the west at Paddington station, cross mid-city at Tottenham Court Road, and slant northeastwards through Stratford Town (not Shakespeare's Stratford). Both lines would stay north of the river. The estimated cost was £2 billion.

"While [the Jubilee Line Extension] was important," Bayliss

explains, "we thought that underpinning the existing commercial centres was probably more important than providing a new railway out to Docklands to assist a third commercial centre. We determined our priorities accordingly."

But, just as there is more than one way to skin a cat, there is more than one way to determine a priority.

"Considerations other than those purely of transport operators have been brought to bear," Bayliss notes. "The plans were not quite torn up, but set on one side. Olympia & York, a very influential group, and Paul Reichmann, a very influential man, were able to get the ear of government at the very highest level. . . . I find the whole thing a very curious arrangement."

He adds, "It was supposed to be a bold signal of the way in which government wanted planning to go in the U.K., with the private sector leading the way and providing some of the funding. The weakness was that there was no systematic way of securing the private contribution, and it was done on a haphazard and uncertain basis." And again, "They [the Reichmanns] had an entrée at No. 10 Downing Street that overruled everything else."

Once they had decided to chip in, O&Y asked for contributions from others, and that led to an auction as to where the line would go after it left Canary Wharf. The two bidders were British Gas, with a substantial piece of property on the Greenwich peninsula, just across the river from the Isle of Dogs, on which they are building a huge housing scheme, and a Swedish firm with a major office development northeast of Canary Wharf. British Gas has a substantial real-estate arm, and a 263-acre site where it hopes to build and sell a mixed retail, commercial, and residential scheme, which will include 5,850 homes. [16]

They were not voluntary bidders; when the government approached British Gas and asked for a contribution, the energy company had said no. So the line was drawn to the north, missing the company's land holdings entirely.

Bayliss recalls: "We deposited the bill [to permit construction of the line] with the route missing their property entirely. And British Gas come and say, 'Yes, okay, we'll contribute £25 million if you'll go by way of Greenwich.' The route of the line was in effect a bargaining ploy."

A successful bargaining ploy. The route was changed, in return for a promise of £25 million. However, this would not be paid all in cash but, to a large extent, in the lands required for the subway-line extension. What the Swedes offered has not been revealed; obviously it was something less. There is now no direct access to their project.

"You route the line to the highest bidder's development," is the way Bayliss puts it. "Instead of following the original line further north, we went through the Greenwich peninsula. I happen to think that is the right alignment, but it was more by good luck than good management. That something of such great moment should be determined by whim cannot be a sensible way. You should not build a system on mere whim and opportunity."

While the Central London Rail Study was being prepared, there was suddenly another study under way, the East London Rail Study, funded by the Department of Transport. The work for this was not done by London Transport or the Department; a private consulting firm, Halcrow Fox and Associates, prepared the study instead. This version *began* with the assumption that a tube line direct to Canary Wharf had already been approved. "The best option for a second line to the Docklands is an extension to the Jubilee Line from Green Park via Waterloo, London Bridge and Canary Wharf to Stratford."[17]

That was accompanied into the public arena by a second version of the Central London Rail Study, which concluded that, with the "regeneration benefits" to flow from extending the Jubilee Line to the Docklands, that was the best course to follow.

To get the sequence clear:

- The Central London Rail Study was prepared for release in January 1989, and ruled against the Jubilee Line Extension.
- On January 23, the secretary of state for transport, Paul

Channon, noted in a written answer to Parliament that the East London Rail Study had been established. "The study will include Olympia & York's proposal for a new underground railway between Waterloo and Greenwich peninsula via the Isle of Dogs."[18]

- On July 26, the East London Rail Study recommended the Jubilee Line Extension.
- The same day, the new version of Central London Rail Study embraced the Jubilee Line Extension.

There is no shyness about what changed the entire planning process. Lord Wakeham, Margaret Thatcher's energy secretary when he was plain John Wakeham, and now the Cabinet member assigned to co-ordinate all dealings on Canary Wharf, put it to me clearly: "The original proposals for the Jubilee Line came out at a total cost which was in excess of the value laid down by the Department of the Environment when they did a cost-benefit analysis. On its own, it would never have been approved. The money would have gone to other projects which were better value for money. However, O&Y undertook to produce in round figures £400 million over a longish period, and we said, 'Right. Subject to the private sector contribution, the public sector contribution will be forthcoming.'"[19]

The necessary legislation was drawn in a rather curious way. It had to be done through a private member's bill, not a government bill, and was prepared by London Transport. But O&Y paid much of the shot. "O&Y contributed £2.5 million towards the Parliamentary bill," Bayliss confirms. "If the scheme proceeds, that will be netted off their financial obligation. In a sense, it is an advance payment on the £400 million."

Malcolm Macdonald, head of the London Division of the Department of Transport, says, "O&Y were driving the whole thing. They got a bill deposited in Parliament before any of the other studies got to the serious phase. The case for other developments was stronger elsewhere, but if they were prepared to fund a study and draft a bill, the government thought they'd make more contributions to the construction of the thing.

"Had it not been for the Department of the Environment-led, O&Y-led, pressure, the Department of Transport would have pushed the other proposals. We would have built the Crossrail and the Chelsea–Hackney line, and the Jubilee Line Extension somewhere behind those two."[20]

I asked if this sort of financing could be extended to other departments. Could one, for example, pay some money to the Department of Defence and then pick out an enemy to go to war against? I got a wintry smile.

On November 16, 1989, Cecil Parkinson, secretary of state for transport, deposited the necessary bill in Parliament, and announced that the Jubilee Line Extension would proceed, that it would cost £1 billion, and that O&Y would be contributing 40 per cent of the cost. The bill whisked through Parliament and received royal assent, but, since no money has ever come from O&Y, it remains in limbo. For the line to be built, Lord Wakeham has to tell the secretary of state for the environment that the money is secured; the secretary of state will send a letter to London Transport authorizing construction, and, fifty-three months later, if all goes well, the trains roll.

But the 40-per-cent figure Channon cited when this process was set in motion was studiously misleading. What O&Y agreed to, in a letter of understanding, was to contribute £98 million pounds to begin with, and to pay another £302 million, spread over a period of twenty-five years. The current projected cost of the line is £1.8 billion. As David Bayliss explains, "The whole £400 million will be worth about £180 million in 1992 prices."

Because of the effect of inflation over twenty-five years, Olympia & York would be paying 10 per cent, not 40 per cent, of the cost. London Transport has so far spent over £200 million preparing the way for the line; O&Y's sole contribution to date has been the £2.5 million it handed over to push the legislation to the front of the pile.

And here's another funny thing. British Gas has yet to come up with a penny of the money promised back in 1989. London Transport now says that, if the money is not forthcoming, they will construct the line and the shell of the station on British Gas land, but the station will not be finished until British Gas makes its contribution. The cost of fitting out the station is about £25 million.

The entire planning structure was turned on its head by a combination of the personal clout of the Reichmanns, especially Paul Reichmann, with the prime minister, and a promise of what might have been a dime out of every dollar of the cost of the Jubilee Line Extension. And the mere prospect of that extension set off an outpouring of more than £4 billion in subsidies for a development that proper planning procedures would never have authorized. I could not find anyone, anywhere, in London who believes that Canary Wharf could ever succeed without the Jubilee Line Extension. Indeed, as Eric Sorenson, the CEO of the London Docklands Development Corporation, told me, the entire development might be in mortal peril if the line is not built. "With the Jubilee Line, you could see a way forward through the next five years. Without it, it is very difficult to see a way forward."[21]

The way forward became murky indeed on November 22, 1990, when Margaret Thatcher resigned. Two days earlier, on the first ballot of a vote to see her re-elected as Conservative Party leader, she fell four votes short of a majority. Her nemesis was Michael Heseltine, her former secretary of the environment, who had disagreed with her over her European policy, and had left the Cabinet. John Major, then chancellor of the exchequer, jumped into the race when Thatcher declined to offer herself for the second ballot, and, on November 28, he was prime minister.

Heseltine was back in the Cabinet, and he had been the original enthusiast for the Docklands. But it wasn't the same thing, at all. He was soon over in Foreign Affairs. There is a theory held by many Reichmann admirers that, without Thatcher's defeat, they might have made it. She would have found some way around the requirement that

O&Y come up with at least the first payment on the Jubilee Line Extension. And/or, she would have forced the displacement of bureaucrats from the Department of the Environment and the Department of Transport out to Canary Wharf. Long-term leases with these departments would have been as good as cash in the bank. With that in place, the bankers, who were growing increasingly restive, would have kept the money flowing.

With Thatcher gone, the Conservatives were not in a mood to make any more concessions to interloping Canadians who had gotten away with, let's face it, quite a lot already. To date, the government has poured into the Docklands area £1.349 billion through the LDDC, £525 million through the Department of Transport, £200 million through London Transport, and whatever tax breaks have been turned into cash so far. Leave out the tax breaks, and call it £2.074 billion. O&Y has contributed £148 million to the DLR (£68 million when it took over the Travelstead group's obligation, and another £80 million to extend the line into the Bank Street station). It also paid £2.5 million to help offset costs of preparing the legislation, as we have seen. We subtract these sums from the £2.074 billion. The public sector total so far, then, is around £1.9 billion. But there is still the rest of the Department of Transport's budget to spend, £669 million, and the Jubilee Line Extension money, of which the public-sector share will be £1.3 billion, for a grand total, before even looking at the tax breaks, of £3.8925 billion. Some of this money would have been spent someday; but it was the Canary Wharf project that caused it to be committed years ahead of any sensible planning.

In the mind of the new government, therefore, the equation became quite simple: no Jubilee money, no Jubilee Line Extension. It was economic nonsense, of course. If the line made sense, a payment of £98 million was not crucial. God knows what the actual final costs of a job that has already gone from £1 billion to £1.8 billion will be. If the line didn't make sense, the O&Y injection couldn't redeem it. But this arrangement had never been about economics; it was about politics, and politically the Reichmanns had just lost their powerful friend at court.

Now, they would have to come up with the money, or else. And they were never able to keep their part of the bargain, for the very good reason that, even before the Parliamentary bill was deposited, the company was in deep trouble. Among other things, Robert Campeau was back in action.

PART IV

The Crisis

To be a successful businessman you need extraordinary talents; and
if you have such talents, why waste them on business?

– Israel Salanter Lipkin, 1810–1883

CHAPTER FIFTEEN

Tar Baby

The only way to succeed in the global marketplace is if you strive to be the best in one area, perhaps two.
 – Paul Reichmann, 1990 [1]

$

We last saw Robert Campeau in Chapter Ten, when in April 1988 the chairman of Campeau Corporation was dancing around the bonfires of his victory over Federated Stores, which he had just taken over for $6.64 billion U.S. The Reichmanns had advanced him $260 million U.S. in return for debentures, but felt that they were covered, no matter what happened, because the debentures were secured by his Canadian properties, including Scotia Plaza, of which they owned half.

Campeau spent most of 1988 selling off parts of his new empire, and reorganizing it, with the unsurprising result that morale sank below sea level, and the debt-burdened corporations, Allied Stores and Federated, began to leak like twin sieves, with employees, money, and unsettling rumours all coming out.

Campeau was still spending money, flying over to Austria at frequent intervals to design and oversee the reconstruction of his dream château, on Lake Attersee. Before he was through, this cosy little cottage had two minarets, cathedral windows, seven bathrooms, a full-sized swimming pool on the top floor, and three guest suites, for which he borrowed $4.6 million from his own corporation. Kurt Waldheim, the Austrian president, who lived on the other side of the lake, might pop in. Let others worry about the debts piling up in North America, he was going to get this *right*. The kitchen entrance was redone five times.[2]

In July, the *New York Times Magazine* ran a profile on "The Man Who Bought Bloomingdale's," which contained a paragraph buried well back on the inside pages that began, "What not even his own children knew was that Campeau had been maintaining a second family in Montreal."[3] The second family was news to no one in Canada, where newspaper articles had carried the salient facts months before, but it was in New York.

According to John Rothchild, in his book on Campeau, "In Westchester County, the wife of a Prudential executive turned to her husband and said, 'How could you all have lent $11 billion to a bigamist?'"[4] Campeau had never been a bigamist; he had been a philanderer, but the distinction didn't make much difference. Financial confidence is mostly a matter of psychology – humbug, if you prefer – and the details of Campeau's lifestyle, which were by any measure somewhat unusual, sent his stock plummeting. I mean, it wasn't as if this stuff came out in the *Post*. This was the *New York Times*.

The timing was dreadful. First Boston had structured the Federated takeover on a bridge loan – short-term – which was to be replaced when junk bonds – high-interest, longer-term notes – could be crammed down the maw of the market. Campeau had once publicly scorned junk bonds, but here he was, flogging them. The First Boston team set up a bond issue of $1.5 billion U.S.; when they unloaded this, they would pay themselves back the money they had loaned Campeau to launch his bid, and then another $115 million in various fees. That would be nice.

However, the market was already crowded with other junk bonds, from deals like the staggering $21-billion takeover of RJR Nabisco, and the atmosphere was made a trifle tense by the continuing revelations in the trials of the various junk-bond kings who were being hustled off to the hoosegow throughout this period, starting with Ivan Boesky and Michael Milken. Yesterday's heroes were serving time, and it did not create the right atmosphere. They would soon pop out again, but the publicity was doing the flogging game no good, no good at all. Alfred, Lord Tennyson, might contend that simple faith was more than Norman blood, but it was getting harder and harder to line up people of simple faith who had any money left to buy Campeau's junk, especially when his *old* junk, bonds sold to finance the Allied Stores deal in 1986, were by this time trading for 81 cents on the dollar. The fact that he had promised never to sell Brooks Brothers, and then promptly sold it, also helped to kill the market. Brooks Brothers was the brightest ornament on the Allied chain; indeed, that was why earlier bond issues had succeeded. Now it was apparent that you could neither trust the man's word, nor his wisdom. Wall Street doesn't care so much about words; it does about wisdom.

When the details of Campeau's unusual home life became the stuff of water-cooler jokes, it was game over. The junk-bond issue had to be pulled from the market, and a much smaller issue, of $750 million U.S., was offered on November 1. The interest was as much as 17.5 per cent,[5] enough to persuade a reluctant market to swallow its doubts and the bonds. Unfortunately, it was too much for Campeau, or Federated, to repay. The $750 million didn't cover the bridge loans; First Boston was still on the hook for $400 million U.S. It wasn't going to help any future bond sales when word came out that Campeau Corporation had lost $203 million Canadian in fiscal 1987.[6]

In December 1988, Campeau was back banging on the doors of O&Y (who were, by this time, building Canary Wharf), and the

Reichmanns were persuaded another foot or so along the plank that leads to the water. Documents filed with the Ontario Securities Commission show that O&Y bought 500,000 shares in Campeau Corporation at $15 U.S. This was intended to, and did, keep the Campeau stock from sinking out of sight. The shares, which had hit a high of $30.38 on the TSE in August 1987, were now under $15, and the Reichmanns' $260 million worth of debentures were convertible at $26. Not so good. The $7.5 million U.S. that the new share purchase brought Campeau could be nothing more than a stop-gap, but it meant that the Reichmanns, for the first time, were direct investors in his company. Which continued to leak money.

Federated lost $158 million in the first three-quarters of the 1989-90 fiscal year. Campeau Corporation, in turn, reported a loss of $203 million U.S. for the thirteen months ending January 31, 1990, down from a $61-million profit in the calendar year before.[7] The banks began to pressure Campeau, not merely to cut costs, but to replace some of his medium-term, high-interest loans with longer-term mortgages. He tried to negotiate a $4-billion mortgage on the Federated properties with Prudential Life Insurance Limited, Nomura Securities of Japan (where he might have stacked the cards against himself a trifle by telling the Japanese, "You ought to be grateful to America. It's rare that a conqueror treats a conquered country as well as you have been treated"[8]), and, finally, with JMB Realty, the developers now in partnership with the Reichmanns. No dice. First Boston, to whom he still owed $400 million U.S. in the bridge loan, were beginning to get very nervous indeed. So were the bond markets. By the spring of 1989, Allied bonds were selling for 61 cents on the dollar, and Federated bonds for 87. (People would buy these depreciating bits of paper because the effect of lowering the price is to increase the effective interest. A $1,000 bond, selling for $610, was returning an interest rate of 22 per cent. Gamblers would play.)

Campeau decided to bring his own financial genius to bear, and, bypassing the First Boston experts, dreamt up a scheme in which he would allow a few chosen investors to give him $3 billion in return for a piece of the action.[9] Equity. The Reichmanns had started to do it; it was the basis of their original agreement with the Teachers Assurance and Annuity Association when they borrowed $250 million in New York. But who wanted equity in Campeau Corporation? You do not bid for deck chairs on the *Titanic*. There were no takers.

As the walls began to close in on him, Campeau came to the Reichmanns once more, in April 1989, with a desperate plea for cash; he had to have $150 million at once, or he would go under. They responded by agreeing to lend him $75 million U.S., secured by his half-interest in Scotia Plaza. If anything went wrong, they would own that building for $125 million, since they had already paid him $50 million U.S. for their half. Well, not quite, there was a mortgage of $440 million Canadian, owed to a syndicate of Canadian banks, led by the Bank of Nova Scotia.[10] Still, it would be a good buy.

That deal was still being churned through the lawyers when, on April 27, 1989, James Roddy, the president of Campeau Corporation, and Buck Luce, the key financial strategist, quit. Campeau presented this as another rejuvenating reorganization; in fact, it was a sign of how fed up his own employees were with his erratic behaviour.[11]

The resignation must have come as a shock over at O&Y. Now they had $260 million in debentures, and $7.5 million in shares, and $75 million in loans to Campeau, in addition to the other $50 million they had put into Scotia Plaza, all tied up with a man whose business behaviour was erratic. At this point, and not before time, Paul Reichmann hired a financial investigator to check out Robert Campeau, and, by midsummer, the investigator was back to tell Reichmann something he didn't really want to know.[12] Federated and Allied could not possibly generate enough cash to pay their bills and the mountains of interest piling up on their various issues of junk bonds. Bankruptcy seemed inevitable. Moreover, it turned out that the $150 million U.S. that Edward DeBartolo had advanced to Campeau, so that he could come up with the necessary injection of equity into the Allied deal (which bit of fancy finance we met in Chapter Ten), had been backed by a note on Campeau's Canadian assets.

If Campeau were to go broke, Paul Reichmann now learned, O&Y would not necessarily have first grabs at Scotia Plaza, or any other Canadian property. DeBartolo might come ahead of them.[13] Their investment was much riskier than it had seemed.

You would never have known, by the way Campeau behaved, that anything had gone wrong, or could go wrong. On May 10, First Boston finally structured another Rube Goldberg financial machine, not to provide the mortgage agreement on Federated that Campeau needed, which, everyone was assured, would come later, but to keep the company going until that could be arranged – in return for more handsome fees.

When the *Wall Street Journal* saluted the annual meeting of Campeau Corporation on July 20, 1989, with a piece suggesting that his companies might not be able to service their massive debts, Campeau heaped scorn on them. "We've been tried, we've been hung and given reprieves so many times from all the newspapers and analysts in this country that it's just amazing we're still around."[14] He went on to paint an upbeat, and not entirely accurate picture of his financial status, and, at a press conference, lectured the Canadian government. It was piling up too much debt, he said, and ought to mend its ways. He also commented on the fact that, in the United States, a chap could do much better than he could in Canada, owing to the marvels of free enterprise. For himself, debt was an elixir. "Debt can be a vital instrument to help leverage growth and create additional value to our shareholders."[15] It is not unusual for tycoons to embrace debt for corporations while recommending governments eschew it. Paul Reichmann had also lectured governments on "the tragedy of government deficits" at the official opening of the World Financial Center on October 17, 1985.[16] Got a good round of applause for it, too, although he was on the way to running up a deficit that would make even some governments wince.

It was all a front. In August Campeau flew to Switzerland, where Paul Reichmann was on holiday, to beg once more for an injection of cash. Reichmann, who now had the disturbing report about the real state of Campeau's finances, told him that his best course was to file for bankruptcy protection under Chapter 11 of the U.S. Bankruptcy Code, which might save – a point not without interest to O&Y – the Canadian assets, even if he lost both Allied and Federated. Campeau left, but the two men met again soon after, at O&Y headquarters on Great George Street in London, where, although no one was to know it, things were not going too well for the Canary Wharf project.

Campeau had reached a crucial point. If he didn't raise some more money soon, there would be no merchandise on the shelves of his new retail empire for the Christmas season. If Paul Reichmann wouldn't lend him $250 million U.S., it might be game over. The fact is that O&Y did not have a spare $250 million at this point, but what it did have, still, was its reputation. Reichmann made a deal that resulted in an elaborate arrangement, later filed with the Ontario Securities Commission.[17]

Olympia & York Developments Limited would guarantee a $250 million U.S. line of bank credit through its holding company, Olympia & York CC Limited, so that Campeau's stores could stock their shelves for Christmas. Campeau, in return, would give O&Y another $250 million in debentures, backed by a number of Campeau assets, including his interest in Scotia Plaza, Waterpark Place, land at Queen and Yonge streets in Toronto, the London Galleria in London, Ontario, his interest in Campeau Corporation (U.S.) Inc., and notes issued by Allied and Federated.[18]

There was more. On September 19, O&Y bought 15,625,000 warrants (rights to purchase stock in Campeau Corporation), each of which could be turned into shares at an "exercise price" of $16 U.S. For these warrants O&Y paid $150,000 Canadian.

As of September 25, 1989, O&Y, with the debentures and stock previously owned, "May be deemed to beneficially own and have sole voting and sole dispositive power (directly) in respect of 32,344,694 Shares (or approximately 45.3% of the outstanding Shares)."[19] It wasn't Campeau's company any more; for all practical purposes, it was O&Y's.

Considering what happened later, and considering the fact that

Campeau Corporation was already headed for the chute, one might wonder why O&Y went into this arrangement. Campeau himself would later come up with his own reason: he thought the Reichmanns were trying to take Scotia Plaza away from him. It seems more likely that they had no more choice than he did. They already had more than half a billion dollars in U.S. funds invested in Campeau. They simply could not afford to write that off, as they would have had to do, if he were forced into bankruptcy. The only thing they could do was to use their own credit to keep him going, while playing for time; they had to have control of Campeau Corporation, if they were to have any chance to turn it around.

The agreement provided for that, too. The "Purpose" set out in that document was "that OYDL [Olympia & York Developments Limited] increase its investment in Campeau and provide its assistance in connection with a major restructuring of Campeau and its subsidiaries to address certain liquidity needs and to ensure orderly operations while pursuing a financial restructuring of Campeau and its subsidiaries to reduce leverage."[20]

Campeau was to be brought to heel. A new board of directors of Campeau Corporation was set up to oversee the restructuring, with three Campeau nominees, three O&Y nominees, and four nominees from the minority shareholders of Campeau. The O&Y nominees were Lionel Dodd, the manager of the Reichmanns' investment portfolio, Gil Newman, their company money man, and Albert Reichmann. The minority nominees were headed by a Reichmann ally, Conrad Black, and a restructuring committee, appointed to sort out the mess, was to be chaired by Lionel Dodd. Campeau was not on the committee. The Reichmanns were now running, besides their own beleaguered empire, a retail empire in the United States. The maiden, vowing she would ne'er consent, consented.

The Reichmanns had just gained control over a black hole.

News that the Reichmanns were firmly in charge caused all the right-thinking people on Wall Street, who may not be as smart as they think they are, to heave a huge, collective sigh of relief. This would soon be sorted out; the stock market responded with the blind stupidity for which that place is known by giving a nice little jump to Campeau shares, from $13.50 on September 13, to $14.75 on September 19. "Wall Street figured," writes John Rothchild, "that the richest developers in the world were too smart to be throwing good money after bad, and therefore that Campeau's predicament must not be as dire as it looked."[21] This was true; Campeau's predicament was not as dire as it looked. It was much worse.

Retail sales were dropping, as North America headed into a severe recession. The debtload would have crippled Allied and Federated in the best of times, but in these times they stood no chance. By September, clothing manufacturers who shipped goods to the chains were beginning to wonder if they would get paid. By November, some had started to hold back. On December 6, Dun & Bradstreet Corp. advised clients not to ship goods to Campeau,[22] and, by January, they had their answer: they would not get paid.

In the meantime, on October 26, the junk-bond market went into a tailspin, and Allied bonds fell to 32 cents on the dollar. Campeau had destroyed the name, reputation, and finance of two retailing chains that had been solvent for seventy-five years, and not all the Reichmanns' horses nor all the Reichmanns' men could do a damn thing about it. Attempts to sell off more of the chains got nowhere – the prices offered were not high enough to rescue the remainder – and stocks in all the companies went into freefall. In mid-December some of the bankers who had large amounts at stake called on the Reichmanns to inject more money, and became pretty bitter when they refused. So did Campeau's small circle of allies. The *Globe and Mail* quoted an unnamed "former director" of Campeau's as saying, "I feel very strongly that they [the Reichmanns] had the opportunity to do something. But nothing was done and it has been a complete waste of time, effort and money."[23]

The Reichmanns might have replied that they were running out of cash themselves, but that might not have been prudent in the circumstances. There was also a bitter personal dispute with Campeau, who was not inclined to let anyone tell him what to do with his company, which ended with the disbanding of the restructuring committee four months after it was set up.

Campeau flew off to Austria to celebrate Christmas at his château, but there was little to celebrate back in New York. And when the manufacturers and jobbers who supplied the Christmas stock to his chains came to get paid on Friday, January 12, 1990, they found themselves in long line-ups at stores like Bloomingdale's, just to get their cheques. The smart ones rushed those cheques to the issuing banks at once, to get the money out. The less nimble deposited the cheques in their own banks, where they were held over the weekend for clearance. That was a long weekend – Martin Luther King's birthday – and on the Monday, Federated and Allied filed for bankruptcy protection; the cheques bounced.

The Allied/Federated joint bankruptcy, worked out in Cincinnati, represented $8.2 billion U.S. in debts. There were 50,000 creditors, a bankruptcy record.[24] The cutbacks to try to keep the companies going resulted in the loss of 8,000 jobs. By the time the two companies filed a reorganization plan that was acceptable to their creditors, in April 1991, $70 million U.S. had been spent for lawyers, accountants, and "work-out specialists" that might otherwise have been wasted on salaries, or on payments to suppliers. The 8,000 people fired, at an average salary of $20,000, saved $160 million, less than the $200 million spent on fees alone in each of the takeovers. This failure pushed Campeau Corporation into insolvency, as well.

The Reichmanns watched the shares in Campeau Corporation drop from $26 U.S. to 50 cents, and to make it worse, had to listen to Campeau blaming them for not working harder and spending more to save him.

They couldn't. And they couldn't tell the world why they couldn't. They had taken on too much. When they had begun to get involved with Campeau, they had not yet finished the World Financial Center, or even given a thought to Canary Wharf. But, in 1987, they had finished the first and started on the second, and both were a heavy cash drag. The inducements required to lure tenants into the New York property, while they might come back in the end, meant that the World Financial Center was a drain, not a source of cash, at this time. And the leasings at Canary Wharf were not going well. Rentals had fallen, because of the City's decision to allow more building. Enticing businessmen into hazarding their bowlers on the Riverbus or the Docklands Light Railway was proving to be uphill work. In 1986 and 1987, stories about how remote the place was – some of them quite wrong, some correct, all damaging – added to the problem.

To help the *Telegraph* pick Canary Wharf for its quarters, O&Y had paid out a one-time cash inducement of £20 million, which was all very well for Conrad Black, the paper's owner, but it rather cut into O&Y's cash flow. The Reichmanns had injected £1.6 billion into Canary Wharf, some of it pulled through various parts of their empire, and they would have to inject more.

The building was not going as well as expected, and, in March 1990, O&Y fired the project managers on the main tower, giving them one day to clear their desks. Even if the banks were still blithely shoving the stuff over the counter, they might have pulled back a trifle if O&Y were suddenly to announce that it didn't have any cash to spare for Robert Campeau. The first rule of banking, as we know, is never to lend money to anyone who doesn't already have it, and while it is possible to kid the banks along, if you actually say you haven't got it, the flow gets turned off at the mains.

There were other problems. Abitibi-Price was not turning around and, along with Gulf Canada, was a cash sponge instead of a fountain of dividends. Not long before Campeau appeared at the door with his tin cup, the Reichmanns had negotiated a $2.5 billion U.S. loan (in the later bankruptcy proceedings, this would always be referred to, in hushed tones, as "the Jumbo Loan") with a syndicate of twelve international banks, led by the Hong Kong and Shanghai Bank, for the Canary

Wharf project.[25] No one outside a small circle knew about this loan, but it would have to be serviced, for somewhere over $250 million annually in interest costs alone. What would happen to this if the Reichmanns pleaded poverty as a reason for rebuffing Campeau?

So, when Paul and Albert Reichmann met with senior officials of Citibank in New York on two occasions in December 1989, they downplayed their connection with Campeau. Citibank had a number of loans out to both O&Y and Campeau's companies; they thought it would be pleasant if the former, which they knew to be rolling in the stuff, shared some out, if only to protect their own interests. At both meetings the Reichmanns stressed how little actual equity they had tied up with Campeau. They declined to play.[26]

Within three weeks of the last meeting with Citibank, Allied and Federated were in bankruptcy, and it is hardly surprising that the Reichmanns drew some harsh looks. They had, after all, taken over Campeau Corporation, and then they had done very little. To anyone who didn't understand their own predicament, it looked not merely heartless, but self-defeating.

The *Globe and Mail* ran an article under the heading "BANKERS DISMAYED THAT O&Y LEFT CAMPEAU TALKS,"[27] which fairly bristled with angry quotes, all from unidentified sources. One banker was quoted as saying, "Clearly the Reichmanns are doing everything they can do to distance themselves from Campeau's troubles. We're still waiting to see if Paul Reichmann is going to come out of the hole he's hiding in and do something for Campeau." This man was identified as "a banker to both the Reichmanns and Campeau." Hard not to be; every major Canadian bank except Toronto Dominion was in that category.

The story went on to justify the headline: "Bankers said they were dismayed by the withdrawal because it was the Reichmanns' intervention last fall that encouraged them not to take any action on some Campeau loans that were technically in default."

Here we have, I think, some indication of why the banks got themselves in so deep with the Reichmanns and then got so sore because the

Reichmanns got them in so deep. As we know, when he began to get uneasy about Campeau, Paul Reichmann sicced a financial investigator on to him, who soon told him that Campeau was in deep trouble. The banks, having backed Campeau for billions, were reassured because the Reichmanns, whose own financial status by this time would have given them a few shocks, had they cared to probe, had become further entangled with the man. Then they became "dismayed" because the Reichmanns, who by this time knew far too much, didn't want to pour more good money after bad. Another unidentified banker complained in the same article that "the Japanese are irate." (He didn't mean the Japanese generally, just Japanese bankers.) "They feel the Reichmanns betrayed them."

It was the apparent position of the banks that the Reichmanns were wilfully standing by and watching Campeau founder, when all they had to do was come to the rescue. Since Paul Reichmann was, at this time, a director of the Canadian Imperial Bank of Commerce, he might have been in a position to explain all this, except that he couldn't, not without seeing the cash window slammed on his own fingers.

The Campeau debacle ended the notion of the Reichmanns as financial geniuses. The *Globe* commented, "The apparent retreat signals a rare financial defeat by the Toronto Reichmanns, who have nurtured a sterling reputation with lenders around the world." [28] And they couldn't even defend themselves, they could only look on helplessly as the Campeau empire was taken apart, block by block. They had tangled with a tar baby; they got stuck at the very first touch, and the more they struggled, the worse it got.

The National Bank went to court to try to recover the $150 million it had loaned Campeau to buy his own company's shares, and seized the shares, which gave it the right to two seats on the board of directors; it now had three seats, the same as O&Y. [29] It then joined with the O&Y directors to hoist Campeau from his roles as chairman and chief executive officer.

Then the Bank of Montreal seized shares for an unpaid loan, and the Bank of Nova Scotia, not wishing to be left out, filed a claim for $10 million it had given Campeau for a mortgage on his Bridle Path mansion. Campeau left for Austria again, and refused to talk to reporters or receive any court depositions "on the advice of his physician."[30]

The company was reorganized, again, with Stanley Hartt, who had been Prime Minister Brian Mulroney's chief of staff, as chairman, and in May 1991, Campeau Corporation, stripped of Campeau, sued him for $12.7 million and asked him to return paintings and cars that belonged to the company. About half the money owed was for the château in Austria,[31] which Campeau doesn't own – it belongs to a private foundation, called a "stiftung," in Switzerland. His wife owns the place on the Bridle Path.[32]

But you can't keep a good man down. Campeau came bounding back to Canada and, at the 1991 annual meeting of Campeau Corporation, put himself back on the board. He had the right, under his original arrangement with O&Y, to name three directors, so he named himself.

On October 22, 1991, O&Y moved to pick up the other half of Scotia Plaza, since Campeau was unable to make any payments on the debentures he had given them, in return for writing off some of his debt to them.[33]

Two months later Campeau Corporation had a stake driven through its heart. At a meeting of shareholders and creditors at the Harbour Castle Hilton, formerly the Harbour Castle, which Campeau had built, for Pete's sake, the company was renamed Camdev Corporation, and Campeau was stripped of his seat on the board, and all but 2 per cent of his shares. The creditors accepted this arrangement, and the company, lighter by $2.2 billion in debts, came out of bankruptcy protection. O&Y wound up with 65 per cent of Camdev, which was dealt off, two days later, to Albert Reichmann for an undisclosed price.[34] (Going by the share price on the market, it should have been about $38.6 million.) Camdev began to shed properties and debt, in an attempt to rebuild itself as a more-modest, but less-debt-ridden, corporation.

Three weeks later Federated Department Stores Inc. emerged from bankruptcy in Cincinnati; the new company is an amalgam of the old Federated and Allied chains, all the parts that are left, anyway.[35]

This second round with Robert Campeau left the Reichmanns badly battered, although not much of the bruising showed in public. Their investment, of more than $600 million Canadian, was worth almost nothing, and they could not afford to take that kind of financial shellacking at this time. They had picked up some assets, including the London Galleria in London, Ontario, the other half of Scotia Plaza, and, of all things, the Blue Bonnet racetrack in Montreal, but they also picked up more debt.

Just as important was the blow to their image as shrewd managers who seldom put a foot wrong. Their judgement was called into question. Their reputation might have been exaggerated, it *was* exaggerated, but, in the world of high finance, Who steals my purse, steals trash, but he that flitches from me my good name plays hell with my bond ratings, and may make it impossible for me to borrow at all.

The Street, that harsh and daffy judge, was beginning to wonder, If the Reichmanns were so smart, how did they get tied up with someone like Robert Campeau? Well, now we know, but nobody knew then, and it was not a subject the Reichmanns were anxious to explore.

If there was one thing they didn't need right now, it was more trouble. So that, naturally, is just what they got.

CHAPTER SIXTEEN

A Sinking Feeling on Canary Wharf

The major banks will not move away from the gossip, and the gossip
will not travel down the road to Canary Wharf. You have to run into
somebody in the street or a restaurant.
– Peter Rees, Director of Planning, City of London, 1990 [1]

$

If you want to have a look at Canary Wharf some time, and it is well
worth a look for anyone travelling to London, the best way to get there
is to take a tube from wherever you are to either Tower Gateway or
Bank Street station. Tower Gateway is right beside the Tower of London; you leave the station and follow signs that take you along a path
and up a flight of stairs to the platform for the Docklands Light Railway. This was the first connection constructed. At Bank Street you
don't even have to leave the station, the "dear little railway" rolls right
up inside. London Transport passes and fares are accepted; a £1.25
ticket from anywhere downtown will get you right through. The three-
car trains, very attractive, new and clean, are driverless, completely
automatic, but there is a conductor aboard to check your ticket. The

sides of the red-and-blue cars are almost entirely glass; you will be able to see everything.

You roll across London's East End, not a pretty sight, swing across the Limehouse Link, and find yourself staring at a series of magnificent new buildings rising out of a sea of council flats on the edge of the development. Disney World meets Don Mills. Even before you get to the Canary Wharf station (four stops, or about fifteen minutes, from Bank Street), there are small signs that not all is well. Some of these are, literally, signs, in apartment buildings along the way. They read "No Noise," and other less-printable variations on the theme that it is no fun having an elevated railway whiz past your sixth-floor apartment every eight minutes all day long. Other indications are less forthright. You pass by wide expanses of hole, with bits and pieces of concrete pilings sticking up, and a couple of silent cranes standing where they stopped when work on Phase Two was suspended. There are pools of water here and there, piles of debris, and odds and sods of construction equipment and planks. Also, one huge excavation with a handful of parked cars scattered about among the pools. Very unlovely.

Then you pull into Canary Wharf station, with its vaulting glass roof, and muted brown-marble walls; it is full of light and welcome. An escalator takes you down to the doors that lead outside; but first, you take another escalator down one floor further, where the signs point you to One Canada Square. Just fooling. The doors on this level are chained, and most of the windows, in what will someday be a basement shopping plaza, are papered over.

Back upstairs, you find another way into the tower, but you can't go up unless you have an appointment with someone. For a time visitors were allowed to zip up to an observation area on the fiftieth floor, but then two bombs planted by the Irish Republican Army were discovered by alert guards, and that ended that. You wander back through to a visitors' centre, where there is a model of the development, a lot of photographs of construction, and some carefully worded bumph about Olympia & York. G. Ware Travelstead doesn't get a mention. Crossing the street into Cabot Square, you find a selection of very nice shops and restaurants, and a number of empty spaces where more shops and restaurants will be, one day. Most of the shops appear to contain goods at prices that only the heads of the companies who lease here could afford, and they shop on Bond Street. One assistant is sound asleep behind her counter. Don't disturb. What do the secretaries and other underlings here do at lunchtime? They go outside, for a stroll. You follow them.

There are walks and parks and promenades, a couple of restaurants on ships, pubs, more parks, more promenades. Everything is new, well-designed, open, dare you use the word "planned?" right down to the 132 full-grown trees of thirteen varieties, 6,000 seasonal bedding plants, 67,500 bulbs, including 16,000 narcissi, scattered among the parks.[2] The overall effect is soothing, and if it weren't for the eerie feeling that you and a handful of others are the last persons left on earth, it would be very restful indeed. One thing will strike you only later; no children. You can walk for a mile and never see a child, a dog, or a cat. That's a little eerie, too. Behind you looms the tower, tall, grey, and handsome. Quite a lot of it is empty. There is a rank of taxis on one side of the road that leads past One Canada Square, and two London double-decker buses wait just down the other way. A lone scooter rambles right down the middle of the road. No need to worry about traffic jams.

Back to the DLR station again, and you ride to the end of the line, at Island Gardens, a lovely park just across the Thames from Greenwich, where the Mean Time gets its meanness at the observatory. On this leg of travel, past Heron Quays, South Quay, Cross Harbour, and Mudchute, you see the flocks of other new developments lured here by the LDDC, and, at South Quay, you zip past the offices of the LDDC itself. You realize that it is only Canary Wharf that blots out everything else on its block of land. The other new developments have been thrust into the midst of communities that have been here for a couple of hundred years. And look it.

Canary Wharf is attached to one end of a peninsula otherwise pulsating with life. Unemployed life, a lot of it, but life none the less. On the return journey, you get out at Crossharbour and walk around. Mean streets. Small, cramped houses, jammed up against each other, blocks of flats, a monstrous, North American-style superstore, with a huge parking lot, and, beyond this, more narrow streets, small houses, broken fences, and a library, a run-down, hopeless-looking thing, which has a good many fewer books than any school library you can remember. The LDDC may be rich, Canary Wharf may represent billions of dollars, but the local communities are dirt poor, and the library shows it. After a disheartening tour, you go wandering again, and find a young man leaning against a doorway. You ask him if he'd be willing to answer a few questions about Olympia & York, you know, the developers.

"Jesus," he says, "them buggers. I worked over there. Leave me be." He glowers.

It seems wise to pass on, around the corner, and there, by God, is a pub. In the pub, over a pint of bitter and a pub lunch likely to give your cholesterol count a goosing – sausages, fried egg, chips, beans, and half a fried tomato – the subject of development comes up.

"Daft," the landlord pronounces.

"Who? Olympia & York? The LDDC?"

A middle-aged man, nursing a small Scotch, replies, "All of them. Christ, what we couldn't do with some of the money they pissed away on that lot over this way."

A younger man looks up from a newspaper and waves his fork. He's having the pub lunch, too. "It was Maggie did them in," he says. "Maggie got them here and then she was gone and left them up the creek. Serves them right."

An older man, a pensioner by the look of him, holds out his empty glass. "Never mind that," he says. "They were all right. There was money in here when things were going. They paid good wages, and they did a lot for the schools. My granddaughter, she thinks the world of them. The people who don't like them," he adds, "are mostly Labour types. Lefty loonies, I call them." He waves the glass gently, suggestively. "Lefty loonies."

This brings up a nice point of etiquette; if you buy him a pint, is that cheque-book journalism? Better to leave, with principles intact.

Back at Canary Wharf, sitting on a park bench nursing a cup of coffee while you await your next appointment, you can't help thinking about what a bloody silly waste it all is. Someday, this development will be finished, and fully occupied. Anyone can see that. London has no place else to grow, except by sticking on yet more suburbs to the north and west. So, it will come east. It will come here. But, if it is to come successfully, the order of events will have to be reversed. It takes ten years, at least, to prepare the infrastructure before you dump a hundred thousand workers into one small area: time to build the roads, time for the communities to regroup, if you bother to let them know what you have in mind, and to think about what the impact will be on themselves.

Because no environmental-impact studies were done – all of that was wiped out with the establishment of the LDDC and the sidelining of the local authorities – there was no warning before the cranes and bulldozers moved in and the air was filled with dust and dirt and all sorts of pollutants, including a ceaseless, godawful din. It would save time, they said, if there were no public inquiry into this aspect beforehand. Now ten thousand local residents are taking legal action against the LDDC and O&Y because of the continual noise, dirt, and disruption created at Canary Wharf during Phase One.[3] How much time will those lawsuits waste? Between 1981 and 1990, the LDDC spent £622 million on administration, roads, and utilities, and £147 million on housing.[4] The roads are much nicer than the houses.

When Canary Wharf rises again, perhaps it will be done the other way around. First the plan, then the development; first, not to make any bones about it, the damn tube line, and then the place the tube line is going to. First, some provision for the housing and schools to make a community, and then provision for the commuters in the big towers. La Defense, the giant development in downtown Paris, worked it that way around; the government provided the infrastructure, then the private side got its chance. Those crazy Frenchmen.

But it was not just the reversal of priorities that did in the Reichmanns and their bright dream, there were a number of other factors besides.

The two years between the time Robert Campeau sought bankruptcy protection and the Reichmanns followed him were full of one damn thing after another, in Canada, the United States, and Britain.

In January 1990, the Reichmanns wound up Olympia & York Enterprises Inc., which had been the holding company for the stock portfolios, and restructured Olympia & York Developments Limited, OYDL, the firm that actually held O&Y Enterprises. Like the old company, it was 100 per cent owned by members of the family. Then they created GWU Holdings Limited, which, again, was wholly owned by the family, with two subsidiaries, GWU Investments Limited, entirely held by GWU Holdings, and GW Utilities Limited, 89.34 per cent held by the family. (The rest was traded on the stock market.) GWU Holdings Limited had been created in 1988, as a subsidiary of a subsidiary of a subsidiary of a subsidiary of Olympia & York Enterprises Inc.

The shares of all the Edper-group companies owned by the Reichmanns, which at this time amounted to 50.01 per cent of Carena Properties, which in turn owned 50.21 per cent of Trizec, and the Reichmanns' 13.92 per cent holding of Trilon Financial Corporation, were all dealt off to OYDL. The stock investments were divided into two groups, with the resource investments going into GW Utilities and the rest into GWU Investments, both held by GWU Holdings, which, as mentioned, the family owned directly.[5] All of this, besides making money for lawyers and registrars, made things much neater, and set the stage for another move six months later.

Gulf Canada was still struggling, burdened with the debts incurred in its original acquisition and the decline in oil prices. On March 30, 1990, Dominion Bond Rating Service looked over the Reichmanns' stock portfolio and declared that it was worth about $6.6 billion. That was the good news. The bad news was that the agency downgraded the company because of the dragging effect of the Gulf stock. DBRS reduced the rating on $160 million U.S. worth of floating rate notes that had been issued against Gulf Canada Square in Calgary, from AA to A.[6] This was not a crushing blow, by any means, but it was a knock on the knee. The agency calculated that the Reichmanns were making annually about $163 million from their portfolio, which was bound to strike outsiders as a very poor return (crudely figured, about 2.5 per cent). Moody's Investment Service also downgraded most of the company's paper, because of "Gulf's weak earnings outlook."[7] The second downgrading was worrisome, and the Reichmanns responded with one of their zippy stock manoeuvres, but this one didn't entirely succeed. They set up a complex deal to upgrade the share value, not only of Gulf, but of related companies.

Then, in June 1990, the brothers sought to "take private" GW Utilities, the company into which they had funnelled their resource holdings. They owned 89 per cent of GW, and offered to buy the remaining 11 per cent of shares held by the public. The aim of the move was "to better realize the value of the company's underlying assets"[8]; that is, by selling some of them. They already had an offer from British Gas for GW's share of Consumers' Gas, and a deal through which Gulf Canada was to buy a chunk of Interhome Energy from Imperial Oil. The idea was to combine GW Utilities and O&Y, which would then hold a company called Oilco, made by combining their stakes in Home Oil and Gulf and their majority share in Interprovincial Pipeline, while selling their Consumers' Gas holdings for $908 million. They would get some money, and the remaining package would be worth more. However, the minority shareholders had to agree, and so did the Ontario Energy Board, and the deal came unstuck, even after they raised their offer to the minority shareholders from $36 to $40.

They went ahead with the Consumers' Gas sale anyway, and then sold their holdings in Allied-Lyons, collecting $1.22 billion by paying themselves dividends through GW Utilities, the beneficiary of the sales. These moves brought in money, but shed assets, and the money, it now appears, went straight out again to help pay the rising bills at Canary Wharf.

The gloomy news continued to pile up. In July 1990, Abitibi-Price reported that it was still losing money, and it would wind up losing $45 million Canadian over the year.[9] This was bad on two counts: the first was that it hit dividend income to O&Y, the second was that Abitibi shares had already gone out as collateral on loans. As the shares fell in response to the reports of losses, so did their worth as collateral.

But perhaps the most startling development on the Reichmann front in Canada was the emergence of Philip Reichmann, Albert's son, the vice-president of Olympia & York Developments Limited, when that company replaced O&Y Enterprises. He invited a group of real-estate brokers up to lunch at First Canadian Place in November 1990, and told them what a tough time it was to be in the realty business.[10] Downtown office vacancy rates in Toronto had soared to 12.7 per cent, from less than 3 per cent two years earlier, and nearly 20 per cent of the seventy-two-storey tower at First Canadian Place was empty. (O&Y was one of the companies that had moved out; it shifted over to the twenty-eighth storey of the Exchange Tower. Its floor in First Canadian Place is now occupied by Price Waterhouse, the O&Y auditors.) The financing of First Canadian Place was not yet in danger, but the building had produced extra cash for O&Y for years, and that was indeed in danger.[11] The vacancies over at the Exchange Tower, the smaller building, were about 10 per cent. Dominion Bond Rating Service had downgraded the paper secured by both buildings, and Philip Reichmann had called in the brokers to explain to them that O&Y was now changing tactics.

It was now willing to slash rates and offer incentives, something it had done in New York and England, but never at First Canadian Place. Another 2.7 million square feet of office space was coming onto the market in the downtown area. Some of O&Y's best clients were leaving, some to go to the new BCE Place, where prestige space was renting for less than the $47 per square foot then charged on the top sixteen floors of First Canadian Place. The message Philip wanted to get out was that O&Y was willing to compete with anybody for tenants. The other message that came out, unintentionally, was that O&Y was in trouble.

Before long a rumour was circulating that OYDL, the major holding company, had defaulted on a loan payment to Citibank. The company and bank both denounced the rumour, which Citibank called "patently ridiculous," but the fact that it was believed, for a time, showed that the bond-rating services weren't the only ones getting edgy about the company. Everybody was.

Things were not going any better across the border.

In 1989, as if they didn't have enough on their plates, the Reichmanns explored the notion of purchasing the world's tallest building, the Sears Tower in Chicago. That came unstuck, and the reason given was that there were tax problems with the transaction, but it happened to coincide with the tottering of the Campeau empire. Whatever the reason, it was a retreat and a defeat. They had also begun work on a 4,500-acre island development off the coast of South Carolina, being built by the Harry F. Guggenheim Foundation, with O&Y as the construction overseers. [12]

Clearly, they had too much on their plates, and at the end of the year they hired John Zucotti, a real-estate lawyer who had been deputy mayor of New York, to the presidency of Olympia & York (U.S.). He would look after the Manhattan real estate, among other things, while they got on with Canary Wharf, a $30-billion project in Tokyo harbour, and Yerba Buena Gardens in San Francisco, which still hadn't jelled, although it was undertaken in 1980. There was also a $100-million office building in Budapest, begun after an Albert Reichmann trip to Hungary, where the brothers were now spending millions in support of local education and religious projects. None of these would ever come off.

Early in 1990, they added another large project to the mix, when Albert Reichmann flew to Moscow with a group of Canadian businessmen and came home with plans to build a sixty-storey skyscraper in the heart of Moscow. They were going to have to keep him home. The Moscow project, a $250-million U.S. development, would be the highest building in the former Soviet Union. It would never happen, either.

In New York, the financial centre of the empire, the place where funds would have to be generated to service Canary Wharf, tenants were moving out of O&Y buildings faster than they were moving in. The faint outline in glue of the words "Drexel Burnham Lambert" was all that remained of one of the best leases in Manhattan, a fifteen-year agreement with the giant stock brokerage on twenty-three floors of 60 Broad Street. Drexel, Michael Milken's firm, had gone bust, and earned itself author Nicholas von Hoffman's pithy epithet, "The criminal conspiracy."[13] The twenty-three floors were empty by the end of 1990, and would stay empty. That was only the beginning. The vacancy rate in downtown Manhattan hit 20 per cent early in 1991,[14] and, at 2 Broadway, above papered-over windows on the ground floor, where there used to be retail outlets, 42 per cent of the office space was standing empty. Merrill Lynch used to live here, but O&Y had persuaded Merrill Lynch to move across to the World Financial Center, without being able to find anyone to replace them. As mortgages came due it was harder and harder, and more and more expensive, to replace the funds with new money, so costs kept going up while income kept dropping.

Olympia & York had formed partnerships with JMB and other companies, but these only made borrowing more difficult, since the titles were complicated by the joint ventures. The city was beginning to believe that the Reichmanns had already borrowed too much; two agencies slashed credit ratings on $548.3 million U.S. in notes against 55 Water Street, and Standard & Poor Corp., the arbiters of such matters, downgraded $630.5 million U.S. worth of bonds the company had issued in 1986.[15] Soon after, $200 million U.S. worth of Euronotes borrowed against 59 Maiden Lane were similarly cut.

These downgradings were a clear signal to the finance industry that a real concern existed, for the first time, as to whether O&Y's New York buildings could continue to service the debts the Reichmanns had rolled up against them to finance their various ventures. The company put on a brave face, as it had to, and John Zucotti, the new president of the U.S. company, was shoved out in front of the curtain to murmur, "New York doesn't represent a problem to speak of to the Reichmann brothers."[16]

That was an interesting choice of words. What does "to speak of" mean, exactly? New York real estate represented more of the Reichmann assets than any other element in the family holdings. The fourteen Manhattan towers hold just under twenty-three million square feet of office space – six times that of First Canadian Place, twice that of Canary Wharf. If these buildings were losing some of their value, which is what the bond ratings were now saying, and if the Reichmanns had borrowed more against them than they were going to be worth, that was a problem, whether you wanted to speak of it or not.

They had also purchased a block of Sante Fe shares in 1987, as we have seen. This is another conglomerate, with railway, oil, and real estate combined, all of which were being pummelled, driving down the value of their shares.

By September 1990, the cash-strapped Reichmanns were moved to the unthinkable; on Wednesday, September 19, word hit Wall Street that the family was looking for a buyer for its 20 per cent partnership in the U.S. real-estate portfolio. The world learned, for the first time, that the real estate was held 80 per cent by the company and 20 per cent by the family. It was this second part that was to go on the market. Official O&Y spokesmen would not comment, but "some company sources," which, if you want to know, means O&Y spokesmen talking without attribution, said the reason for unloading this portfolio was "succession planning by the company's owners, Paul, Albert and Ralph Reichmann, to free up money for their 14 children."[17] This was hard to accept. Why would anyone in his right mind sell into a declining market real estate that had been built up since 1977, unless he had to? The money was needed over in Britain, where, in another change of direction, the Reichmanns were no longer going to finance the Canary

Wharf project themselves. They had already begun negotiations with a group of banks to raise £500 million. [18]

Canary Wharf could not begin to return cash until lessees moved in in 1991, but money could be raised on the prospect of leasing. The stock sale would provide some breathing time, if it went well.

But it didn't. There was no interest whatever shown by the American market. "Who wants to buy real estate at this time?" asked one investment banker.

We have already seen that matters were not going well at Canary Wharf itself. The sudden dismissal of the Anglo-Canadian consortium of construction companies actually doing the work, in March 1990, was revealed, a month later, to have been brought about because the project was six months behind schedule. [19] There was, in fact, less and less reason to hurry, except for the desperate need for cash, because vacancy rates had doubled and rental rates had halved in the past year. More and fatter incentives were being laid at the feet of potential lessees, but, so far, almost no British clients could be persuaded to sign up (if you don't count the *Telegraph*, owned by Canadian Conrad Black's Hollinger Inc.) for any substantial space. Moreover, American companies like Texaco and American Express, who had agreed to long-term leases, were beginning to have doubts. O&Y had promised millions of dollars worth of extras to both these companies; but would there be any millions with which to do the work?

It was against this background of unrolling disaster on two continents that Paul Reichmann condescended to give an interview to the *New York Times*, on November 28, 1990. [20] It was a crucial interview. By this time, the Reichmanns had borrowed heavily to support Canary Wharf, and would need billions more. Loans are based on confidence, not numbers; with a number of mortgages, bonds, and notes coming due in the next year, lenders were going to have to be persuaded to hold onto their notes. That would be accomplished by belief, nothing more.

Whenever I think of the Reichmanns – with a good deal of

sympathy – at this point, I am reminded of a story I read as a child in *Boy's Own*, or one of the other British annuals we all got for Christmas when I was a kid. A boy, about ten, discovers by accident that he can fly, and takes great pleasure in soaring around. But he is careful never to let anyone see him. Then, one day, when his school goes on a picnic, a classmate becomes trapped on top of a cliff. The boy flies up and brings him down, to the enthusiastic applause of his fellows. Then the rescued child discovers that he has left his hat atop the cliff, but our hero tells him not to worry, and soars up to get the hat. He has it in his hand when a master comes around the corner, looks up, and says, "Little boys can't fly." Upon which, the poor little bugger comes crashing down.

An act of faith is what keeps bonds turning over, instead of being cashed in when they come due. The holder has two choices; he can present the bond and say "Pay up," or he can persuade himself that it is a good enough investment to leave the money where it is. As long as the paper is earning money, and the interest payments are being met when they fall due, the inclination is to leave it alone. But if there is the slightest concern that the bond, when presented, will not be redeemed, you cash it in. That is why we have bond-rating agencies. Paul Reichmann had to convince the world that O&Y's debts would be paid off as they came due. And, by golly, he did.

Despite the steady string of disasters that had dogged O&Y over the past two years, he sent Richard D. Hylton, the *New York Times* reporter, away with a story that said that little boys can fly. The article, entitled, "Reshaping a Real Estate Dynasty," began, "The Reichmann Family built a fortune by attacking while others were in retreat."[21] It was illustrated with a photo of Margaret Thatcher and Paul Reichmann examining a scale model of Canary Wharf in an admiring way. The interview took place in the O&Y office on Park Avenue at 45th Street, and resulted in an assurance to all those nervous Nellies out there that "the Reichmann brothers – Paul, 60 years old, Albert, 61, and Ralph, 59 – are making changes that will provide more financial security and make operations less interdependent and able to function without a

Reichmann at the helm." Bringing in John Zucotti was part of the strategy; the U.S. empire would function under his guidance. You might chose to read this as meaning that money would not be diverted from the United States to pay the mounting bills at Canary Wharf; you would be wrong. The article said that Zucotti was the first non-family member to head an O&Y company. That was wrong, too. Mickey Cohen had been president of Olympia & York Enterprises.

Paul Reichmann ran the reporter around his empire, where everything was going, he said, just about according to plan, except for a few minor glitches caused by the temporary lull in world markets everywhere. And, in the line quoted in the prologue to this book, he dismissed as "children who don't know what they are talking about" those who speculated that the company was pressed for cash. The reporter was duly impressed. The Reichmanns were going to expand their empire, he noted, not pull back. Expand where? Were they going to take over the Klingons? The *Times* noted that, when construction was finished at Canary Wharf, which was then gobbling money at an alarming, but undisclosed, rate, the short-term loans that were causing such a headache would be replaced by a lower-cost, long-term mortgage "from a pension fund or insurance company."

In short, there was nothing to worry about; the writedowns by the bond-rating agencies were understandable, in the circumstances, but you and I and other, more sophisticated, thinkers realized that all this short-term stuff would soon give way to longer term, cheap money from a pension fund or an insurance agency (the Teachers Assurance and Annuity Association was, at this point, bringing its case against O&Y into court, so that was a nice touch).

His world might have been coming apart at the seams, but Paul Reichmann, redoubtable, "usually reclusive," as the *Times* called him – working-in the necessary phrase – was still able to plug the holes, for now. He had just plugged a big one with a rolled up issue of New York's finest newspaper.

It couldn't last.

CHAPTER SEVENTEEN

The Thousand Cuts

"Sorry, I was held up at our Docklands site."

"Ah," said Jobson. "The never-never land. If you ask me that whole set up's a . . ."

"Bubble that could burst. Oh, I dare say. And a lot of people are making a mint of money."

– Penelope Lively, 1991 [1]

$

For the Reichmanns, the early part of 1991 was taken up, as we have already seen, between trying to put some distance between themselves and the collapsing Campeau empire, and in getting Canary Wharf launched at last. It was to open in July; by early April less than half the space for Phase One, which should have been nearly full by now, had been let, [2] and Phase Two prospects were grim indeed. London office rents were still dropping, and in the Docklands area itself rents near Canary Wharf were as low as £10 per square foot. O&Y needed at least three times that, just to break even. "The market is atrocious," Roger

Nield, manager of the Docklands office of a London realty company told *Maclean's*,[3] "the odds are stacked against Canary Wharf." A number of financial institutions had signed up, including Crédit Suisse First Boston, Morgan Stanley, and Manufacturers Hanover Trust, but not a single *British* financial firm was committed. If Canary Wharf was supposed to have been on the way to becoming London's new financial centre, it was a disaster.

Michael Dennis, the managing director of Olympia & York Canary Wharf Limited, insisted that "things are going to turn very soon." He said that the Gulf War and high interest rates had discouraged companies from making any major commitment, such as a long lease at Canary Wharf, but, with rates down and Iraq crushed (ho, ho), major new tenants would soon be knocking at the door. It was not to be; indeed, Canary Wharf's occupancy rate never got above 55 per cent during 1991, and the leases for Phase Two barely made it past 20 per cent before the project was called off.[4]

Dennis, who would not talk to me, despite an invitation to meet him any time, anywhere, is apparently very bitter about what he saw as the boycotting of Canary Wharf by the City. He told friends that British snobbery, the old "club and pub" argument, had much to do with the failure of the project. There is undoubtedly something in this, clearly indicated by a headline on the tribulations of Canary Wharf that I glimpsed on a newsstand in London, just after the collapse, that read, "ONCE AGAIN, HOME TEAM 3, VISITORS 0." Dennis, according to his friends, also found the British civil service pig-headed and antediluvian, because of a reluctance to move a couple of thousand bureaucrats out to Canary Wharf – a lifeline that might well have kept the project going for at least a time.

But there were other factors at play, including an imperfect understanding on the part of some of the O&Y people of the *amour propre* of Britons. Malcolm Macdonald, an influential strategist in the Department of Transport, told me that he had meetings every two weeks with Olympia & York, and found them much too bumptious.

"Michael Dennis used to stroll into the secretary of state's office with none of the usual deference. He would complain about the lousy lifts. Well, you just don't do that."

In Dennis's defence, it should be said that most of the civil servants I spoke to admired him, while agreeing that he was, indeed, bumptious. It should also be said that the lifts at Two Marsham Street, where the Department of Transport is, mainly, housed, are lousy.

Just the same, Olympia & York undoubtedly came into London with an attitude that they would show the locals how things are done, how a really top-notch, well-organized North American firm could run rings around them. It was not surprising that, when things turned against the intruders, there was no disposition on the part of British companies to rush to their assistance. The Reichmanns had insisted that they didn't need any help; they wouldn't look at a British partner for the Canary Wharf project. Well, then, let them get on with it.

"They made a lot of unnecessary enemies," says David Bayliss, director of planning for London Transport. "There was already a well-developed property industry here, and they just brushed them aside. They had a reputation for arrogance."

With the business sector thoroughly soured, the Reichmanns did the same thing with the bureaucracy. When the Department of Transport was overruled, along with London Transport, and a private consultant was brought in to push the Jubilee Line Extension, the result was to create an unintended, but unavoidable, resentment in the breasts of the Department of Transport. You could not chuck out that department's carefully laid, and expensive, plans for a decade of growth in London, substitute another plan which made no sense except that it would trigger some phantom private financing, and expect the bureaucrats to like it. O & Y didn't care whether they liked it; it wasn't up to them to like it, but to do it. Not wise.

While the offended bureaucrats were nursing their grievances, Fate was preparing to sock the Reichmanns on the occiput with a blackjack.

The blow fell on May 1, 1991, when Dominion Bond Rating Service – boy, they were getting to be a drag – released a report stating that

O & Y had lost $1.25 billion in the value of its stock portfolio in the past year.[5] Gulf Canada Resources, accounting for almost a third of the company's portfolio, was on a rating alert, Abitibi-Price was still drooping, and Campeau Corporation shares, which had been valued at $120 million to O & Y, were now worth no more than $3 million. Most of this portfolio had already been pledged as collateral for various loans extended to O & Y.

In the following months, Paul Reichmann scoured the world looking for investors, or bankers, or anyone, who would advance the funds that would keep the whole operation going until the famous long-term, low-cost mortgages could be secured. He hated travel, but he travelled almost constantly, to England, Japan, Hong Kong, Toronto, anywhere he could lay his case before financial men, sometimes sleeping on the company's Gulfstream jet. And everywhere he travelled he carried a handsome collection of pictures of Canary Wharf, now open for business. He would haul them out in the middle of a financial meeting and begin to show them around, to the bafflement of others present; just like a proud new grandpa, showing off pictures of the kid. If only people could see what a beautiful set of buildings they were, the money would come forth. But it didn't; or, at least, what money did trickle in was expensive. By now more than $2 billion had been spent on Canary Wharf,[6] with very little in the way of rent money to offset it. It didn't help matters that Paul Reichmann was fast gaining a reputation for wanting to redo deals that had, as the other side thought, been settled.

He kept reassuring everyone, even close aides within the company, that it would all work out; the money would be in place in due course, there was nothing to worry about, it was only a matter of time. And then time ran out.

Olympia & York had made a deal with Morgan Stanley for the building at 25 Cabot Square. The bank paid for the structure as a way of advancing funds to O & Y, with an agreement that it would be repurchased at a price of $231 million U.S., through a subsidiary of O & Y, Rochemoor Limited, which was established solely to buy and hold the

building. The way Morgan Stanley understood the deal, it could close
any time after November 1991, and the money would then be paid over.
Robert Greenhill, president of the banking firm, accepted a variation
of the contract, in which the money could be delayed until January.
This new arrangement was made on the telephone, in December, and
Reichmann and Greenhill faxed their signatures to each other to con-
firm it.[7] But Reichmann apparently had quite a different understanding; he thought the money was not now due until June 1992, and that
he was within his rights in refusing to pay.

Morgan Stanley was miffed, and launched a lawsuit in January
1992. There was another consideration that strengthened O&Y's position, if a court chose to accept its view of the matter. The Morgan Stanley deal was in the form of a "put"; that is, the bank had the right to
require O&Y to go through with the purchase any time over a period of
three years, beginning in November 1991. It moved on the put as soon
as it could, for the very good reason that there was some doubt about
where the money to make it work was to come from. Morgan Stanley
had also signed a separate side deal, under which it was to arrange the
financing that would allow the purchase. The bank arranged for, and
collected, a retainer fee towards this deal; it would have collected
another fee on its completion, but, after six months of effort, no satisfactory arrangement could be made.

Morgan Stanley had the right to make O&Y buy its building – that
was one deal. The bank agreed to find the money that would allow
O&Y to buy its building – that was the second deal. O&Y's understanding, broadly put, was "As soon as you guys at Morgan Stanley raise the
money, we'll be happy to buy your building from you." The question
was, were these two deals linked? If Morgan Stanley couldn't persuade
someone else to come up with the money, was the whole arrangement
delayed or disrupted? Olympia & York argued that it was; Morgan
Stanley argued that they were two separate matters, and that it had the
right to proceed with the put no matter what happened on the financing. The court would have to decide that one, and O&Y wouldn't like

the answer. No one but the principals would know about this mess until May, the worst possible time.

That was strike one.

A month later, in early February, O&Y was running out of money to pay some of the short-term commercial paper it had out, and a consortium of Canadian banks provided $275 million in emergency financing. The banks were beginning to get a little edgy by this time, but they came through with the money.

On the heels of this, on February 13, DBRS struck again, with another report downgrading both the IOUs being floated by O&Y as commercial paper and $475 million worth of notes on First Canadian Place.[8] The main reason? "The lack of any financial information on O&Y, which created doubts in the mind of the investor." At this point, First Canadian Place was 28 per cent vacant.[9]

Strike two.

More notes were coming due almost every day, part of the flotilla of loans O&Y had sent out to sea in the heady days when things looked so rosy, and the company had to have cash on hand to meet them. Accordingly, in the early afternoon of February 28, a group of bankers and lawyers met with senior officials of O&Y in the offices of Davies, Ward & Beck, the company's longtime law firm, on the forty-fourth floor of First Canadian Place. The banks represented were the Gang of Four – the Canadian Imperial Bank of Commerce, the Royal Bank, the Bank of Nova Scotia, and the National Bank – who were owed, collectively, about $3 billion[10] by this time, although they had not yet given any indication that the amount was anything as large. The meeting was to get the banks to come up with an emergency loan of $240 million to tide the company over – but that is not what happened. The obligatory cups of coffee had not yet begun to cool when Robert Hall, senior vice-president of Royal Bank, told his banking colleagues that he wanted to meet with them privately. "One of the nice things about the Davies, Ward & Beck offices," I was told, "is that they have these conference rooms all over the place."

In another room, Hall told the other bankers that, over the past three days, O&Y had depleted a $60-million line of credit with his bank to pay off investors in short-term company bonds, and that another $800 million in commercial paper was coming due within the next month. (In fact, it was $1.1 billion.) [11] If you are a holder of one of these notes, on the due day you present it to the paying agent named on the note, and the paying agent, usually a bank or trust company, pays you the principal and interest out of an account the debtor has set up for this purpose. If the investors wanted to cash these notes, Hall said, O&Y could not come up with the money.

A stunned and solemn group of bankers straggled back down the hall to tell O&Y that, no, there would not be any $240-million loan. [12]

You think that's it, don't you? Not at all. The Reichmanns simply rolled with the punch and kept on going.

On March 2, a run on O&Y commercial paper began, which is one way of saying that holders of the notes were dumping them as fast as they could, even at a sharp discount. [13] At this time there were reportedly three sets of notes coming due: $400 million against O&Y Commercial Paper II Inc., $300 million against Exchange Tower, and $416 issued by GW Utilities.

It is worth quoting, I think, from the DBRS report of April 28, 1992, a major research paper on O&Y's troubles, which notes an outstanding assortment of running sores under the heading "Reasons for the Run."

1. The rating cuts on the O&Y Commercial Paper II program and First Canadian Place (bond rating), which were released on February 13, 1992.
2. General concern with real-estate companies by the investor.
3. The lack of any financial information on O&Y, which created doubts in the mind of the investor.
4. A series of specific events which affected O&Y, and became quite significant on a cumulative basis:
   a. Strong negative rumours from Tokyo.

b. Continuing negative rumours from New York.

c. As things progressed, in the week of March 9-13, O&Y was repaying commercial paper as it fell due between 5:30-6:30 p.m. at day's end, as it scrambled to secure funds. When news of this situation hit the marketplace (about March 10 or 11), any chance of issuing new commercial paper became virtually impossible.

d. Banks were extremely sensitive to real-estate lending, due to fears about their own credit ratings, plus they also had never seen the financial statements of O&Y, and did not know what they were facing. Thus, banks were reluctant to give additional support to O&Y.

Well, that does it for me, how about you? The prose style of DBRS might be slightly lacking – the whole thing might have been boiled down to WATCH IT! in about thirty-point type – but the content was riveting. If the lads were rushing over with the day's take at the last minute to pay off the notes, if there was no way they were going to be able to float any more loans, and if, plus and gulp, the banks had been sluicing out all this dough without ever having a real look at O&Y's consolidated books, it was time to float the lifeboats. Gary Klesh, of the investment house of Klesh & Co., in London, would be moved to remark that it wasn't any one thing that was bringing O&Y down – "This thing is dying from a thousand cuts."[14] DBRS had just inflicted about a dozen of them. But, over at O&Y, nothing visible happened.

One of the batches of notes that came due on March 3, 1992, a Tuesday, was payable through the CIBC, but when noteholders turned up at the bank, they were told there was no money in the O&Y account.[15] After a mad scramble, this money was found, but a certain edginess, to put it no stronger than that, was stealing over the market.

Two days later O&Y announced that it was selling its shares in Inter-provincial Pipeline for $655 million, which it would use to pay off some of its debt. This brought a small sigh of relief, and when rumours of an impending bankruptcy began to make the rounds, an O&Y spokesman was able to say, on March 6, that the company was "current on all its obligations." Which was true, but not half the story.

At this time O&Y began to hold meetings every morning at eight a.m., with its lawyers, accountants, company managers, and consultants, to see what could be done about the crisis. There was no panic; on the other hand, nobody knew what was coming next.

More trouble was what was coming next.

Canary Wharf was teetering on the edge of bankruptcy by now; although O&Y had been scrupulous about keeping its contractors and subcontractors paid up to date, there was still work to be done, and no money to do it with. The trouble with financing the development the way the Reichmanns had, which was to dig up the credit they needed as they went along, was that the greatest demand for cash came before the buildings could be leased. When the credit markets dried up, as they did when the recession hit, they couldn't get the necessary cash by converting the short-term notes to mortgages. It's called "financing out." They couldn't finance out of the completed buildings to provide working capital to keep the project going, and without the working capital, there was nothing to do but hope and pray.

About the middle of March, Donald Fullerton, then chairman of CIBC (he was due to retire within months), took to the telephones to persuade the other banks in the Gang of Four, and Citibank, to advance another £50 million to Canary Wharf to keep it from falling off the dock. [16] This one would rebound.

Just about the time Fullerton was popping his dimes into the telephone, Olympia & York failed, on March 15, to pay promissory notes on the Exchange Tower, which came due that day. They amounted to $299,713,770.24. The fat was now fairly in the fire. A committee was immediately set up by the management of Royal Trust, the trustee for the noteholders, to take action on their behalf.

But no action was taken, because the whole thing was being looked after. According to the transcript of a later meeting of the committee, quoting Richard Pound, a lawyer with Stikeman Elliot, who was on the board of Royal Trust, "The Trustee received assurances from Olympia & York that its problem was a temporary shortage of cash flow, due to its inability to issue further paper, and that the position of the noteholders was now fully secured." And why was it secured? "Management of the Trustee was advised by Olympia & York, on an extremely confidential basis, that a proposed sale for refinancing of the Exchange Tower complex had been all but fully negotiated, involving certain banks, with support from the Ontario government and the federal government."[17] The Reichmanns were going to sell the Exchange Tower, and the government would back the notes that would be paid. A bailout.

The notes being in default, the appropriate action to take was for the bondholders to issue a notice of default. But if they did that, Pound stated, "the government-sponsored financing would definitely disappear, with the result that commercial paper markets generally would be destabilized and that the value of the real estate owned by Olympia & York, including the Exchange Tower, mortgaged as collateral for the noteholders, would be diminished."[18]

Royal Trust checked with both governments and was given assurances, Pound said, by both banks and government officials, that "completion of the financing only required final approval from the governments involved."[19]

However, there was no "government-sponsored financing" to speak of. What there was was an awful lot of talk in Toronto and Ottawa about whether to ride to the rescue – which governments were doing with monotonous regularity when companies got into trouble – one more time. There were certainly "contingency plans," and press conferences at which senior politicians indicated that they were "considering" a rescue plan, and memos passed back and forth about how to stick the other government with the cost, but any bailout of the magnitude required here would be a political decision, not a bureaucratic one. And the decision, not to put too fine a point on it, was going to be Ixnay, or *jamais de ma vie,* according to choice.

Never mind; for the moment, the bondholders were breathing easier, and easier still when, on March 23, in the face of continuing
rumours, O&Y announced that it was going to "restructure its debt" to
meet a "liquidity crisis." This was the first public acknowledgement
that the company was unable to meet its obligations. News stories put
the debt at between $12 billion and $20 billion.[20] The restructuring,
which was demanded by O&Y's bankers, would put Thomas Johnson,
a former executive with Manufacturers Hanover and Chemical Bank
in New York, in Paul Reichmann's chair as president of O&Y (Albert
was chairman by this time). Johnson had a reputation as a numbers
man, whereas Paul Reichmann had been known to say that, if you
depended too much on numbers, you never got anything done. The
banks wanted to depend on numbers from now on; they were lonely
for them, and were now in a position to start calling the shots.

The story announcing the new arrangement was headed "REICH-
MANNS CALL IN CAVALRY: U.S. BANKER TO HEAD O&Y,"[21]
which missed the point by a mile. A more appropriate head would
have been "Bankers call in sheriff: Reichmann NOT to head O&Y." One
of the ubiquitous unnamed spokesmen for O&Y said, "Nothing
changes as far as the top executive leadership is concerned, which
remains with Paul and Albert. Putting this group in place allows Paul
to spend more time on Canary Wharf." Great kidders, these PR men.
Certainly the bankers *intended* to make changes as far as executive
leadership was concerned, and, indeed, all the way down the line, or
the transfusions would cease. Johnson's hiring was combined with the
formation of a restructuring committee, just to make sure the restructuring was real, and the engagement of three companies, J. P. Morgan
& Co. Inc., James D. Wolfensohn Inc. of New York, and Burns Fry Limited of Toronto, as financial advisers (that is, they were to try to dig a
tunnel to daylight).

Steve Miller, a vice-president of Wolfensohn (the company had
former Federal Reserve chairman Paul Volcker as its chairman; we are
talking class), would work on the restructuring committee, which

would be chaired by Johnson, a bald, bespectacled, thoroughly respectable number-cruncher whom Paul Reichmann couldn't stand.

Johnson would last exactly nineteen days.

You are entitled to one of two theories as to why Johnson fled so quickly; I think there is something in both. The first is the story put out by Johnson's allies and the banks (Johnson himself went to ground, and has not spoken on the subject). According to this theory, Paul Reichmann simply would not move over to make way for Johnson, and the whole point of his presence was so that he could work things out with the banks, so he bowed out. The other theory is the one put out by O&Y's allies, and it is that Johnson wanted to get paid first, in effect. "He had negotiated a severance package and wanted O&Y to put the money in escrow. O&Y didn't have the money, and the banks wouldn't put it up. They wanted Paul to pay it personally, but his position was that, if the banks wanted this, they should pay for it. Johnson walked away."

That was simplifying things a little too much. CIBC had, at first, offered to provide a $3-million letter of credit to cover Johnson's first year of pay, which was to be $1 million U.S., plus a bonus of $2 million U.S., if the restructuring worked. Johnson, obviously, thought he might wind up with nothing if it didn't. The Bank of Commerce was passing the hat to other banks to help to put the $3 million in the pot, but received nothing but angry rejections, so the bank pulled back. Johnson resigned, demanding a severance package, and was offered a "token sum" by Paul Reichmann. He promptly hired a public-relations firm in New York, Hill & Knowlton, one of the biggies. This seemed to indicate he was about to go public about the matter, so the "token sum" was fattened up to $2 million in a personal cheque signed by Paul Reichmann. Johnson took it and went.

He would be well out of it. Three days after Johnson's resignation, reclusive, media-shy Paul Reichmann was playing the *Financial Post* like a zither. The paper announced breathlessly that "the Reichmann empire is in sound financial condition, despite cash-flow problems,"

on the basis of "financial statements released exclusively to the *Post*."[22]
There was a front-page article, by the FP's editor, Diane Francis, and
inside, a column by Francis, entitled "Reichmann empire on secure
footing," and an editorial, "Calm approach needed on O&Y," all carrying the same message: "The Reichmanns are in great shape," which is
how the Francis column began. Zounds! All that fuss, and there was
nothing the matter, after all. Apparently, the *Post* figured the empire's
soundness on the basis of real-estate evaluations that showed the family holdings to be worth much more than its debts – "a $6 billion equity
cushion," which sounded terrific, were it not for the regrettable fact
that the evaluations were not negotiable at the bank.

Still, it perked up everybody's spirits for a while, especially when
the *Globe* weighed in with an editorial declaring that the Reichmann
debts might be $20 billion, but their assets were worth $30 billion. The
Globe had had a peek at the same numbers.

Bankers, alas, are a hard and cynical bunch, and they were not prepared to let the whole thing ride on the basis of a couple of news
reports, so the very next day, at a meeting in Toronto between O&Y
officials and twenty of its large lenders, a "bank advisory committee"
was established to look over the Reichmann shoulder. It was headed by
CIBC, Citibank, and the Hong Kong and Shanghai Bank.[23] There were
two items of business on the agenda of this new committee. In the first,
O&Y made it clear that it expected the banks to roll over their notes as
they came due, to which the banks replied that they would have to
reserve their position on that one. In the second, a meeting scheduled
for the following week in Toronto was put off to April 13, so that all the
O&Y lenders could attend. This now included ninety-one financial
institutions, showing what a busy boy Paul Reichmann had been – the
very number startled some of the bankers.

When the $440 million U.S. note on Scotia Plaza came due on
April 1, the day after the Toronto meeting, the banks refused to roll it
over,[24] which rather answered that point. This debt was originally
shared by Campeau Corporation, but since O&Y had taken over the
other half of the building, it took over the other half of the debt. You

have to think of these things. At the same time, however, the banks did not serve notice that the note was in default. It was in limbo, which is a nice little condo next door to default.

And the day after that, the board of directors of the CIBC accepted Paul Reichmann's resignation from the board. He did not attend, but resigned by letter. "Insiders said Reichmann made the decision a week or so earlier, for conflict-of-interest reasons," the *Financial Post* reported.[25]

Conflict of interest is an interesting phenomenon in bank circles. It is, and always has been, standard practice in the banks to put their major borrowers on the board. Encourages the chaps to come to the right place for their money. It also raises, inevitably, a conflict, real or perceived, when directors vote on where the money should go. As far back as the 1978 Royal Commission on Concentration, this had been pointed out to the banks, who paid absolutely no attention.[26] Paul Reichmann had been on the CIBC board for six years, when it was dealing with all sorts of matters that must have touched his interests. I was so curious about this aspect that I wrote to the CIBC – who had already said they wouldn't speak to me in this life or the next, but might consider my questions – to ask what conflict of interest had suddenly arisen when O&Y was in money troubles that did not obtain between 1986 and 1992. And do you know, the sons-of-guns never even wrote back. They're probably still thinking about it.

The next few days were given over to statements from O&Y trying to calm everybody down, and from various government spokesmen in Ottawa and Toronto explaining that they were still contemplating a rescue package, but don't rush them. After that, things began to hot up.

On April 6, O&Y missed a payment of $62 million U.S. due on an $800 million U.S. bond issue, secured by the package of Manhattan real estate.[27] This was not necessarily fatal, given that Johnson supposedly had just taken over, and there was no need for the bondholders to declare a default yet, so they didn't.

April 7 brought the first public knowledge of the fact that O&Y had missed a bond payment, and on April 8 came word that the company had sold most of its holding in Trilon Financial Corporation for about $65 million to the Ontario Teachers' Pension Plan Board. Since O&Y was using this Trilon stock as collateral, it had to substitute other shares. Boy, life can get complicated.[28]

April 9 wasn't any better. On the one hand, John Major's government was re-elected in Britain, which might help. The Canary Wharf issue had come up during the election, but it was rather complicated by the fact that the Labour Party, whose instinct was to knock the Jubilee Line Extension, had a number of ridings down that way which might go Tory if they thought jobs were at stake. Call that one a draw.

But the news out of New York was scary. A $5.5-million interest payment on a $930-million U.S. bond, secured by three New York office buildings, was made only hours before the issue would have been declared in default. You could not escape the mental image of O&Y personnel scrambling around in taxis with satchels full of borrowed cash to be unloaded at the last minute to avoid defaults. Not a regular way to do business.

Things did not look good for the fateful meeting on Monday, April 13, when bankers would fly in from all over the world to determine the Reichmanns' fate.

CHAPTER EIGHTEEN

The Grenade Goes Off

It's moving well.
   – Paul Reichmann, April 13, 1992 [1]

$

It was like a Royal Visit. The security at the Sheraton Centre Hotel on Queen Street in Toronto – just across the road from the bankruptcy-court office, as a matter of fact – was tight. The meeting was scheduled for 1:30 p.m., and a stream of limos began to pull up at the hotel's recessed main entrance off York Street about half an hour before that. The circling horde of reporters and photographers was asking the disembarking lords of finance who they were, but most just strode on by. It seemed appropriate that the four hundred moguls were going to gather in the hotel's large, ritzy ballroom, and there were a lot of jokes about who was going to dance with whom, and sweet music, and that sort of stuff. As the fatal moment neared, there were more and more guards, mostly in suits, with walkie-talkies grafted onto their heads, circling the area. The real cops were outside, although there were doubtless some inside, in plain clothes.

To get into the ballroom you had to have a special blue card issued by mine host, Olympia & York, and the scruffy mob of journalists, having no such entrée, could only stand by while the bankers trudged past, and make smart remarks. Paul and Albert Reichmann fooled almost everybody, rolling up to a fire exit in their limo and scampering down a little-used stairwell before dodging into the meeting. One photographer did get a shot of Paul, however, wearing his skullcap, black suit, white shirt, dark tie, and a smile that had apparently been fixed in place by a plastic surgeon. The lips were curved, but the teeth were gritted.

The great advantage of holding these things without the rude public and the even-ruder press in attendance – the same thing applies to many parts of a Royal Visit – is that the actual events, as they transpire, can be somewhat modified before word is circulated to the yammering multitudes. This meeting, for example, produced a headline in the *Financial Post* that read "BANKERS GET LOOK AT O&Y DEBT PLAN," with a subhead, "Recovery will take some time – Paul Reichmann."[2] Sounded smooth enough, for a meeting that had been billed as a showdown.[3] It was not until weeks later, when all the accounts of a wide range of participants had been put together, that it was possible to see what a disaster the meeting had been from the Reichmanns' point of view.

Paul Reichmann and his money man, Steve Miller, did the talking for O&Y, and they laid before the bankers a proposal that was breathtaking in its audacity. Reading from financial figures that were at least a year out of date,[4] Miller put the company's debt at $14.3 billion, but its net equity at about $5.5 billion.[5] There was a shortage of immediate cash, but no long-term problem.

Then came the proposal for restructuring that everyone had been waiting for. What the banks had to do, they were told, was to be patient. Just keep rolling those notes over as they come due, and all will be well. In the meantime, O&Y needs another $300 million or so to get on with the great work, and to relieve the temporary liquidity crisis. Kindly leave your contributions in the hall.

It did not go well, and the obligatory squad of unnamed bank sources was soon out howling for blood. "It's the same Olympia & York arrogance as always," one of them complained. "They want concessions, but they won't let us see what's behind the curtain."[6] What was behind the curtain was Paul Reichmann, telling everybody to have a little more faith.

But it was Steve Miller who was delegated to put the boot in. "If there were a massive refusal by the banking groups to do as the company suggests, O&Y would have to go through a series of filings in several countries."[7] That was plain speaking. Lay off, and give us more money, or we will file for bankruptcy protection, which would mean that a number of banks would have not only to disclose their huge loans, but to write at least part of them off. There had been a number of stories suggesting that the Reichmanns might give up some of their empire, by converting debt to equity (that is, exchanging bonds for shares, as Campeau had done) and/or by selling some of their buildings to reduce the load. This was not going to happen, the meeting was told. Pay up.

The *Independent*, a British newspaper that had been following the Reichmann saga through Canary Wharf, later commented that Paul Reichmann "wanted to play hardball with his creditors on the grounds that they had too much to lose not to support him. . . . The rescheduling proposal attempted to divide the creditors and to make as few concessions (such as equity participation) as possible. O&Y also gave out very little information about itself, which infuriated the banks."[8] The Reichmanns were determined to bring the banks into line, rather than vice versa. The banks would, in due course, take their revenge.

The day after this disaster, O&Y had another new president, Gerald Greenwald, who had been Steve Miller's boss when both worked for Lee Iacocca at Chrysler. They knew all about crises. Greenwald was much more acceptable to Paul Reichmann – but then, it was rapidly becoming clear, even to that imperturbable man, that he could not go on as before.

The next stage in this saga didn't become public until December 1992, when Jacquie McNish, in a detailed, two-part piece in the *Globe and Mail*, laid it bare. Just after the Toronto Sheraton meeting, McNish reported, there was a meeting of a score or more of international bankers in the private dining room of Osler Hoskin & Harcourt – in First Canadian Place, of course. "Over the catered lunch with French wine," the bankers were also trying to digest a confidential O&Y memo, detailing secret deals struck with various lenders weeks before March 23, when the company first admitted that it had run out of money. The document showed that O&Y's five main banks, CIBC, Royal, Nova Scotia, National, and Citibank (the Gang of Four plus one), had hidden what they knew of conditions at Canary Wharf from their colleagues, and tried to scoop assets to salvage bad loans.[9] In one deal, the Gang of Four had exchanged a $131-million note for mortgages on four Toronto office towers only two weeks before the March 23 announcement. If true, this suggested that the international banks were being asked to advance more money by the Gang of Four at a time when O&Y's prime assets had already been pledged to the Canadian banks. Moreover, the same collateral had been transferred to some of the Gang of Four's weakest loans to O&Y, thereby increasing their security, while downgrading the security of other banks. This is called "cross-collateralization," and it is frowned on.

These revelations led to a lot of finger-pointing and a shouting match. It would also lead, later, to a claim by the international banks that the Gang of Four had rushed in ahead of their fellows to try to get a place in the lifeboat, and legal action by two of the foreign banks, Crédit Lyonnais and the Hong Kong and Shanghai Bank, to try to get the cross-collateralization reversed. An unnamed (naturally) banker at that meeting declared, "It bordered on morally repugnant, and we were outraged," according to the *Globe*.

At a meeting of the major banks in the O&Y boardroom at the Exchange Tower on April 15, where the company was asking for a measly $8 million to keep the kettle boiling, there was a furious battle among the bankers, and the meeting was adjourned.

That was the Wednesday before Good Friday. On Easter Sunday, at yet another meeting in the O&Y boardroom (which started badly when security guards seized the coffee and pop some of the bankers had brought along with them, because you could only have edibles that came from the kosher kitchen), the foreign banks proposed that loans to O&Y, even small ones to keep it going, would come to a dead halt unless cross-collateralization ceased, and unless all the banks would come to a "standstill" agreement, a pledge by all of them that none would declare any O&Y debts in default. The reason for such an agreement was obvious: if any one bank moved against the company, trying to get in under the bankruptcy gun, there would be a godawful rush to seize assets, an unseemly scramble in which anything might happen, such as the wrong people getting repaid.

Scotiabank announced that it could not stand still, because it had served notice, on April 15, that $200 million U.S. was in default, and now it was going to take action. Scotiabank was persuaded to pull back, but the message the foreign banks came away with was that it was now a matter of every man for himself. O&Y would get enough money to keep it ticking over, and not a penny more.

The bankers had finally got it through their thick heads that they ought to learn something about the finances of the company to whom they had loaned so much money, and the CIBC asked its own auditor, Peat Marwick, to take a close look at Canary Wharf. Peat Marwick duly reported that O&Y had made so many side-deals to lure tenants in that the whole financial edifice was in danger. To cover all the tenant inducements, Canary Wharf would need another £600 million, more than four times the amount Paul Reichmann had asked for on April 13. Obviously, the CIBC did not know about these side-deals when its chairman was out telephoning the other banks in mid-March to induce them to unbuckle their wallets one more time on behalf of the British project.

The atmosphere was now poisoned. The banks were mad at each other and at O&Y. Olympia & York appeared to be pursuing a policy of divide and conquer, dealing with small groups of banks in turn, and taking a very tough stance.

The hammer blows continued. On April 21 the consortium of

banks agreed to lend O&Y $23 million, not the requested $300 million, to meet bills. On April 22 Ontario premier Bob Rae met Paul Reichmann, and emerged from the meeting to tell reporters that the province would not partake in any scheme to bail the company out. This effectively killed *any* chance of a bailout, although Ottawa would not announce its refusal until later.

The same day, that dratted DBRS placed some O&Y debentures on "Rating Alert with negative implications, because the shares in GW Utilities, Trizec and Trilon backing the securities are near lows for 1992, and if Home Oil is sold, GW Utilities may very well be liquidated, and all cash distributed to shareholders."[10] At the same time, $475 million in bonds on First Canadian Place were reduced in rating to BBB from A.

This triggered a move by which O&Y's shares in Abitibi-Price and Gulf Canada Resources were placed in the custody of the Toronto Dominion Bank. These shares formed part of the collateral for the famous Jumbo Loan of $2.5 billion U.S., and they went to Toronto Dominion because that bank was the only one that did not have any large O&Y loans. It had refused to play when it couldn't get enough information from the company to satisfy its lending officers. Sensible fellows. (TD did have one loan to O&Y, for a small development at Deerfield Beach, near Miami. The loan was to the U.S. company, for $12 million U.S., and the bank has launched a lawsuit to try to recoup.)

Rolling right along, on April 28 Robert Campeau filed a $1.25-billion lawsuit against the Reichmanns and the National Bank, claiming breach of promise, because, he alleged, O&Y had promised to lend him at least $800 million, and that this would have saved his U.S. companies. He also alleged that O&Y and National Bank directors had worked together to oust him from his own company.

The outlook was grim, and some of the men around Paul Reichmann were now desperately trying to persuade him to give up the ghost and file for bankruptcy protection, but he brushed the suggestion aside. Olympia & York could still pull through, he said, and anyone who held another opinion would be proven wrong.[11] Just the same, some of the company advisors began to seek legal opinions on what was the best way to go, if push came to shove.

It did. In Britain, the consortium of eleven banks that were the major lenders to Canary Wharf advanced another £5 million, walking-around money, but would not unbend any further. That was, appropriately, on May Day. The next day, in New York, Chemical Banking Corp. placed $125 million U.S. in loans to O&Y in the category of "non-performing loans." They were going to have to write them off, because they had given up hope of collecting.[12]

The Reichmanns were now being pummelled in three countries at once. Back in Canada, a $17-million interest payment on mortgage bonds secured by First Canadian Place was missed on May 4. Royal Trust, acting for the bondholders, declared O&Y in default. The situation was now rather different from when Royal Trust was hoping for a government bailout in the case of the Exchange Tower bonds. In Ottawa, Finance Minister Don Mazankowski had just announced that there would be no government-guaranteed bank loans.[13]

The next day, May 5, Royal Trustco Limited, as trustee for the bondholders on the loan secured by First Canadian Place, served notice that the debt must be met within seven working days. If payment was not made by five p.m. on May 14, the bondholders would be able to seize First Canadian Place. This was the end of any "standstill agreement." If the rush for the lifeboats was not exactly on, the starting time had been set for May 14. Royal Trust was moving in part because it had learned that O&Y was buying up "a substantial principal amount" of its notes, "in its effort to stave off defaults."[14]

Paul Reichmann calculated that, if it was not yet time to throw in the towel, it was at least time to wave a washcloth. Accordingly, on May 7, a marathon meeting of the banking group's leading lenders was called in the boardroom on the thirtieth floor of One Canada Place, at the heart of the Canary Wharf development. The bankers could look out one glass wall to the west, towards the City, across the completed buildings of Phase One, a view that the wags called "the Avenue of the Triumph of Capitalism," or, to the east, across a wasteland of building sites, derelict warehouses, and blocked roads, "the Avenue of the Defeat of Capitalism." The bankers probably spent most of the time looking down at their notepads and shaking their heads, because a new rescheduling plan, laid before them by Paul Reichmann, Gerald Greenwald, Steve Miller, and Michael Dennis, represented only a minimal and grudging retreat.

Gone was the notion that the company would never give up equity, and, in its place, O&Y offered the banks up to 20 per cent of the equity in the company and up to 30 per cent of Canary Wharf in return for a five-year suspension on loan payments and $645 million in new money. However, the shares involved would be non-voting; ownership, but no voice or control.

The bankers listened to this and then, according to Jacquie McNish's recounting, Paul Farrar, a senior vice-president of CIBC, said, "We aren't going to put another penny into Canary Wharf. This turkey won't fly."[15] That was an interesting and provocative turn of phrase, especially coming from a bank that had gambled more than $1 billion on that turkey's prowess in the air – and, indeed, had persuaded other banks to back a flight.

The meeting ended, late at night, with the bankers agreeing to "consult" the wider group of banks, who would turn it down. Eight of the bankers, representing Barclays, Citibank, Crédit Lyonnais, the CIBC, the Bank of Montreal, and the Bank of Nova Scotia, went straight from this meeting to another conference in the tower, involving only Canary Wharf lenders, who were owed £1.4 billion in all.

Over the vigorous objections of the CIBC, Paul Reichmann persuaded them to put up another £21 million to keep the project alive through May. Apparently, the CIBC had gone from being O&Y's strongest proponent to head cheerleader for the funeral.

There have been at least a dozen printed versions of these meetings, but the most detailed, in Jacquie McNish's two-part series in the *Globe*, contains a story, told for the second time, which has a strange ring to it.

As he left Canary Wharf about 11:30 that May evening, Mr. Farrar's primary concern was how to get back to his hotel in central London. It was a blustery, damp night and cabs were nowhere to be seen in the remote Docklands.

Tired and freezing, Mr. Farrar huddled outside with his lawyers at the foot of the Canada Square Tower, the centrepiece of the multi-building complex. The men couldn't take their eyes off a giant maroon Daimler Benz, Mr. Reichmann's car.

As they waited for their cab to arrive, the group stared enviously at Mr. Reichmann's chauffeur, who was warming himself inside the luxury car. Their taxi finally arrived after more than a half-hour wait. [16]

Tells you all you need to know, doesn't it? These birds were trying to build a business centre in the middle of nowhere. No wonder the turkey wouldn't fly.

The trouble with the story, which I have no doubt the *Globe* got down exactly as it was told (although, the first time the newspaper told it, in May 1992, the Daimler swept by, with Reichmann inside), is that it makes no sense. In the first place, you don't have to stand outside One Canada Place (not Canada Square Tower), there is a huge foyer where you can stand in the warm, and watch your taxi roll up. In the second place, the Docklands, as we have already seen, is anything but remote. In the third place, all the gang had to do, if there were no cabs in the rank across the street, was to walk down to the bus stop, where a twenty-four-hour bus service would whisk them back to civilization. And in the fourth and final place, try getting a cab sometime in the middle of the City at 11:30 at night, and see where it gets you.

What the story tells us, I think, is how the war of words was going between the banks and the Reichmanns, with all the sniping from behind the cover of anonymity in stories floated out to the newspapers, to make it more damaging and dangerous.

The litany of doom rolled on. On May 11 O&Y managed to meet another $6-million interest payment on notes secured by three

Manhattan office towers only hours before the deadline. The next day, J. P. Morgan & Co. led a group of banks in declaring O&Y in default on a $160-million U.S. note. The New York bank said it was going to seize interest-rate swaps it was holding as collateral. J. P. Morgan at this time was O&Y's financial adviser in New York; it was attacking its own client.[17] This raised the spectre of hordes of small creditors jumping in to grab assets before the inevitable collapse. What worried the Reichmanns in particular was the possible loss of their rich New York properties.[18] The policy of raising money on commercial paper, which is normally renewed every sixty or ninety days, was blowing up in their faces as the noteholders clamoured for payment.

Back in Toronto, on May 13, there was another tense meeting at First Canadian Place, where the banks recommended that O&Y file for protection under Chapter 11 of the U.S. Bankruptcy Code, to protect the company assets before they were gnawed down by mice. This was the same advice Paul Reichmann had given Robert Campeau, but he wouldn't take it, not yet.[19] The banks then refused point blank to lend O&Y the $17 million it had to have by five p.m. the next day to meet the interest on the First Canadian Place bonds, or lose the centrepiece building of its empire.

A London court chose the next morning, May 14, the worst possible moment, to rule against O&Y in the case brought against it by Morgan Stanley in connection with the purchase of their building. The court ruled that the two deals between the two firms were not connected. Olympia & York might very well have a claim for damages against the bank for a breach of its undertaking to raise the money for the purchase of its building, if it chose to sue over that matter, but that did not invalidate the put deal. Olympia & York was directed to pay Morgan Stanley International $231 million U.S. for 25 Cabot Square, and, if it couldn't come up with the money by May 21, Morgan Stanley could seize the building.

A novelist might hesitate to use the crude coincidence of the honourable, disdainful family receiving its final wounds from bonds floated on its proudest creation, its ally plunging in the knife, and a lawsuit launched by the firm that started it on its way to the Docklands in the first place, but that is what happened.

At this point bondholders could seize First Canadian Place, because of the missed payment there, the J. P. Morgan group in New York could seize the American assets, because of the $160 million default, and Morgan Stanley could seize the British assets. The struggle to stay afloat was over. Paul Reichmann finally gave the word.

With commendable speed and organization, once the decision was taken, it was implemented.

That afternoon, in Toronto, the Reichmann brothers met at First Canadian Place to discuss the details. Shortly before five p.m., a call was placed to Bruce Zirinsky, their New York lawyer.

At five p.m., Zirinsky called Cecilia Lewis, a bankruptcy-court clerk, at her office in the Manhattan bankruptcy court, asking for permission to deliver papers to her home in Chappaqua, New York, that evening.

Just after seven p.m., two lawyers from O&Y arrived at the Lewis home with a stack of papers, seeking protection under Chapter 11 of the U.S. Bankruptcy Code. The papers were signed at 7:22 p.m., and the companies were shielded.[20] In the United States, about $6 billion in debt was still exposed, but creditors were reluctant to push O&Y into bankruptcy, as long as some money was still being paid.

About the time the lawyers were driving away from Cecilia Lewis's home in Chappaqua, more O&Y legal counsel were gathering to appear before Mr. Justice Blair in Toronto, which they did at eight p.m. They filed for protection under the Companies' Creditors Arrangement Act on behalf of O&Y and twenty-eight other companies (they are listed in Appendix 1). After a three-and-a-half-hour hearing, Mr. Justice Blair signed the papers and granted a stay of proceedings until October 21; the assets of the twenty-nine firms were safe for five months.

When news of O&Y's collapse hit the newspapers the next day, they all carried a nice little note of optimism from Steve Miller, who had been working so frantically to keep this from happening. Don't take all this too seriously, Miller said, a little bankruptcy protection won't hurt: "It's as though you're walking down the street, you notice it's raining, you open your umbrella and you keep going."[21]

If he really meant this, O&Y had apparently learned nothing. The lesson was going to be brought home all over again, in the coming months.

CHAPTER NINETEEN

Sisyphus, with an Attitude

This is not a bankruptcy. This is not a liquidation. This is not the end of O&Y. This is a restructuring.

    – Gerald Greenwald, president, Olympia & York, May 17, 1992 [1]

$

Sisyphus, in case you've forgotten, was the ruler of Corinth in classical mythology, who was punished for his excessive trickery by being condemned forever to roll a huge rock up a hill. As soon as he got it to the top, it would roll down again, and he had all that weary work to do over. The working out of the O&Y bankruptcy was much like that, and it wound up with the bizarre sight of Cyrus Vance, the sometime U.S. secretary of state, being flown in, after his failure to end the war among Serbian, Croatian, and Muslim forces in Bosnia, to act as mediator between the company and some of its creditors. He did better in Bosnia.

Olympia & York applied for bankruptcy protection on May 14, 1992, as we have already seen. A plan for reorganization was accepted by most of its creditors in two weeks of voting, between January 11 and

January 25, 1993. The reorganization proposal was taken before Mr. Justice Robert Blair on February 1, and accepted on February 5.

In between, we heard the anguished voice of Richard Orzy, lawyer for one group of bondholders, complaining, "Eight months and $50 million later, we're back to where we were."[2]

There were four major effects of the successful application on May 14:

- The Reichmanns remained in charge of their companies, but could not borrow any more, or dispose of any assets, without court approval. The company's board lost its power.
- The payment of both principal and interest on all loans was suspended while the protection lasted. The companies would continue to pay their employees and suppliers, but this action immediately removed $600 million in interest payments, now overdue, from the table, as well as everything else that would come due during the next eight months.
- The "Applicants," as the O&Y group were properly referred to, were required to prepare and submit an arrangement between themselves and their secured and unsecured creditors "before July 13, 1992, or such other date as may be ordered by the court."[3]
- All "proceedings, suits, and actions against the Applicants" were stayed, suspended, and restrained – three words meaning the same thing – until otherwise ordered. This included the "rights of creditors to take possession of, foreclose or otherwise deal with the assets of any Applicant."[4]

The U.S. subsidiaries would continue to struggle along, paying what they could, while going deeper into the hole every day. U.S. law is much more favourable to the debtor than is Canadian law – so much so that Laurence H. Kallen, a leading American expert on bankruptcy law, has written that "many a conservative, antiregulation industrialist would come to realize that not only could he survive with his company in bankruptcy, he could get downright *comfortable* [emphasis in the original] in the protective embrace of Chapter 11."[5] This would prevent the U.S. creditors from making a dash for the courtroom, at least until the Canadian mess was sorted out.

In Britain matters were more complicated. In England the Insolvency Act removes the owners from control of the assets at once, and puts a court-appointed administrator in their place. o&y hoped to avoid that, for the very same reason that, if you had to undergo a serious operation, you would rather have it performed by a doctor of your choice than one plucked out of a matched set stored somewhere at the back of the hospital.

The day after the balloon went up in New York and Toronto, Prime Minister John Major appointed Lord Wakeham, the newly minted Lord Privy Seal, as Cabinet co-ordinator of the crisis, and he began to meet regularly with the banks.

Lord Wakeham's main task was to make sure that the commitment to put in the £98 million that o&y had promised as its first payment towards the Jubilee Line Extension came across the table, if not from the company, from the banks. And they were balking. The banks reasoned that, since the sum represented such a small share of the total, surely the government could be pressured into putting it up rather than throwing away the £200 million that had already been invested by London Transport. Lord Wakeham told me, "It was quite a long time before the banks had to face up to reality. They had a feeling that the government was going to find their share of the money, but we weren't. And it took a long time for the penny to drop, or the dime to drop."

There was an added difficulty in that, by law, North American banks were required to write off on their own books not only the debts that were not being serviced, but any new money, such as the £98 million down-payment, as long as o&y was in receivership. This led to the North American banks saying to the European banks, "Oh, you do it," and the European banks saying, "The hell we will," although, of course, in much more bankerly prose.

This shy dance continued well into 1993, but I will be astounded if it ends in the government giving way. It would be a terrible political blunder, for one thing. For another, it was not only that the banks had government in a bind; the reverse was true as well. Lord Wakeham, again: "The banks had security on the project, and if they wanted to realize on it they had to complete the Jubilee Line. If you've put some money on a person's house and he hasn't put a roof on it, you've probably got to put a roof on it if you want to realize on your security."

On May 20, 1992, flying what was by now a well-worn trial balloon, a senior official from the Bank of England told the eleven main lending banks at a meeting that the government was thinking seriously of moving two thousand civil servants to the Docklands. So, c'mon guys, why not put up the money? The story promptly appeared in the London papers, but the banks wouldn't bite. First, move 'em, then we'll talk, they said.

Lord Wakeham was scheduled to meet the bank representatives at two p.m. on May 28, to explain the government's position and get a definite response from the group. This led to another of the acrimonious brouhahas now becoming all too common among the bowler-hatted set, this time in the law offices of Allen & Overy in the City of London's Cheapside district. The eleven main lending banks on the Canary Wharf project were: Barclays and Lloyds from the U.K.; CIBC, Royal, and National from Canada; Commerzbank from Germany; Crédit Lyonnais of France; Crédit Suisse of Switzerland; Kansallis-Osake Panki of Finland; and Citibank and Manufacturers Hanover from the United States. It was necessary to come to a unanimous decision, but only four banks – Crédit Suisse, Citibank, KOP, and Crédit Lyonnais – were in favour of putting up the money. Lord Wakeham was told not to come to the meeting; there was no point in it. Instead, he phoned Major to tell him that the deal was off.

Thereupon the banks refused to advance the £500 to £700 million it would take to complete the construction already under way and pay for the tube extension. This left Olympia & York with three choices: liquidation, receivership, or Administration. They opted for the third, as the most likely to give the project some chance to recover. The banks blamed the government. "The government's silence cratered the project," said another of those unnamed bankers.[6] However, it is hard to escape the conclusion that the crater was created when O&Y's grenade went off.

Later that same day, O&Y filed for Administration with Britain's High Court. Also that day, back in Toronto, the *Globe and Mail* reported yet another "source within one of O&Y's major banks" as saying that "Paul Reichmann is finished. Paul Reichmann and the entire Reichmann empire are going to lose all of it."[7] Do we begin to detect a certain animus here? Steve Miller, the man in charge of working things out for O&Y, had lost a little of the bouncy optimism that had stood him in such good stead so far, and described the move to Administration as "a serious setback."[8]

Administration is not, as in his metaphor concerning the Companies' Creditors Arrangement Act, like raising an umbrella. It is more like a garrotte.

The accounting firm of Ernst & Young became the administrators of Canary Wharf because, among other reasons, it was the only major firm with enough insolvency staff left to handle it, what with all the other insolvencies then plaguing Britain, starting with the late Robert Maxwell's. Within weeks, all but a handful of the London-based employees of O&Y were out the door, all construction work had stopped at Canary Wharf, and the Reichmanns had lost all control over that part of their empire.

Stephen Adamson, one of the three Ernst & Young insolvency experts now running the British companies, told me, "It is extremely unlikely that Canary Wharf will ever be finished by the Reichmanns." His job, the grey-haired, handsome, chain-smoking Adamson told me, was "to get on and do it. . . . Some people say Administration is analogous to Chapter 11 in the States, but the major difference is that, there, the debtor remains in possession. Here, the administrator has full powers to run the company, and it is he who puts the proposals to the creditors, not the debtor."[9]

The whole point of the U.S. law appears to be to do the least possible harm to the people who piled up the debt in the first place, of British law, to move them out of the way as quickly as possible, and of Canadian law, as usual, something in between. Decapitation if necessary, but not necessarily decapitation.

The *Independent* newspaper became a trifle testy with a number of attempts, chiefly in Britain, to pretend that life would go on much as usual under Administration. "O&Y tried to present the move as the logical extension of a carefully prepared strategy to sort out the company's financial affairs," the paper puffed. "It was nothing of the sort. Rather, it was the logical extension of a series of arguments, infighting and distrust that scuppered O&Y's earlier attempts to reach agreement with its bankers."[10]

The same paper noted that a Gallup survey of pension funds, insurance companies, and private firms showed that more than 60 per cent of them had no interest in the Docklands, one in eight was planning to cut back on its exposure to developments there, and only 2 per cent had any plans to increase investment.[11]

Back in Canada the papers filed with the CCAA protection notice showed O&Y's assets to include a $3.8-billion investment in Canary Wharf, along with $3.1 billion in shares, $3 billion in Canadian real estate, and $5 billion in U.S. real estate. The usual problem arose: how could one know that the real estate was worth that much? We would soon find that it wasn't.

The infighting continued. The group of banks that had been so irritated by the way the Gang of Four Canadian banks moved to improve their own hold on assets filed a motion before Mr. Justice Blair complaining that the Gang of Four were guilty of "fraudulent preference." This was one of many motions that would be swallowed up in the morass of other proceedings; it may or may not ever reappear.

Once the court tussle had begun, the Canadian banks began to reveal, for the first time, the extent to which O&Y had managed to get into their ribs. Scotiabank was the first to provide a figure. It had made about $600 million in loans and other commitments. The Bank of Montreal then stepped forward to list $318 million in loans to O&Y as "non-performing" (which means no interest or principal payments have been made for ninety days). The Royal Bank disclosed its total exposure as $780 million, of which $510 million was non-performing. [12] The exposure included $217 million to Canary Wharf and $250 million in U.S. funds, Royal's contribution to the famous Jumbo Loan. The CIBC reported that it was taking a $1.2-billion loss provision against bad loans for the second quarter of 1992, especially against their loans to O&Y, which totalled $860 million; about half of this was on Canary Wharf. Finally, the National Bank weighed in to announce that it had loaned O&Y $473 million.

Five Canadian banks had forked out $3.03 billion to Olympia & York. And what had caused the decline that put all this money at risk? According to Paul Reichmann it was "irresponsible press speculation" that brought on the liquidity crisis, which in turn brought his company down. [13]

It seems to me that the simplest way to follow the ups and downs of the succeeding months is in the form of a diary.

May 30, 1992 – In London, Prime Minister John Major says the British government won't bail out Canary Wharf. [14]
June 1 – Frederick Copeland, head of Citibank's Canadian operations for the last five years, resigns suddenly. "He expressed a desire to pursue other interests," a spokesman for the bank says. [15]

In all, a Citibank Canada-led syndicate loaned O&Y $600 million, backed by shares now worth $172.6 million, leaving the syndicate with a shortfall of $427.4 million. Copeland might well find, in the circumstances, that other interests were the very thing he wanted to pursue.
June 2 – The *Financial Times* of Britain reports that two potential bidders for Canary Wharf have decided separately that it is only worth about one-fifth of what it cost to build. The Anglo-American conglomerate Hanson plc and the Peninsular & Oriental Steamship

Company (the same one that owns part of the Riverbus) did separate evaluations. Hanson plc told Lord Wakeham that the company would only bid if banks wrote off most of Canary Wharf's debt. The two companies conclude that the project is worth about £600 million, although at least five times that amount has gone into it so far.

In Toronto, on the same day, the first meeting of O&Y's unsecured creditors takes place. As the largest of these, CIBC expects to be named chair, but the other banks, ticked off at the bank's switches, names CIBC as co-chair with the Royal. There are fifteen banks on the committee.[16]

June 3 – In New York, J. P. Morgan tries to get a small principal payment from O&Y on the $160-million loan that has been in default since April. O&Y refuses. "How can O&Y pay principal to Morgan and ask for a moratorium from other creditors?" asks an unnamed company source. The company is asking the American lenders to hold off while it tries to sell assets.[17]

June 5 – Mr. Justice Blair rules against an O&Y proposal to lump all the real-estate lenders into a single group. The point is that 75 per cent of the creditors must agree by October 21 on a rescue plan to get the company out of bankruptcy, and those with first mortgages object to being stuck in with others. The judge splits "project lenders" from other real creditors, as he sets up six committees to draft a rescue plan.

The same day, in New York, O&Y's 32,502,317 shares in Sante Fe Southern Pacific Corp. of Chicago go on sale, priced at $12.25 U.S. The sale will bring in $379.6 million after expenses, all but $15.7 million of which is already pledged to creditors, and goes straight to them.[18]

June 8 – The *Wall Street Journal* reports that lenders to O&Y have greater exposure than shows in court documents, because of interest-rate swaps, on which the company has lost money.

June 19 – Court documents show that the bill for lawyers and financial advisers will run to $20 million by the end of October. In the end, the total tab will exceed $50 million.[19] This is in Canada; the American legal costs are running at $600,000 a month and other costs at

$200,000 a month, according to the same document filed by Price Waterhouse, the court's "Information Officer."

June 26 – The Teachers Assurance and Annuity Association case, which has been marching through the courts since the early 1980s, comes clanging down. A New York judge, Herman Cahn, rules that an O&Y subsidiary is liable for breaking off the $250 million U.S. loan agreement. A decision on the damages is deferred until later, and will no doubt be appealed. Teachers claimed that it lost $120 million when Paul Reichmann suddenly reneged and took out another loan, at lower rates, with a U.S. bank. In his defence, Paul Reichmann said there were "several irreconcilable disputes" over the loan, but the court finds against him. Judge Cahn, in a thirty-page decision, rules that "testimony does not support that the parties were at an impasse." Reichmann had informed Teachers, in January 1984, that he would terminate the loan agreement within ten days unless the association finalized the negotiations and agreed to forward the money. The judge found he had "no right" to do this, because the previously scheduled closing was more than a year away.[20] The judge was careful to say that Paul Reichmann's testimony was "credible and persuasive." The judgement was a matter of law, not of Reichmann breaking his word, but the end result was that his company had committed "an anticipatory breach of the commitment agreement."[21] Few read the judgement; what came across was that, as Michael Lesch, the lawyer for Teachers, told me, "he walked away from this deal without any justification, and that's what the court held."[22]

July 2 – Creditors and O&Y strike a deal over the costs of the CCAA action itself to the end of August. The lenders will supply part of the estimated $8 million required monthly, while O&Y will supply the rest from dividends from shares held in Abitibi-Price, Gulf Canada, and Carena Properties Inc. The Reichmanns will personally pay $5 million on a note due in 1996, as their contribution to the restructuring. O&Y will try to sell as much of $70 million in unpledged assets as possible to help with costs. The Gulfstream jet that whisked Paul Reichmann around the world in his search for transfusions of cash is on the block. (It will sell for $7,748,000. It was bought for $9 million.)[23]

In New York, the U.S. Olympia & York has hired Lazard Frères as a financial adviser to "focus on raising capital for O&Y's U.S. operations."[24] This is part of the increasing distance being put between the Canadian and American operations as time goes by.

Also on the same day, O&Y abandons the Yerba Buena project in San Francisco, swallowing the $20 million U.S. it has already spent there. It retains an option to step back in later, but don't hold your breath.

July 8 – In New York, financier Li Ka-Shing notifies O&Y that it is in technical default on a $57.5-million mortgage on 60 Broad Street. He has a 49 per cent interest in a partnership with O&Y there.[25]

July 9 – In Toronto, Mr. Justice Blair gives O&Y, which is required to come up with a restructuring plan next week, an extension to August 21.[26]

July 10 – Another of those time bombs from the past goes off, as O&Y's audited statements for 1991 are filed in court. The pile of debt from the twenty-nine associated companies was "approximately" $8.6 billion, but the total long-term debt of the empire as of January 31, 1992, was $16,373,753,000.[27] Call it $16.4 billion. The debts attributable to Canary Wharf were comparatively small – just over $1.2 billion – because the work had been paid for as it went along, out of the income of or loans to the rest of the company. The long-term debt of Olympia & York (U.S.) Holdings Company was just over $3.2 billion in Canadian funds, while O&Y's interest in Trizec, Gulf Canada, and Abitibi-Price accounted for the rest of the long-term debt (except for a minuscule $36 million owed by companies owned by O&Y, but not subject to the court restrictions).[28]

The audited statements show that O&Y lost $2.1 billion in 1991, most of it in writedowns of $1.4 billion – $218 million on Canadian real estate, $335 on the preference shares of various real-estate companies, $231 million on Campeau Corporation, $135 million on GWU Holdings, $125 million on Sante Fe Energy Resources, $99 million on Trilon

Financial, $160 million on Gulf Canada, and $45 million on Abitibi-Price.[29] A few hundred millions here, a few hundred millions there, it soon adds up to real money.

The company's assets are valued at $22.05 billion and so, accounting practice being what it is, are the liabilities. But there is a problem. Price Waterhouse, the auditors, in a note that is the auditor's equivalent of a bellow of outrage, complain that O&Y is carrying Canary Wharf as an asset worth $3.57 billion. "In our opinion, the value of the development has been impaired. Generally accepted accounting principles require that the amount of the impairment in value should have been estimated and provided for in these financial statements."[30]

Reichmann family shares in O&Y have plummeted in value from $2.1 billion in fiscal 1990 to *minus* $134 million this year.

At a press conference called to try to take some of the sting out of this, O&Y proposes that its creditors exchange their debt for special preferred shares, called "distress preferreds," which are exempt from tax. The shares were introduced as a change in the Income Tax Act in 1978 to help companies avoid liquidation. These will do nothing for foreign lenders, since they have no Canadian taxes to set them off against, nor for debtors who are unprofitable. Individual bondholders do not get the benefit, either.[31]

The proposal is quickly rejected by the banks.

July 22 – In London, unnamed "sources" say Paul Reichmann has teamed up with CBS chairman Laurence Tisch in a consortium to make a joint offer to take over Canary Wharf. The sources are obviously among the bank lenders. The consortium would put in £350 million to finish the project, in return for 50 per cent of the equity. This is one of six bids under consideration by the administrators, and another unnamed banker calls it a "non-starter."[32]

August 13 – Hanson plc pulls out of talks with Canary Wharf administrators.[33]

August 14 – After a meeting in the boardroom of a Toronto law firm on the sixty-second floor of Scotia Plaza in Toronto, Steve Miller of O&Y says, "Well, if someone will open the window, I'll leave now."[34]

In the meantime, Paul Reichmann is flying all over the world to get a deal, and the bankers and O&Y are sniping at each other from behind the bushes. In London, a banker complains that the new proposal is a LIFO deal, "last in, first out." In Toronto, unnamed O&Y executives complain that the CIBC had been "petulant" in pushing O&Y into administration in England.[35]

August 20 – In Toronto, O&Y holds a press conference to release details of its restructuring plan, which will be filed in court the next day. Steve Miller and Gerald Greenwald do the presenting. Basically, the project lenders, each of which has been offered a different restructuring plan, are asked to extend the maturity in return for some direct equity in the buildings.[36]

As part of the plan, O&Y will become a public company, after decades as a private one. The family will donate its 20 per cent interest in O&Y's indebted U.S. operations, along with a company owned by Ralph Reichmann. This would add about $100 million to the coffers. This is a considerable retreat by O&Y, but not nearly enough.

August 21 – The plan is filed in Toronto at two p.m. It is not well received, spawning quotes like, "We need to see some meat on the bones."[37]

August 27 – This is the initial deadline for a proposal to be laid before creditors in London, but it is put off.

September 8 – O&Y agrees to relinquish ownership of 55 Water Street in New York to creditors in exchange for cancelling the $548.3-million U.S. debt on the building.[38]

September 11 – In Toronto, Mr. Justice Blair extends protection to O&Y to December 31 from October 21.

September 15 – O&Y sells its empty office tower at 320 Park Avenue to Mutual of America, which held a mortgage for $147 million U.S. on the property.[39]

September 18 – In New York, O&Y creditors react with rage to a report which reveals, correctly, that the Reichmanns have a personal stake in the World Financial Center through a secret partnership with the

Bronfmans. The U.S. company has been denying for more than a year that the family had such an investment. [40]

September 22 – In Toronto, the Toronto Stock Exchange announces that it will launch an investigation into the revelations of September 18, particularly the fact that two public companies in the Edper group failed to disclose that they were shareholders in the World Financial Center through Battery Park Holdings Inc. The Edper holding is through Carena Developments Limited, which is controlled by Hees International Bancorp Incorporated. In turn, the Reichmann family owns shares in Carena. The company's explanation is that their secret stake in the deal, which started out at somewhere above $150 million U.S. and is now worth about $138 million U.S., was not "material compared with Carena's $14 billion assets." Therefore, they were not required to reveal it to the banks who are so sore, now, that they didn't. [41]

The eleven main lending banks in London agree at last to put up the £98 million needed to get the Jubilee Line Extension going, but some details are still to be worked out. This causes hearts to soar in London, but only temporarily. The negotiations to pin down who will pay what drag on for months. [42]

September 28 – In Toronto, the other shoe drops on the World Financial Center–Carena imbroglio when it is revealed that the Reichmanns have already sold off their share of the relevant holding company. [43] The O&Y creditors are outraged anew. So are the Bronfmans.

September 30 – In New York, O&Y's U.S. affiliate presents a proposal to seventy-five U.S. creditors at a meeting in One Liberty Plaza. The Reichmanns are not there, in order to underline the independence of the U.S. company. The proposal is the same as one turned down months ago in Canada: O&Y asks for a five-year moratorium on debts, and offers no equity in return. [44] Creditors at the same meeting learn that O&Y (U.S.) lost $230 million U.S. in 1991. This is a bitter blow, since most lenders assumed that the U.S. companies, at least, were still making money. [45]

October 2 – In London, four senior directors of Canary Wharf, including Michael Dennis, the chief executive, are laid off by the court administrators in London. The others are Robert John, Peter Dale, and Charles Young.[46]

October 27 – In Toronto, O&Y proposes yet another complicated settlement with its creditors, under which the company would be divided into three parts and the creditors would get substantial control. The assumption behind the proposals is that property values will be restored and O&Y will repay most of its debt out of the increases. In return, the creditors are to hold off for five years. The proposal is born dead. Within hours the banks indicate that it will not be accepted.[47]

November 18 – O&Y makes a new proposal, entirely different in character, to its main creditors in Canada. This one assumes that the company will become, in essence, a management company, running the projects others will own. The change will take place over a period of five years, and debt repayment remains suspended for that entire period. The secured creditors are given the right to seize the collateral, including the buildings, at any time, but it is assumed that most will not, since the equity in the buildings will not cover the debts now, but it may by the time the plan is completed. The unsecured creditors have the right to exchange their debt for equity, and could end up with as much as 90 per cent of O&Y itself.[48]

November 20 – Their old allies, the Bronfmans, turn on the Reichmanns, as Battery Park Holdings Inc., an equal partnership between Carena Developments Ltd., controlled by the Bronfmans and J. Richard Schiff, sue to have a receiver appointed for the World Financial Center.[49] This will drag on.

December 16 – O&Y submits its plan to the Toronto court for emergence from protection under the CCAA. The plan is essentially the one bruited three weeks earlier, under which debt repayments are suspended for five years, and creditors will be able to seize the collateral securing their debt at any time, on giving thirty days' notice. The properties not seized will go into a new company, O&Y Properties, which will be owned 9 per cent by O&Y Developments Limited and 10 per cent by the Reichmann family. In return, the Reichmanns are protected from lawsuits arising out of their actions over the period before the bankruptcy. Gradually, O&Y will evolve into the management business, managing buildings it used to own for fees of about 3.5 per cent of the leasing costs.

This plan will be voted on by thirty-five classes of creditors, beginning in mid-January. As in all CCAA cases, the plan must be accepted by a majority in each class, representing 75 per cent of the debt, for the arrangement to be binding. But this time there is an added wrinkle. All the unsecured creditors are put into a single class, which effectively gives that class a veto, since the unsecured debt represents so much (about half) of the total owed.[50]

December 23 – O&Y sells its stake in Sante Fe Resources to Sarlos Trading Limited for $82.65 million. Most of the money goes directly to creditors.[51]

December 29 – Two creditors file suit in New York in connection with one of the insolvent O&Y buildings, 59 Maiden Lane. Dickstein & Co. and Third Avenue Fund Inc. allege that 59 Maiden Lane is insolvent, because the $200-million U.S. worth of bonds due in 1995 and secured by the building is far in excess of the property's fair market value.[52]

December 31 – Ownership of Aetna Canada Centre in Toronto is transferred to Prudential Insurance Co. of America, making it the first O&Y building to be handed to a creditor.[53]

January 11 to 25, 1993 – Thirty-five classes of creditors file through a series of meeting rooms in L'Hôtel, a swank establishment on Front Street in Toronto. All but eight classes approve the plan laid before them by O&Y, and the restructuring will be accepted on February 5. There are several days when it appears the vote will go against the Reichmanns, as various lenders unload their anger and disappointment, but for most of the groups, especially those with secured loans, the pleasure of being able to push the company into bankruptcy is more than balanced by the fact that the only real chance of collecting a substantial portion of the money owed is to keep O&Y in existence. Who better to manage the buildings? So, grumbling, they consent.

It had taken months to penetrate the layers of defences the Reichmanns and their lawyers had thrown up in an attempt to keep control, but control had gone, at last, to the creditors. The restructuring will dismantle much of the Reichmann empire, over time, although avoiding liquidation. The final version accepted by the court on February 5 called for the creation of a new company, O&YDL Inc., out of an amalgamation of the insolvency wing of Coopers & Lybrand, a major accounting firm, with O&Y. The Reichmanns are left with Olympia Floor & Wall Tile Company and O&Y Properties, a Toronto-based management firm. The five-year restructuring plan will be run by Robert Lowe, head of insolvency at Coopers & Lybrand. There is a three-member board, consisting of Albert and Paul Reichmann and Lowe, but Lowe will have final authority, since all decisions must be unanimous. The long, always-acrimonious, sometimes harrowing, increasingly expensive, process was over, at least in Toronto.

Then, of course, all hell broke loose in the United States, where the American subsidiary of the Canadian firm was trying to restructure $6 billion U.S. in debt without going through a formal bankruptcy. When the creditors took charge in Canada, the Canadian board of directors lost their powers – among them, the power to appoint the board of the U.S. company. John Zucotti, the president of that company, wanted to name his own directors, but Lowe, the Canadian administrator, insisted that he had to have the right to fire them. This led to a long, complex battle, with gangs of lawyers parading before U.S. bankruptcy judge James Garrity to argue the interests of various affected parties. In the meantime, no major decisions could be made, because there was no board to approve them. Some of the U.S. creditors began to mutter about forcing the U.S. company into bankruptcy after all.[54]

The stalemate led, in mid-May 1993, to the company hiring Cyrus Vance to mediate the dispute, one month after he withdrew as the United Nations' peace envoy in the civil war that was in the process of destroying the former Yugoslavia. He finally worked out a compromise, which involved the establishment of a neutral body to sort out all disputes among the various parties. A nine-man board, seven of whom are independent U.S. businessmen, was agreed to; John Zucotti and Lowe got the other two seats. The U.S. restructuring lurched forward.

It was time to take stock, and see what lessons had been learned.

Don't Cry for Them, Financial Post

It's been a long day, but we're very, very happy.
    – David Brown, the leading O&Y lawyer, February 25, 1993[1]

$

Two days after the restructuring of O&Y was approved, Paul Reichmann announced that he was launching a new, Toronto-based partnership, Reichmann International, with New York financier George Soros. A new real-estate investment company, Quantum Realty Fund, hopes to raise $525 million from mutual-fund shareholders, and the two men will add another $75 to $100 million to that sum. They will invest in "undervalued North American commercial developments," which could well include some of the properties O&Y's various creditors are trying to sell.[2] The king is dead, long live the king.

It soon became clear that Reichmann International, which involves two generations of Reichmanns – not only the three brothers, but a number of their offspring – is likely to become a major international company. Soros, whom the *Financial Post* calls "the selfish saint,"[3] runs a number of investment funds with a collective value of more than

$5 billion. His latest, the Quantum Realty Fund, has as its investment adviser his old friend Paul Reichmann. The fund was capitalized at $600 million U.S., and will no doubt be closely connected to Reichmann International.

Like the Reichmanns, Soros comes from Hungary. He was born in Budapest in 1931, the son of a Jewish lawyer. His family escaped persecution during the war by living under false identities, and he moved to London two years after the war, and later to New York, where he made a fortune in investments. Also like the Reichmanns, he has contributed generously to a number of worthy causes all over the world. He earned $650 million U.S. in 1992, making him the highest-paid person on Wall Street, so I guess he can do just about what he wants.

His clippings read quite a lot like the stuff the financial writers used to churn out by the yard about the Reichmanns, come to think of it. They may be churning it out again. While the Reichmanns' creditors were still sniping at them and at each other in early 1993, Albert and Paul Reichmann began work on a series of schemes in Mexico City, which will be Reichmann International's development debut. Some details of the project were released in June,[4] and suggest that the Reichmanns have put in bids on at least three separate sites: one in the historic Alameda section of Mexico City, one along Paseo de la Reforma, and one in the Sante Fe development on the western edge of the city.

Albert Reichmann has already established a close working relationship with Mexican president Carlos Salinas, and has met the president's two most-likely successors. The Mexican banks have indicated an interest in helping with some of the finance, and there is a clear need for high-quality business space in the Mexican capital. All this has a hauntingly familiar ring; however, we are to believe that this is not Canary Wharf with enchiladas on the side. For one thing, vacancy rates are less than 1 per cent in Mexico City, and, for another, rents are about twice as high there as they are in the depressed markets where O&Y has been working in recent years. Finally, the Reichmanns would be working with local partners, not on their own, as was the case in

London. It is hard to miss the message that the Reichmanns have emerged from their ordeal bloody but unbowed (to say nothing of unbankrupt), and the corollary message is that shedding a few billion dollars, while inconvenient, is hardly fatal to businessmen of daring.

It would be ironic, but not entirely surprising if, on the strength of a new success in Mexico, the Reichmanns were to take on Canary Wharf once more. A number of the senior officials I spoke to in London suggested this as a possibility, provided the Reichmanns also take on a British partner. The Jubilee Line Extension, which has been "officially approved" at least three times, is, as I write this in mid-1993, soon to be officially approved, signed, and started. It will take fifty-three months to complete. During that time most of the other infrastructure required to make the project work – chiefly, the roads – will be finished, and in, let us say, five years, the Mexico City project will be well under way. Sounds about right.

In the meantime, as the brothers began to re-emerge onto the world financial scene in mid-1993, there was blame to be apportioned, and it tended to be flung about liberally.

The Reichmanns blamed the media, for spooking the investment community and causing a run on their commercial paper, but we know better. We know that Dominion Bond Rating Service kept issuing bulletins that said, Yoo-hoo, hey look, over here, for months before the run on O&Y paper began in February 1992. We of the media were, if anything, too kind, or too dumb, to do the Reichmanns much harm until they were already in serious trouble.

Peter Wade, the O&Y community-affairs man, blames the City. "I think what's happened here is that the City kicked the teeth in of a foreign investor, particularly because it was a Canadian investor." He has an unkind word for the media, as well. "They really gave us a drubbing from day one. They just never let up."

Peter Corfield of Ogilvy & Mather, who now heads a support group for Canary Wharf called the London Docklands Business Initiative, blames the banks, who "totally misjudged the situation." The

Reichmanns took the long view, he says, and, in the long view, Canary Wharf will work. There was, he says, "a loss of faith," which is characteristic of our time. As for the City, "They never look east, they never look beyond their noses; they think we live in a different time zone." Corfield would welcome the Reichmanns back tomorrow, with a red carpet.

Stephen Adamson, one of the administrators now responsible for cleaning up the London end of the mess, doesn't blame anyone, but he does say, "I think that what happened was that the minute Canary Wharf became a serious threat to the City, the planning restrictions were released, and people started putting up millions of square feet of space. When the recession hit, there were far too many buildings and far too few people willing to rent. It exacerbated what would already have been a difficult situation, and the only thing that kept things going as long as they did was the quality of the buildings. I am astonished that they [the Reichmanns] couldn't see that this was bound to happen."

Andrew Sarlos, the Reichmann ally, thinks the problem was essentially one of an expanding ego. "Paul Reichmann got to thinking he could walk on water, and he couldn't."

American analysts seem to think it was just a question of pushing a good thing too far. A typical comment was that of Paul J. Isaac, chief analyst with Mobon Securities of New York.[5] "The Reichmanns were very over-aggressive, and you can say that they committed real errors in judgement, in retrospect. But the Reichmanns were people with a hot hand and a particular vision who just pushed too hard. They were guys who were willing to push the edge of the envelope, and they pushed it past the time in which that particular strategy worked."

The banks, of course, blame the Reichmanns, although almost always from the safety of a thicket of anonymity.

Peter Foster, who has written two books about the Reichmanns, and seems to think they are finished forever, blames the whole mess on Paul Reichmann's ambition and the banks' fecklessness.

Paul Reichmann's fatal flaws were excessive belief in his own powers, corporate acquisitiveness, and a penchant for larger and larger gambles. What ultimately killed the Reichmann empire was Canary Wharf. The seeds of destruction lay in Paul Reichmann's unquenchable ambition. However, he could never have taken his empire to the size it ultimately achieved – and the disaster it ultimately threatened – without the willing cooperation of a mesmerized banking community.[6]

Quenchable ambition is okay; the unquenchable kind not so. If Foster is right, what we need is a course in some community college somewhere to distinguish the difference. It will be a tough course to teach, almost as hard as explaining how "corporate acquisitiveness" is a bad thing to budding executives who have spent a lifetime learning that it is the only thing. Apparently, Albert Reichmann, the chairman, is blameless, along with Ralph. And, apparently, all you need to get a few billions out of the banks is a course in hypnotism.

It certainly is true that the Reichmanns were sparing of information. David Bayliss, the London Transport planner, told me that, when it appeared that O&Y would be advancing money for the Jubilee Line Extension, his group tried, in vain, to get hard numbers from them. "My chairman [C. W. Newton, chairman of London Transport] is on the board of a number of banks, including the Hong Kong and Shanghai Bank, which had loaned money to O&Y. So, when this deal came up, we asked to see the security that would back it, before we started the project, and we were told that the money was secured by the company's unlimited liability. Of course, there's no such thing; it's just a phrase. We managed to get an auditor's certificate from their Canadian auditors, but it was not very satisfactory. It was based entirely on a series of assumptions about the numbers being accurate. We know now what that security was worth."

The banks were in the same position as London Transport. They might ask for financial details, but that didn't mean they would get them. In those circumstances the duty of the banks was straight-forward enough: they ought not to advance the money on incomplete information. But they did, and they will again, because the money to be made on deals as large as those offered by O & Y is so great that greed swamps common sense, every time. Ask Northland Bank, or Canadian Commercial Bank, or any of the thousands of savings and loans associations that were swept into oblivion in the 1980s, while the costs were transferred onto the taxpayer's back.

The banks have sent out the signal, through a number of stories in the media, that they are taking a long, hard look at their standards of risk, at last. Al Flood, the new chairman of CIBC, told his shareholders' meeting that the bank is now taking "a more conservative and disciplined approach to the granting of credit." Canary Wharf would not have met the new standards, he said.[7] There are those who believe the banks have learned their lesson, just as there are those who believe that every leprechaun knows the location of a crock of gold. A leprechaun who belonged to the Albany Club could probably float a sizeable loan against the crock. For myself, I doubt it. The banks got massacred in loans to almost any country that owned an oil well in the 1970s, and jacked up all their charges to whittle down those losses; they got clobbered in U.S. real estate, and came home to pour their treasure, our treasure, into the laps of Olympia & York. What really appears to have happened on the heels of the O & Y and other real-estate debacles is that small businesses were badly hit; their loans were called in unprecedented numbers, while companies like the Edper Empire kept right on borrowing until they, too, were threatened with collapse. Then the banks got fussy. This is the way they have always behaved; why should we expect them to change?

For those who cling to the status quo, the comforting thing about all the available explanations as to what went wrong with Olympia & York is that they all follow the "one-bad-apple" school of argument. The system is fine, working well, distributing rewards according to market theory to those with just the right ambition, but not too much.

It is rather like the argument advanced by the athletics industry in March 1993, when Ben Johnson was barred for life after testing positive for a banned substance. "Now this former athlete, alone, must assume the burden of this latest embarrassment," said Paul Dupre, president of Athletics Canada.[8] Sportswriter Stephen Brunt commented, "Their haste to hustle Johnson out of the sport without even a hint of due process has everything to do with their desire to get back to business as usual. There's nothing wrong with the system, folks, there's nothing wrong with sports. Just one bad apple who has now been excised."[9]

Business writers have the same problem with the one-bad-apple argument that the sportswriters do. The adored system seems to go out of its way to encourage and reward the very characteristics that push success over the brink to failure. Business as usual has produced the same results with central figures as disparate as Michael Milken, Ivan Boesky, Donald Trump, and the Reichmanns. Doesn't that tell us something? The one-bad-apple argument is, pardon me, applesauce.

One of the things this saga has shown, surely, is that the Reichmanns did play by the rules, almost all the time, certainly more of the time than a majority of their business fellows. They strove to do what almost everything we see and read and hear tells us is the only worthwhile thing to do, to grow bigger and bigger and bigger. We carry lists of The World's Wealthiest, and are astounded when people bust a gusset trying to stay on the list. Apart from inheritance, there is no way onto that list, or the other lists and honours that come, in our world, to those whose greed has no bounds, except by being over-aggressive. Bound to lead to trouble, I would think.

We have set up, in Canada, Britain, and the United States, a system that increasingly wants to substitute private for public planning, and to allow entrepreneurs to buy into the development, not merely of projects, but of provinces. The NDP government of Ontario, cross-dressing in Thatcherite skirts, is going to build new roads where the highest tolls can be collected, and public transit where developers can be persuaded to kick in a few millions along the route. McDonald's can buy time in our classrooms, via closed-circuit newscasts, complete with ads, that our children are required to watch. Business students at the School of Management at the University of Toronto pay for computer time on terminals in place of the books they used to read, because most of the books have been shipped off to the archives. You can't make money on a library, but you can on a computer. And, of course, we all know that justice is fairly encapsulated in that old *New Yorker* cartoon in which a lawyer is shown asking a client, "How much justice can you afford?"

The corporate system that is at the heart of the modern economy works on the principles of ever-expanding power and ever-diminishing responsibility. When Canada changed its tax laws in 1971 to allow companies to write off the interest of their investments in other companies, it not only gave the conglomerate official blessing, it reached into the public purse to help that noxious form of business organization on its way. We have made it almost painless for companies to grab instead of build, and we have established a system of bankruptcy laws that makes it, at least for very large companies, the main duty of the legal system to keep in business the firm that goes off the rails.

The Companies' Creditors Arrangement Act is of no use to the ordinary Canadian business person, who pays, in his or her taxes, the millions of dollars it costs to administer the law. It is not an act for the creation of millionaires, but for their protection against the outcome of their own follies. Uwe Manski, president of the Canadian Insolvency Practitioners' Association, calls the CCAA "Canada's own do-it-yourself Chapter 11." He has very little regard for Chapter 11, which he calls "An unmitigated disaster for anyone other than the O&Ys of this world. The costs are staggering. You have all these creditors and all these committees and they all have lawyers and they're all feeding at the trough. If there is enough money, you can keep it up, but very few smaller companies ever emerge."[10]

Bankruptcy, under this and other laws, is becoming a matter of defence, reorganization, even convenience. Companies go bankrupt to shed their unions, or to slough off debt, or to avoid litigation for having produced a product that has massacred or crippled a few thousand customers. If a company is large enough, and in debt enough, it can even use the threat of bankruptcy to bring its creditors to heel. Drop your interest charges, or I'll blow us all up.

As for the banks, they can take these gambles, because the Canada Deposit Insurance Corporation will protect all but a small portion of their customers against any loss, thus neatly removing the market from the equation. Why bother to shift your accounts from a bank that has been identified as an incautious lender, when you are protected anyway? Moreover, the people who run the banks have everything to gain, personally, when the big loan deals are signed, and very little to lose when they go belly up. Senior executives win praises and bonuses for bringing in fat new loans; ever hear of one who got fired when a loan went sour? It was, remember, the 2,500 tellers and other lowlifes who got shoved out the door at CIBC in the cutbacks imposed by that bank after the O&Y fiasco. Citibank lost its Canadian president, to be sure, but we have the bank's own word for it that that had nothing to do with imprudent loans to O&Y. We are left with the alternatives that the bank is a liar, or that making imprudent loans is perfectly all right, so far as the bank is concerned.

Uwe Manski says, "The glamour of the big loan is sometimes so endearing to the lenders that they lose sight of the normal lending criteria and become blinded by the opportunity to make a large, perceived low-risk loan to a pre-eminent enterprise. Here is a chance to make a quarter of a point against big bucks. Sometimes, of course, there is also the opportunity to charge sizeable fees to put big deals together."

Seen in this light, what happened to O&Y has less to do with the personalities of the Reichmanns, who are, God knows, about as unlike Robert Campeau or Donald Cormie as they can be, than it has do with the laws governing incorporation, taxation, banking, and bankruptcy.

One of the mottos of our age is "Go for it," and the other is, "Pay for it," and the Reichmanns, aided and abetted by as eager a bunch of bankers as ever bankrolled a gambler, went for it. As long as it worked, they were worshipped, and when it came apart, as every venture that presumes that there is no limit whatever to growth *will* come apart, well, they didn't suffer much. They are far better off than they were when they founded Olympia & York, far better off than you or I, far better off than all but a tiny scattering of humanity, certainly better off than any of the thousands of people, from their own employees to the bank employees who were ditched to help pay for the mess, who felt the impact of their collapse.

The physical legacy of Olympia & York looks impressive, a collection of really lovely, functional buildings in cities from Toronto to Los Angeles, New York to the Isle of Dogs. What the economists call the "opportunity cost" of their works will never show on the record, because there is no way to calculate whether the billions in public funds used to help them along their way would have gone to schools and housing, public transport, health and education, or any of the things we need so much more than we need another nice building.

And that, surely, is the only real lesson in all this. If society is concerned, first and foremost, with doing only those things that pay off, we can hardly complain when we find private hands in the public till. If everything is for sale, nothing has any value. If we have no standard but the accumulation of wealth, we will continue to see successes, and failures, exactly like the Reichmanns', as well as those of far-more-disreputable business men and women.

Appendix 1
The Companies Under Protection

In the Canadian Action

1. Olympia & York Developments Limited
2. Olympia & York First Canadian Place Limited
3. Olympia & York ET Limited
4. Olympia & York Exchange Tower Limited
5. Olympia & York SP Corporation
6. SPE Operations Ltd.
7. Olympia & York ACC Limited
8. Olympia & York AMCC Limited
9. Olympia & York FAP Limited
10. Olympia & York (Fifth Avenue Place) Limited
11. Olympia & York GCS Limited
12. Olympia & York (Gulf Canada Square) Limited
13. Olympia & York (Shell Centre) Limited
14. Olympia & York 240 Sparks Street Limited
15. O&Y CPI Credit Corp.
16. Olympia & York Commercial Paper II Inc.
17. Olympia & York Eurocreditco Limited
18. Olympia & York European Holdings Limited
19. Olympia & York Realty Credit Corp.
20. Olympia & York Resources Credit Corp.
21. Olympia & York Resources Corporation
22. O&Y Energy Holdings Limited
23. O&Y Forest Products Holdings Limited
24. Olympia & York Realty Corp.
25. O&Y Equity (Canada) Ltd.
26. O&Y (U.S.) Development Canada Ltd.
27. Olympia & York SF Holdings Corporation

28. GWU Investments Limited
29. 857408 Ontario Inc. (formerly Olympia & York CC Limited)
    (Source: Court filings)

Of these, five also filed in New York State

1. Olympia & York Developments Limited
2. O&Y Equity (Canada) Ltd.
3. Olympia & York Realty Corp.
4. O&Y (U.S.) Development Canada Ltd.
5. Olympia & York SF Holdings Corporation.

Appendix 2
Shareholders in Olympia & York Developments Limited as of May 14, 1992

Shareholder	Class A Preferred Shares	Class C Preferred Shares	Common Shares
Albert Reichmann	102,043.38		106,097.3060
Egoshah Reichmann	197,283.32		62,375.1800
The Philippe Reichmann Trust	34,059.55		41,583.7850
Paul Reichmann	87,744.55		90,503.4420
Lea Reichmann	186,037.49		46,781.6270
The Vivian Reichmann Trust	19,868.07		24,257.0710
The Rachel Reichmann Trust	19,868.07		24,257.0710
The Lillian Reichmann Trust	19,868.07		24,257.0650
Ralph Reichmann	87,744.55		90,504.4410
Ada Reichmann	186,037.49		46,781.6270
RRF Corp.	14,901.05		18,192.8005
The Steven Reichmann Trust	14,901.05		18,192.8005
Abraham Reichmann Trust	14,901.06		18,192.8030
Rochelle Reichmann Trust	14,901.06		18,192.8030
Reichmann Trust	116.25		473,261.5800
Trustees appointed under the will of the late Renée Reichmann		57,389.772	
Total issued shares	**1,000,275.00**	**57,389.772**	**1,103,430.4020**

(Source: Court filings)

Appendix 3
The Empire at its Height, 1991

1. The Companies

Statistics Canada's *Inter-Corporate Ownership, 1992* lists 165 companies in "The Reichmann Group." They are:

608863 Ontario Inc.

695160 Ontario Inc.

695161 Ontario Inc.

80395 Alberta Limited

80600 Alberta Limited

903009 Ontario Inc.

 Subsidiary companies:

 Counsel Corporation

O&Y DMML Ltd.

 Subsidiary companies:

 M. Zagerman & Company Limited

Olympia & York Developments Limited

 Subsidiary companies:

 168883 Canada Inc.

 633319 Ontario Inc.

 6853474 Holdings Ltd.

  Subsidiary companies:

  Hergy Construction Co. Ltd.

  J&B Shelterplex Ltd.

 720497 Ontario Inc.

 750423 Ontario Inc.

 851489 Ontario Inc.

 Abitibi-Price Inc.

Subsidiary companies:
Abitibi-Price Finance Inc.
Abitibi-Price ReFinance Inc.
Abitibi-Price Sales Corp.
La Cie Gaspesia Ltée.
Grand Falls Central Railway Company Limited
The Jonquière Pulp Company
Logging Development Corp.
Mattabi Mines Limited
The Price Company Limited
Terra Nova Explorations Ltd.

Caddiford Investments Limited

Campeau Corporation (this was before it became Camdev)

Subsidiary companies:
397330 Ontario Ltd.
734495 Ontario Ltd.
755368 Ontario Ltd.
Campeau Pacific Corporation
Campeau SPE Real Estate Corporation

Subsidiary companies:
SPE Operations Limited
Hippodrome Blue Bonnets Inc.

Subsidiary companies:
Imprimerie Experta Inc.
Logo Computer Systems Inc.
Place du Saguenay Inc.
Power Pry Corporation

Caramat Holdings Limited

English Property Corporation

Subsidiary companies:
Star Great Britain Overseas Holdings Limited
Star Properties (No.16) Limited

Grenoble Developments Ltd.

Gulf Canada Resources Limited
  Subsidiary companies:
  150433 Canada Inc.
  156911 Canada Inc.
  Asamera Inc.
    Subsidiary companies:
    Asamera Espana Inc.
    Asamera Minerals Inc.
    Asamera Oil Inc.
      Subsidiary companies:
      Gasamat Inc.
    Asamera Oil (Indonesia) Ltd.
    AsameraCan Inc.
    Chucuri Exploration Inc.
    Helpful Expansion Limited
    Rio Meta Exploration Inc.
    Vacusan Systems Ltd.
  Beaudril (1987) Limited
  Beaufinco Equipment Holdings Ltd.
  British American (Quebec) Inc.
  Canadian Gulf Oil Company
  Canadian Oil Debco Inc.
  Cansulex Ltd.
  Carnduff Gas Limited
  Glen Park Gas Pipe Line Company Limited
  Gulf Alberta Pipe Line Co. Ltd.
  Gulf Canada Brunei Limited
  Gulf Canada Frontier Exploration Limited
  Gulf Canada Hurghada Limited
  Gulf Canada Jambi Limited
  Gulf Canada Limited
    Subsidiary companies:
    Nottingham Gas Ltd.
    The Tenstar Corporation

Gulf Canada Malaysia Limited
Gulf Canada Petroleum Inc.
Gulf Canada Properties Limited
Hibernia Management and Development Company Ltd.
Hiram Walker Resources Ltd.
Interprovincial Pipeline Inc.

   Subsidiary companies:
   Hiram Walker Resources Ltd.
   Home Oil Canada Limited

      Subsidiary companies:
      Home Oil Alaska Limited
   Home Oil Company Limited

      Subsidiary companies:
      158433 Canada Limited
      Federated Pipe Lines Ltd.
      Home Exploration Limited
      Home Hydrocarbons Inc.
      Home Oil (Asahan) Ltd.
      Home Oil Australia Limited
      Home Oil (Brunei) Ltd.
      Home Oil Far East Ltd.
      Home Oil International (Ecuador) Ltd.
      Home Oil International Ltd.
      Home Oil (Mediterranean) Ltd.

         Subsidiary companies:
         Home Oil Philippines Limited
      Home Oil New Zealand Limited
      Home Oil (South Sumatra) Ltd.
      Independent Pipe Line Company
      Panarctic Oils Ltd.
      Progas Limited
      Scurry-Rainbow Oil Limited

         Subsidiary companies:
         Minerals Ltd.

        Interprovincial Pipe Line (NW) Ltd.

        Interprovincial Pipe Line (Alberta) Ltd.

    National Petroleum Inc.

    Peace Pipe Line Ltd.

    Redwater Water Disposal Company Limited

    Rimbey Pipe Line Co. Ltd.

    Sandalta Energy Ltd.

    Syncrude Canada Ltd.

    Tuba 4 Transport Ltd.

GWU Holdings Ltd.

    Subsidiary companies:

    GW Utilities Limited

        Subsidiary companies:

        755992 Ontario Inc.

            Subsidiary companies:

            Interprovincial Pipeline Inc.

        922229 Ontario Inc.

        940421 Ontario Inc.

        Bayal Investments Ltd.

            Subsidiary companies:

            648789 Ontario Limited

        Kahlantine Holdings Inc.

Maple Leaf Ceramic Industries (1967) Ltd.

    Subsidiary companies:

    Flextile Ltd.

O&Y (CPI) Credit Corp.

O&Y Equity (Canada) Ltd.

O&Y (U.S.) Development Canada Limited

Olympia & York CC Limited

Olympia & York Contractors Limited

    Subsidiary companies:

    826244 Ontario Inc.

Olympia & York Creditco Holdings Corporation

Subsidiary companies:
Olympia & York Commercial Paper II Inc.
Olympia & York Commercial Paper Corp.
Olympia & York Eurocreditco Limited
Olympia & York Exchange Tower Limited
Olympia & York First Canadian Place Ltd.
Olympia & York (Gulf Canada Square) Leasing Limited
Olympia & York (Gulf Canada Square) Limited
Olympia & York Queen's Quay Terminal Limited
Olympia & York (Shell Centre) Ltd.
Olympia & York 240 Sparks Street Ltd.
Olympia & York 5140 Yonge Street Leasing Limited
Olympia & York 5140 Yonge Street Limited
Olympia & York European Holdings Limited
Olympia & York (Fifth Avenue Place) Limited
Olympia & York (Fifth Avenue Place) Leasing Limited
Olympia & York Realty Corp.
>   **Subsidiary companies:**
>   Olympia & York SF Holdings Corporation
>   >   **Subsidiary companies:**
>   >   Olympia & York Realty Credit Corp.
Olympia & York Resources Credit Corp.
Olympia & York Securities Corp.
>   **Subsidiary companies:**
>   Olympia & York Financial Limited
Olympia & York SP Corporation
>   **Subsidiary companies:**
>   SPE Operations Limited
Sante Fe Southern Pacific Corp.
Trilon Financial Corp.
Westcana Carpets Limited
Olympia & York Enterprises Inc.
>   **Subsidiary companies:**
>   825684 Ontario Inc.

> **Subsidiary companies:**
> Carena Properties Inc.
> Trizec Corporation Ltd.

R. Investment Corp.
   Subsidiary companies:
   695162 Ontario Inc.

2. *The Real Estate*

i. CANADA

a. Toronto

Aetna Canada Building
Bell Canada Data Centre
Blue Cross Building
Canada Wire Building
First Canadian Place
Foresters Building
Global House
MonyLife Building
Nestlé Building
North York Medical Centre
Ontario Federation of Labour Building
Queen's Quay Terminal
Scotia Plaza
Shell Canada Data Centre
Sunoco Building
Texaco Building
Toronto Star Building
Xerox Building

b. Calgary

Amoco Building
Esso Plaza
Shell Centre

c. Edmonton

City Centre Building

d. Ottawa

Amoco Building
Brewer Hunt 11 Business Park
Bristol-Myers Building
Dashwood Building
C.D. Howe Building
L'Esplanade Laurier
Ottawa Citizen Building
Place de Ville
Place Bell Canada

e. Oshawa

Oshawa Executive Centre
Oshawa Shopping Centre

f. London

London Galleria

g. Kanata

Kanata Town Centre
Bell Northern Building

ii. UNITED STATES

a. New York

World Financial Center
237 Park Avenue
245 Park Avenue
320 Park Avenue
425 Lexington Avenue
1290 Avenue of the Americas
60 Broad Street

125 Broad Street
55 Water Street
59 Maiden Lane
One Liberty Plaza
Two Broadway

b. Other U.S. Cities

Exchange Place, Boston
One Financial Plaza, Springfield, Ma.
Olympia Center, Chicago
1999 Bryan Street, Dallas
Olympia Place, Orlando
One Commercial Plaza, Hartford
One Corporate Center, Hartford
400 South Hope Street, Los Angeles
11601 Wilshire Boulevard, Los Angeles
Fountain Plaza, Portland, Or.
Yerba Buena Gardens, San Francisco

iii. BRITAIN

Canary Wharf

(Source: Court filings)

3. *The Stock Portfolio as of May 14, 1992*

	Area	Percentage	$million Cdn.
a. in Canada			
Gulf Canada Resources	Oil & gas	75%	744
Abitibi-Price	Forest products	82%	931
Trizec Corp.	Real estate	35%	382
Trilon Financial	Finance	10%	90
Camdev	Real estate	65%	31
GW Utilities	Oil & gas	89.3%	430
b. in the United States			
Catellus Development	Real estate	15%	101
Sante Fe Energy Resources	Oil & gas	15%	97
Sante Fe Pacific	Holding company	19%	484
c. in Britain			
Rosehaugh	Real estate	8%	10
Stanhope Properties plc	Real estate	33%	26
Total in Canadian $			**$3,326**

(Source: Dominion Bond Rating Service files)

Appendix 4
Key Dates

1898: Samuel Reichmann born in Beled, Hungary, in 1898.

Renée Gestetner born in Győr in 1899.

1921: They marry.

1923: Eva born in Beled.

1925: Edward born in Beled.

1927: Louis born in Beled.

1928: Family moves to Vienna.

1929: Albert born in Vienna.

1930: Paul born in Vienna.

1933: Ralph born in Vienna.

1938:

March 12: Hitler declares *Anschluss* (union) with Austria, and German troops occupy the country.

August 11: The Reichmanns flee to Paris.

1940:

May 10: German troops approach Paris. The Reichmanns flee once more, across the border into Spain, hours before the border is closed. They go to Tangier, Morocco, later this year.

June: Spanish troops occupy Tangier, annex it as part of Spanish Morocco, "to restore order."

1942:

November: Allied troops take over Morocco.

1943:

Renée Reichmann becomes the representative in Tangier of the Va'ad Hatzalah.

1945:

Samuel and Renée Reichmann visit New York.

1952:

> *March 30:* Independence riots break out in Tangier; Reichmanns begin to plan for another move.

1953:

> *August:* French resident general orders Sultan Mohammed V out of the country to prevent civil war, and when he won't go, he is kidnapped and flown to Corsica, and is replaced by his uncle, as France's puppet. Moroccans are outraged.

1954:

> *December:* Edward Reichmann goes to North America to explore possibilities there for the family. He decides to stay.

1955:

> Edward sets up Olympia Trading Company in Montreal, later buys Montreal Tile, and forms Olympia Floor & Wall Tile.
>
> Louis follows to Montreal, leaves for New York.
>
> *August 1:* Riots and demonstrations on behalf of the deposed sultan lead to brutal repression by the French and an attempt on the life of their puppet sultan, Ben Afara. This leads in turn to a French declaration that Moroccan independence will be recognized.
>
> *November 16:* Sultan Mohammed V returns from exile to Rabat. Tangier enters a period of chaos, and vast amounts of gold are shipped out.

1956:

> *March 3:* Moroccan independence recognized.
>
> *Midsummer:* Ralph Reichmann moves to Canada to take over the tile company.
>
> *September:* William Zeckendorf unveils his plan to transform downtown Montreal, centred on the Place Ville Marie.
>
> *October 29:* The International Zone of Tangier is dissolved.

1957:

> Paul Reichmann joins Ralph, and they move the tile business to Toronto. The brothers decide to build a warehouse on Colville Road, but the bids by contractors seem too high. Paul decides to contract the building himself. The building is completed for

$70,000. Paul decides to leave the tiles to Ralph and go into building full time.

1958:

York Developments, named after the surrounding county, is set up to handle real estate.

Webb & Knapp (Canada) and the Rubin brothers buy the Fleming Estate, just off the Don Valley, in Canada's largest single land transaction at the time. The development there is called Flemingdon Park.

1959:

Samuel, Renée, and Albert move to Toronto.

Early 1960s:

The Reichmann construction business expands rapidly, building one-floor offices and warehouses.

1965:

May: Webb & Knapp goes bankrupt and the Reichmanns buy Flemingdon Park. They immediately begin building on the property, with the MonyLife Insurance building at the southeast corner of Don Mills Road and Eglinton as their first multi-storey building.

1969:

Olympia & York Developments Limited is incorporated in Ontario, and a head office set up in the Toronto Star building at One Yonge Street, which the Reichmanns built.

1973:

First Canadian Place, tallest building in the Commonwealth, begun in heart of Toronto.

1974:

Olympia & York Developments, by the end of this year, has completed thirteen office buildings with three million square feet of space, and has built the largest suburban office space in Canada at Flemingdon Park.

1975:

May 18: First tenants move into lower twenty-two floors of First Canadian Place, on schedule.

1976:

> *October:* Reichmanns visit New York to study Uris Package, begin to negotiate.

1977:

> *September 19:* Uris Package deal signed in Manhattan.

1979:

> *March 15:* Olympia & York takes control of English Property, large British real-estate developer, for $157.3 million, after a bidding war and eventual accommodation with Trizec.

> Reichmanns purchase 10 per cent of Canada Northwest Land Limited.

1980:

> Reichmanns win contract to build world's largest financial centre in New York.

> *August:* Robert Campeau approaches Ken White to buy into Royal Trust.

> *September:* Olympia & York begins to buy shares in Brinco.

> About the same time, O&Y moving on Abitibi-Price Inc., the world's largest paper company. Same month, buy 9 per cent of Royal Trustco, holding company for Royal Trust, for $33 million, increasing share to 23.9 per cent later.

> Win contract to redevelop twenty-five acres in downtown San Francisco, a deal that is still not done thirteen years later.

> *November:* Win the contract to build the World Financial Center in New York.

1981:

> *March 6:* After a bidding war, in a deal financed by CIBC, O&Y takes 16.8 million shares of Abitibi-Price, for $32 a share. One of the largest takeovers to date, at $534 million.

> *April:* Olympia & York pays $214 million to buy 20 per cent of MacMillan Bloedel, another forest-products giant. They trade some of this into a purchase offer being made by Noranda – now controlled by Brascan, and thus Edper – and wind up with about 10 per cent of MacBlo and a stake in Noranda.

May: Begin buying shares of Hiram Walker.

June: They are buying into Bow Valley Industries, an oil company with wide interests, partly owned by Cemp Investments, the holding company of Sam Bronfman's children.

July 2: In England, the London Docklands Development Corporation begins work.

Paul Reichmann sends an intermediary to Hiram Walker to suggest that, since by this time O&Y has 10 per cent of Hiram Walker, he should have a seat on the board. He is rejected.

July 31: In three days at the end of July, O&Y pays $120 million to acquire 5.9 per cent of Hiram Walker – 3.8 million shares.

Paul Reichmann begins negotiations with Teachers Assurance and Annuity Association for a $250-million loan for Tower A of the World Financial Center.

December: Ground breaking for the World Financial Center in New York.

By end of 1981, the Reichmanns have spent over $1 billion in two years diversifying into paper, oil, finance, and resources.

1982:

March: American Express signs to rent the largest Battery Park building for thirty-five years in "largest real-estate transaction in history," worth $2.4 billion.

In New York, O&Y sells off two Uris buildings, re-mortgages 245 Park Avenue, its headquarters, for $308 million.

In London, Geoffrey Howe, then chancellor of the exchequer, sets aside several hundred acres of Port of London Authority land on the Isle of Dogs as an Enterprise Zone.

1983:

Deal is struck with Teachers, for $250 million U.S. at 14 per cent, plus 25 per cent of the gross income from the tower. The money is to be repaid over thirty-five years, and the signing helps O&Y attract other lenders.

October: Paul Reichmann visits Pittsburgh to explore possibility of buying the Canadian subsidiary of Gulf Oil, then going through a takeover battle and a series of scandals. There is no interest in selling to him at the price he offers. He will be back.

1984:

January: Paul Reichmann writes Teachers, saying that the money must be forthcoming and the deal finalized within ten days, although it is not scheduled for payment until 1984. Reichmann then terminates the deal and gets a new loan from Manufacturers Hanover, at much lower interest. Teachers sues, a suit that will explode in June 1992.

March: Olympia & York raises $970 million U.S. through the largest mortgage in history.

In New York, a bidding battle for Gulf Oil is won with the entry of a white knight, Standard Oil Co. of California, also known by its brand name, Chevron.

June: Olympia & York buys 16.2 million shares of Cadillac Fairview for $232 million.

August 24: In New York, a deal with Merrill Lynch & Company is announced for World Financial Center.

1985:

February: Federal government announces that Chevron acquisition of Gulf Canada can only go through if it is put on the block "for sale to Canadian-controlled purchasers." Deadline of April 30 is set; after that, Chevron is free to do what it likes.

March 19: The Reichmanns make an offer, which Chevron accepts, to purchase Chevron's 60.2 per cent of Gulf Canada. The deal is conditional on a favourable tax ruling from Ottawa.

Spring: "Little Egypt Bump" approved for Gulf takeover.

August 2: Olympia & York signs deal to pay $2.8 billion for Chevron's 60.2 per cent of Gulf Canada.

August 17: Globe and Mail breaks "Little Egypt Bump" story.

August 31: "Little Egypt Bump" deal between O&Y and Norcen signed.

Summer: Michael von Clemm and Archibald Cox visit Canary Wharf, decide to bring in G. Ware Travelstead to develop a new financial centre there.

September 30: Gulf's Ontario and Western refining and marketing assets sold to Petrocan, while Quebec and Maritime assets are sold to Ultramar, a British Company.

October: Mickey Cohen becomes president of Olympia & York Enterprises, the holding company for O&Y's public investments.

October 17: In New York, official opening of the World Financial Center.

1986:

Paul Reichmann joins board of directors of CIBC.

Early March: Robert Campeau begins secretly buying shares of Allied Stores.

March 11: The City of London, seeking to counter any attempt to undercut the Square Mile, announces that it will change planning restrictions to allow construction of additional office space.

March 17: Gulf board is told that it is going to make a bid for control of Hiram Walker Resources, borrowing $1.2 billion for the purpose. They agree.

March 19: Albert Reichmann calls Bud Downing, chairman of Hiram Walker Resources, on vacation in California, to inform him that Gulf Canada is making an offer for the shares of his company that morning.

March 26: Hiram Walker board recommends rejection of Gulf offer.

Over the Easter weekend, a series of meetings among Allied-Lyons, their lawyers, Walker, and Interprovincial and the Reichmanns. Interprovincial decides to sell its shares to O&Y, in return for getting Home Oil.

March 31, Easter Monday: Hiram Walker announces creation of Fingas, with $2.2 billion of capital, $2 billion from Walker, and $200 million from Allied-Lyons. Fingas offers $40 a share for 50 per cent of Walker shares. Walker will sell its liquor interests to Allied for $2.6 billion.

April 1: At a meeting of the Interprovincial board, hostile Hiram Walker directors are ordered to leave before the vote on Interprovincial joining the O&Y bid.

April 2: Court battle begins in Toronto over injunctions O&Y is seeking to prevent the sale of the liquor assets and the Fingas offer.

April 4: Bid for Walker shares upped to $35 a share.

April 9: Mr. Justice Robert Montgomery rules against O&Y.

TransCanada Pipelines offers to buy all Hiram Walker shares at $36.50, a total bid of $4.1 billion, the largest in Canadian history.

April 11: Gulf ups its bid for all Walker shares to $38.

April 15: TCPL pulls its offer, which has never been officially made. Golden parachutes for senior Walker executives are filed with the Securities and Exchange Commission in Washington.

April 17: Hiram Walker board approves Reichmann bid, "failing a higher bid." There is none. They are bidding $3.3 billion for the shares they don't already own, but the liquor business is gone – or going.

May 27: Paul Reichmann calls his first press conference, ever, in Windsor. It is a disaster.

June 2: Sir Derrick Holden-Brown, Allied CEO, appears at a Toronto press conference to announce that Allied-Lyons is suing the Reichmanns for $9 billion.

July 9: Ontario Supreme Court upholds Montgomery's decision and upholds the sale to Allied.

July 11: Investment Canada approves takeover of Walker liquor business by Allied-Lyons.

July 29: Interprovincial announces purchase of Home Oil for $1.1 billion.

December 29: Robert Campeau closes deal for Allied Stores, for $4.1 billion.

1987:

May: Olympia & York begins buying shares in Sante Fe Southern Pacific.

June: Gulf restructuring plan implemented.

July 17: In London, G. Ware Travelstead is bought out of Canary Wharf by O&Y.

Olympia & York promises to spend £400 million to help build the

Jubilee Line Extension, and to pay £68 million to improve the Docklands Light Railway and £80 million to connect the DLR to the Bank Street tube station.

Early October: Campeau begins to buy Federated shares through a dummy corporation, at $45.

October 19: Stock-market crash. Federated shares drop to $34, and Campeau decides he will take it over.

November 30: The Reichmanns swap their stake in Hiram Walker for cash and Allied-Lyons shares worth $1.3 billion, and become largest single shareholders in Allied-Lyons.

1988:

January: Project Rose is approved in Toronto by directors of Campeau Corporation – to take over Federated Stores.

January 25: Campeau makes formal offer of $47 a share for all 90 million shares of Federated, a total cost of $4.2 billion.

About the same time, he approaches the Reichmanns to get them to invest in equity. As with Allied Stores, they decline, but buy $260 million in convertible debentures in Campeau Corporation, the proceeds of which can be used for Federated.

March 21: Deal signed between Olympia & York Developments Limited and Campeau Corporation.

April 1: Campeau, in partnership with R. H. Macy & Co., buys Federated for $73.50 U.S. a share. The company is over-burdened with debt and immediately begins to bleed money.

May 11: Prime Minister Margaret Thatcher drives ceremonial pile to start O&Y's Canary Wharf.

December: As Federated and Allied go into a tailspin, O&Y injects more money, buying 500,000 shares at $15 each in Campeau Corporation, which reported a loss of $203 million for fiscal 1987.

1989:

January: Central London Rail Study rules against the Jubilee Line Extension.

January 23: East London Rail Study announced.

April 7: Robert Campeau visits the Reichmanns in Toronto, with a desperate plea for cash. They agree to lend, not invest, another $75 million with his half of Scotia Plaza as collateral.

Paul Reichmann hires a financial investigator to look into Campeau Corporation, and learns, by midsummer, that Federated and Allied cannot generate enough cash to pay bills and interest. Bankruptcy seems inevitable. In August, Campeau flies to Switzerland to meet Paul Reichmann in a vacation chalet, and asks for another $250 million. Reichmann advises him to file for bankruptcy protection, and Campeau goes away to think it over.

July 26: East London Rail Study and new Central London Rail Study recommend extension of the Jubilee Line, with O&Y to pay £400 million of the £1 billion cost.

September 12: Paul Reichmann and Campeau meet again, in London.

September 19: Olympia & York buys 15,625,000 Series A warrants each for one share of Campeau Corporation, and agrees to guarantee a $250-million U.S. line of credit for Campeau. In return, Campeau Corporation is to be restructured.

October 16: Word that things are not going well hits the street, and Allied and Federated bonds floated to support these deals fall in price. Campeau begins to badmouth the Reichmanns, blaming them for not coming up with a fix.

November 16: Jubilee Line Extension announced. The line is estimated to cost £1 billion, of which O&Y will pay £400 million, or 40 per cent.

1990:

January: Olympia & York Enterprises is wound up and Olympia & York Developments Limited reorganized.

January 7: Campeau reorganizes U.S. companies, disbands restructuring committee, and the Reichmanns withdraw.

January 15: Federated and Allied file for bankruptcy protection in Cincinnati.

January 31: Reorganization of O&Y portfolios under OYDL, switching all shares owned by OYDL to GWU Investments Limited.

March: Olympia & York dismisses project managers on main tower of

Canary Wharf, now six months behind schedule, giving them one day to clean out their desks.

March 30: Dominion Bond Rating Service reduces rating on $160 million U.S. of floating rate notes on Gulf Canada Square from AA to A.

September 19: Olympia & York offers to sell 20 per cent of its U.S. real-estate portfolio. There are no takers.

November 22: Margaret Thatcher resigns.

November 28: John Major becomes British prime minister.

In *New York Times* interview, Paul Reichmann dismisses as "children who don't know what they are talking about those who speculated that the company was pressed for cash."

1991:

January: Standard Poor Corp. downgrades $630.5 million worth of O&Y bonds.

May 1: Dominion Bond Rating Service reports that O&Y stocks have lost $1.25 billion in value in the past year.

October 22: Olympia & York takes over Campeau's half of Scotia Plaza.

December: Olympia & York fails to honour agreement to repurchase the Morgan Stanley building at Canary Wharf for $231 million U.S.

1992:

January: Morgan Stanley launches suit in London, although suit remains secret.

Early February: Consortium of Canadian banks provides $275 million in emergency financing.

February 13: Dominion Bond Rating Service in Toronto downgrades O&Y debt issues on O&Y commercial paper and First Canadian Place.

February 28: In Toronto, in offices of Davies, Ward & Beck on the forty-fourth floor of First Canadian Place, bankers meet senior officials of O&Y to discuss a loan of $240 million to save the company. After revelation that O&Y has used up its credit line with the Royal, the loan is refused.

March 2: A run on O&Y commercial paper begins.

March 3: Olympia & York scrambles to meet $40 million of paper due.

March 5: Sale of O&Y share of Interprovincial Pipeline announced. The company says it will use the $655 million obtained to reduce debt.

March 6: An O&Y spokesman, denying rumours of an impending bankruptcy, says the company is "current on all its obligations."

March 10: Olympia & York finds itself unable to roll over commercial paper, with $1.1 billion outstanding in three different programs, most of it coming due within forty-five days.

March 15: CIBC chairman Donald Fullerton persuades other banks to advance another £50 million to Canary Wharf to keep it out of bankruptcy.

March 20: Royal Trust, holding notes on the Exchange Tower, is assured by Olympia & York "on an extremely confidential basis," that a government bailout will soon be announced.

March 23: In the face of continuing rumours, O&Y announces that it is going to "restructure its debt" to meet a "liquidity crisis." This is the first public acknowledgement that the company cannot meet its obligations.

March 24: Thomas Johnson takes over as president of O&Y, replacing Paul Reichmann.

March 25: Olympia & York fails to make payment of $62 million in interest on an $800-million U.S. bond issue due this day. This issue is secured by Manhattan real estate.

March 26: The *Financial Post* declares that "the Reichmann empire is in sound financial condition, despite cash-flow problems," on the basis of "financial statements released exclusively to the *Post.*"

March 27: Meeting in Toronto between O&Y officials and twenty of its large lenders.

April 1: London announcement that the banks have refused to extend a $450-million loan about to come due. The loan is not declared in default.

Paul Reichmann's resignation from the board of directors of CIBC is accepted during a marathon board session.

April 6: Olympia & York misses a bond payment in New York.

April 8: Olympia & York sells most of its Trilon Financial Corp. holding, for about $65 million.

April 9: In England, the Tory government of John Major is re-elected.

In New York, a $5.5-million interest payment on a $930-million U.S. bond secured by three New York office buildings is made, hours before the issue would have been declared in default.

April 13: Toronto meeting with four hundred bankers. O&Y's proposed restructuring plan is not well received.

April 14: International bankers meet in Toronto, accuse Canadian banks of grabbing O&Y assets.

April 15: Olympia & York calls a meeting with bankers in Toronto, to get $8 million. The meeting is adjourned.

April 20: Easter Monday, Passover, another meeting in O&Y offices, another battle.

April 21: Short-term loan of $23 million advanced to O&Y by banks.

April 22: Ontario premier Bob Rae meets Paul Reichmann, later announces that the province will not bail the company out.

DBRS places some debentures on "Rating Alert with negative implications."

Olympia & York places 79 per cent interest in Abitibi-Price Inc. and 75 per cent interest in Gulf Canada Resources Limited in custody of the Toronto-Dominion Bank to secure $2.5 billion U.S. loan to a consortium of international banks. The T-D has no O&Y loans.

April 28: Campeau files a $1.25-billion lawsuit against the Reichmanns and National Bank.

May 1: Banks in London lend O&Y another $16 million to keep Canary Wharf going for another week.

May 2: Chemical Banking Corp. of New York places $125 million in O&Y real loans in non-performing category.

May 4: A $17-million interest payment on mortgage bonds secured by First Canadian Place is missed. O&Y is declared in default by Royal Trust, acting for bondholders.

In Ottawa, the federal government turns down request to guarantee bank loans.

May 5: Royal Trustco Limited, as trustee for the bondholders on the $325-million U.S. loan secured by First Canadian Place, serves notice that the debt must be met within seven working days. If payment is not made by five p.m. on May 14, the bondholders can seize First Canadian Place.

May 7: Olympia & York meets bankers at Canary Wharf, with a new rescheduling plan. Bankers hate it.

May 11: Another $6 million payment on notes secured by three Manhattan office towers is met hours before the deadline.

May 12: J. P. Morgan leads a group of banks in declaring O&Y in default on a $160-million U.S. note.

May 13: In Toronto, at a tense meeting in First Canadian Place, the banks say they will support a Chapter 11 filing, but Paul Reichmann holds out.

The banks then refuse to lend O&Y the $17 million to meet the interest on the First Canadian Place bonds.

May 14: Olympia & York files for bankruptcy protection in Toronto and New York.

May 16: Citibank writes off $100 million of its real-estate loans to O&Y.

May 19: Olympia & York tells holders of $548 million U.S. in bonds secured by 55 Water Street in Manhattan that it cannot meet interest payments.

May 22: Scotiabank becomes first Canadian bank to reveal its exposure to O&Y; it has made about $600 million in loans and other commitments.

May 27: In London, banks refuse any new loans to Canary Wharf. O&Y applies for Administration.

June 2: The *Financial Times* reports that two potential bidders for Canary Wharf have decided separately that it is worth only about one-fifth of what it cost to build.

June 5: Olympia & York's stake in Sante Fe Pacific Corp. goes on sale.

June 26: A New York judge rules that an O&Y subsidiary is liable for breaking off a $250-million loan agreement with the Teachers Assurance and Annuity Association of America.

June 30: Mr. Justice Blair blocks a plan by American Express Co. to tear up its lease for Canary Wharf.

July 2: Olympia & York abandons the project to erect an office building in Yerba Buena district of San Francisco.

July 9: Mr. Justice Blair gives O&Y an extension to August 21 to come up with a restructuring plan.

July 10: Olympia & York 1991 annual report released.

July 13: Another restructuring proposal.

August 12: U.S. investors and British bankers meet in London to explore the possible purchase of Canary Wharf from the lenders to O&Y.

August 13: Hanson plc pulls out of talks with Canary Wharf administrators.

August 20: Olympia & York press conference in Toronto to release details of the proposal to be filed in court the next day. The proposal angers the lenders.

August 27: Initial deadline for proposal to creditors in London. It is put off.

September 5: Canadian banks classify $3 billion in loans to O&Y as non-performing.

September 8: Olympia & York agrees to relinquish ownership of 55 Water Street in New York to creditors.

September 11: In Toronto, Mr. Justice Blair extends protection for O&Y to December 31.

September 18: It is reported that the Reichmanns have a personal stake in the World Financial Center through a secret partnership with the Bronfmans.

September 21: In London, banks reject the bid to buy Canary Wharf for £230 million.

September 22: TSE is investigating the revelations of September 18.

September 22: The eleven main lending bankers in London agree, in principle, to put up, at last, the money needed to get the Jubilee Line Extension going.

September 30: O&Y (U.S.) presents proposal to seventy-five U.S. creditors at a meeting in One Liberty Plaza.

October 2: Four senior directors of Canary Wharf are laid off by the court administrators in London.

October 27: Olympia & York proposes another complicated settlement with its creditors. It is rejected.

November 13: The Jubilee Line funding deal falls through.

November 18: Olympia & York makes a new proposal, entirely different in character, to its main creditors in Canada.

December 16: Olympia & York submits plan to Toronto court for emergence from protection. The plan is essentially the one bruited three weeks earlier.

1993:

January 11: Creditors begin voting by classes on O&Y proposal.

January 25: Voting finished; eight of thirty-five classes of creditors reject the plan, the rest accept.

February 5: In Toronto, court approves the restructuring plan.

February 8: Paul Reichmann announces that he is launching a new, Toronto-based partnership, Reichmann International.

March 5: Olympia & York restructuring plan implemented.

May 12: In New York, creditors threaten to force the U.S. subsidiary of O&Y into bankruptcy in a battle over the appointment of directors.

May 28: Announcement that Cyrus Vance has been named to mediate the dispute.

June 2: Reichmann International is bidding on three major projects in Mexico City, worth $400 million U.S.

Notes

Prologue

1. *Globe and Mail*, December 5, 1992, p. B1.
2. The debt, and its demise, did not come to light until much later. *Globe and Mail*, June 1, 1993, p. A3.
3. Chapter C-36, An Act to Facilitate Compromises and Arrangements between Companies and their Creditors.
4. Ibid., Part I, section 6.
5. Ibid., Part II, section 11.
6. Court filing.
7. Uwe Manski, paper, "Bill C-22: Bankruptcy Act Amendments," 1992, p. 6.
8. *New York Times*, November 28, 1990, p. D1.
9. *Fortune*, September 9, 1991, p. 59.
10. *Weekend*, October 13, 1979, p. 26.
11. The tab, court documents will later reveal, is in the area of $18–20 billion, measured in U.S. funds, about $3.6 billion borrowed from Canadian banks, $15 million from foreign banks and bondholders, and a pile of miscellaneous debts, some of which are disputed by the company.
12. *Globe and Mail*, May 22, 1992.
13. Court filing.
14. We will get to these later; one involved Morgan Stanley, the investment bank, the other the Teachers Assurance and Annuity Association of America.
15. *New York Times, op. cit.*
16. Hungary's gross national product in 1990 was estimated to be $22.9 billion in Bernard Stonehouse's *Pocket Guide to the World* (New York: Facts on File, 1990), p. 308.

17. Canary Wharf, Fact Book, Olympia & York, p. 27

18. Dr. Brian Edwards, *London Docklands: Urban Design in an Age of Deregulation* (Oxford: Butterworth-Heinemann, 1992), p. 70.

19. *Newsweek*, June 1, 1992, p. 64.

Chapter One

1. Jonathan Miller, in Thomas Derdack, ed., *The International Directory of Company Histories* (London: St. James Press, 1992).

2. E. Garrison Walters, *The Other Europe: Eastern Europe to 1945* (Syracuse: Syracuse University Press, 1988), p. 208.

3. Robert A. Kann, *The Multinational Empire: Nationalism and National Reform in the Hapsburg Monarchy, 1848–1914*, vol. 2 (New York: Columbia University Press, 1950), p. 332*n*.

4. C. A. Macartney, *October Fifteenth: A History of Modern Hungary, 1929–45* (Edinburgh: University Press, 1957), p. 18.

5. C. A. Macartney, *Hungary: A Short History* (Chicago: Aldine, 1957), p. 18.

6. Ibid.

7. Elaine Dewar, "The Mysterious Reichmanns: The Untold Story," *Toronto Life*, November, 1987, p. 72. This rambling, discursive, and highly controversial account contains, nevertheless, a good deal of factual information not available elsewhere – and which will probably remain unavailable, since publication of the article effectively silenced the sources that Dewar used within the family. While some of the facts and most of the conclusions reached by Dewar remain open to question, the specifics cited in these notes appear to be correct.

8. Walters, *op. cit.*, p. 141.

9. Ibid., p. 205.

10. Ibid.

11. Macartney, *October Fifteenth, op. cit.*, p. 209.

12. Walters, *op. cit.*, p. 208.

13. Dewar, *op. cit.*, p. 137.

14. Most biographies have Samuel moving from Beled in 1920, between

revolutions, but Elaine Dewar's research, which puts the births of the first three children in Beled, makes this seem highly unlikely. The first official traces of the Reichmanns in Vienna date from 1928.

15. Alan Bullock, *Hitler and Stalin: Parallel Lives* (Toronto: McClelland & Stewart, 1991), pp. 564-9.

16. Dewar, *op. cit.*, p. 136.

17. Ibid., p. 114.

18. Ibid, p. 139.

19. (Quoted in) Peter Foster, *The Master Builders: How the Reichmanns Reached for an Empire* (Toronto: Totem, 1987), p. 9. This book by Foster was first published in hardcover as *The Master Builders: How the Reichmanns Built an Empire* (Toronto: Key Porter, 1986).

20. Dewar, *op. cit.*, p. 144

21. (Quoted in) Dewar, *op. cit.*, p. 74.

22. Dewar, *op. cit.*, p. 76.

23. Gavin Maxwell, *Lords of the Atlas: The Rise and Fall of the House of Glaoua, 1893–1956* (London: Longmans, 1956).

24. Dewar, *op. cit.*, p. 144.

Chapter Two

1. Foster, *The Master Builders, op. cit.*, p. 13.

2. Dewar, *op. cit.*, p. 144.

3. Ibid., p. 150.

4. Susan Goldenberg, *Men of Property: The Canadian Developers Who Are Buying America* (Toronto: Personal Library, 1981), p. 37.

5. Foster, *The Master Builders, op. cit.*, p. 11.

6. Peter C. Newman, *The Canadian Establishment, Volume Two, The Aquisitors* (Toronto: McClelland & Stewart), p. 207.

7. The figures are drawn from the Annual Report for 1963.

8. Walter Stewart, *Towers of Gold, Feet of Clay: The Canadian Banks* (Toronto: Collins, 1982), p. 97.

9. William Zeckendorf, *The Autobiography of William Zeckendorf* (New York: Holt, Reinhart and Winston, 1970).

10. Ibid., p. 49.

11. David Olive, "Owe&Why," *Report on Business*, August, 1992, p. 10.

12. Foster, *The Master Builders, op. cit.*, p. 16.

13. Ibid.

14. Zeckendorf, *op. cit.*, pp. 175–6.

15. James Lorimer, *The Developers* (Toronto: Lorimer, 1978), p. 28.

16. Interview, January 19, 1992.

17. Foster, *The Master Builders, op. cit.*, p. 18.

18. Ibid., p. 19.

19. Peter Foster, *Towers of Debt: The Rise and Fall of the Reichmanns* (Toronto: Key Porter, 1993). In his first book on the Reichmanns, *The Master Builders*, Foster said the deal was "supposedly" signed in the vaults. He has apparently become more sure of himself, although it is hard to know what significance attaches to the exact location. In *The Master Builders*, he gave a price-tag of $25 million. No price-tag is given in the second volume. The price was, in fact, $17.8 million.

20. Stewart, *Weekend, op. cit.*

21. The details are from the Statement of Claim in the Beers' legal action.

22. The Beer brothers sold their business in 1976, but felt so strongly about the lawsuit that they continued it themselves, spending about a quarter of a million dollars to fight it. "The guy who bought from us," said Doug, "wanted nothing to do with it."

Chapter Three

1. David Olive, *Report on Business*, August, 1992, p. 9.

2. Foster, *The Master Builders, op. cit.*, p. 26.

3. The figure given is in U.S. dollars in the *New York Times*, August 17, 1980, section III, p. 9, in an article by Canadian business writer Susan Goldenberg.

4. Foster, *The Master Builders, op. cit.*, p. 29.

5. Goldenberg, *New York Times*, August 17, 1980.

6. Interview, August 28, 1992.

7. *Globe and Mail*, April 18, 1992, p. B1.

Chapter Four

1. Zeckendorf, *op. cit.*, p. 6.
2. Vanessa Letts, *New York* (London: Cadogan, 1991), p. 67.
3. *New York Times*, June 15, 1977, p. D1.
4. Foster, *The Master Builders*, *op. cit.*, p. 34.
5. *New York Times*, May 21, 1976, p. D17.
6. Stewart, *Weekend*, *op. cit.*, p. 30.
7. Foster, *The Master Builders*, *op. cit.*, p. 41. My nomination for the deal of the century, so far, is the one by which the Saudi Arabians traded thirty-six million barrels of oil – cost to them, zilch – for ten Boeing 747 aircraft, valued at $4 billion. That one made it into the *Guinness Book of Records*.
8. (Quoted in) Foster, *The Master Builders*, *op. cit.*, p. 42. He calls the chapter on the Manhattan purchase "The Deal of the Century."
9. Goldenberg, *Men of Property*, *op. cit.*, p. 42.
10. *Independent*, May 17, 1992, p. 15.
11. Olympia & York Developments Limited. Revenue Producing Real Estate. January 31, 1992. Court document.
12. *Wall Street Journal*, September 9, 1992, p. B3.
13. Goldenberg, *Men of Property*, *op. cit.*, p. 29. Actually, the Talmud has a pretty good line to cover quotes like this: "He who learns from another one chapter, one halachah, one verse or one word or even one letter, is bound to respect him."

Chapter Five

1. Stewart, *Towers of Gold, Feet of Clay*, *op. cit.*, p. 123.
2. Court filing.
3. Eric Kierans and Walter Stewart, *Wrong End of the Rainbow: The Collapse of Free Enterprise in Canada* (Toronto: Collins, 1988), p. 52.
4. Ibid., p. 53.
5. *Globe and Mail*, July 3, 1992, p. B3.
6. Bryan Burrough and John Helyar, *Barbarians at the Gate: The Fall of RJR Nabisco* (New York: Harper & Row, 1990).

7. Eric Kierans and Walter Stewart, *Wrong End of the Rainbow, op. cit.,* pp. 90-91.

8. E. J. Benson, minister of finance, *Summary of 1971 Tax Reform Legislation,* p. 50.

9. Patricia Best and Ann Shortell, *The Brass Ring: Power, Influence and the Brascan Empire* (Toronto: Random House, 1988), p. 99.

10. Peter Foster says, "The brothers were held in awe, even in Manhattan, because they could pick up the phone and arrange a $300-million line of credit in less time than it took to order a pizza." *The Master Builders, op. cit.,* p. 65. Not with toppings, I bet.

11. Goldenberg, *Men of Property, op. cit.,* p. 56.

12. Best and Shortell, *The Brass Ring, op. cit.,* p. 97ff.

13. *Globe and Mail,* February 22, 1979, p. B1.

14. Foster, *The Master Builders, op. cit.,* p. 69.

15. Best and Shortell, *The Brass Ring, op. cit.,* p. 101.

16. Ibid., p. 35.

17. There is a detailed, and disturbing, account of the role of Gordon Capital in this scandal in Erik Nielsen's memoir *The House Is Not a Home* (Toronto: Macmillan, 1989).

18. Foster, *The Master Builders, op. cit.,* p. 72.

Chapter Six

1. Best and Shortell, *The Brass Ring, op. cit.,* p. 11.

2. *Toronto Star,* May 25, 1983, p. A1.

3. Best and Shortell, *The Brass Ring, op. cit.,* p. 78.

4. James Fleming, *Circles of Power: The Most Influential People in Canada* (Toronto: Doubleday, 1991), p. 186.

5. *Toronto Star,* February 6, 1993, p. C1.

6. *Financial Post,* December 5, 1992, p. 4.

7. *Financial Post,* January 30, 1993, p. 3.

8. A detailed analysis appears in Kimberley Noble's article "Edper Hees' disastrous prayer," *Globe and Mail,* February 12, 1993, p. B1.

9. Interview, November 13, 1992.

10. Foster, *The Master Builders*, *op. cit.*, p. 80.

11. John Rothchild, *Going For Broke: How Robert Campeau Bankrupted the Retail Industry, Jolted the Junk Bond Market and Brought the Booming Eighties to a Crashing Halt* (New York: Simon & Schuster, 1991).

12. (Quoted in) Patricia Best and Ann Shortell, *A Matter of Trust* (Toronto: Viking, 1985), p. 68.

13. Ibid.

14. *Maclean's*, March 29, 1993, pp. 30-31.

Chapter Seven

1. (Quoted in) Walter Stewart, "Good and Rich," *Weekend*, October 27, 1979, p. 26.

2. Peter Newman, "A Unique Monument to Urban Life," *Maclean's*, March 13, 1989, p. 33.

3. Carol von Pressentin Wright, *Blue Guide to New York* (New York: W. W. Norton, 1991), p. 139.

4. "A Brief History of the World Trade Center," pamphlet, Port Authority of New York, 1992.

5. Wright, *op. cit.*, p. 136.

6. Brendan Gill in *New Yorker*, August 20, 1990, p. 70.

7. Foster, *The Master Builders*, *op. cit.*, p. 44.

8. *New York Times*, July 26, 1980, p. 16.

9. Goldenberg, *Men of Property*, *op. cit.*, p. 34.

10. Wright, *op. cit.*, p. 137.

11. Richard Saul Wurman, *NYC Access* (New York: Access Books, 1991), p. 29.

12. Foster, *The Master Builders*, *op. cit.*, p. 60.

13. Ibid., p. 58.

14. *Independent on Sunday*, May 17, 1992, p. 15.

15. *Globe and Mail*, June 27, 1992, p. B1.

Chapter Eight

1. *Globe and Mail*, February 19, 1993, p. B7.
2. The book was still being reworked when I spoke to Field in late 1992. Edper executives will want to read it, when it comes out.
3. Jonathan Martin, in Thomas Derdack, ed., *The International Directory of Corporate Histories* (London: St. James Press, 1988), p. 245.
4. Foster, *The Master Builders, op. cit.*, p. 82.
5. Best and Shortell, *The Brass Ring, op. cit.*, p. 105.
6. Foster, *The Master Builders, op. cit.*, p. 93.
7. Ibid.
8. *The International Directory of Company Histories*, vol. 2, pp. 262-3.
9. Ibid.
10. Foster, *The Master Builders, op. cit.*, p. 92.
11. (Quoted in) ibid.

Chapter Nine

1. *Globe and Mail*, April 11, 1986, p. 1.
2. Walter Stewart, *Uneasy Lies the Head: The Truth About Canada's Crown Corporations* (Toronto: Collins, 1987), p. 157.
3. Walter Stewart, *The Golden Fleece: Why the Stock Market Costs You Money* (Toronto: McClelland & Stewart, 1992), p. 4.
4. Foster, *The Master Builders, op. cit.*, p. 118.
5. *Winnipeg Free Press*, March 20, 1985, p. 66.
6. *Globe and Mail*, October 22, 1985, p. 1.
7. *Hansard*, October 22, 1985, p. 7869.
8. Ibid.
9. Ibid., p. 7870.
10. Stewart, *Uneasy Lies the Head, op. cit.*, p. 158.
11. Foster, *The Master Builders, op. cit.*, p. 148.
12. *Globe and Mail*, April 5, 1986, p. B1.
13. Ibid., April 11, 1986, p. 1.
14. Ibid., April 12, 1986, p. B1.
15. Foster, *The Master Builders, op. cit.*, p. 211.

16. *Windsor Star*, April 22, 1986, p. 1.

17. *The International Directory of Company Histories*, vol. 2, p. 264.

Chapter Ten

1. *International Directory of Company Histories*, vol. 4, p. 702.

2. Ibid., p. 703.

3. *Business Week*, June 1, 1992, p. 29.

4. Foster, *The Master Builders, op. cit.*, p. 94.

5. *Toronto Star*, October 18, 1985, p. E1.

6. *Maclean's*, August 24, 1987, p. 28.

7. *Maclean's*, December 7, 1987, p. 36.

8. *Fortune*, January 29, 1990, p. 122.

9. Rothchild, *op. cit.*, p. 46.

10. *Toronto Star*, April 7, 1988, p. A3.

11. *Fortune*, January 29, 1990, p. 121.

12. Rothchild, *op. cit.*, p. 57.

13. Rothchild, *op. cit.*, p. 96.

14. Rothchild, *op. cit.*, p. 98.

15. *Report on Business*, May 1990, p. 52.

16. Ibid., p. 147.

17. Ibid., p. 55.

18. Report under Subsection 100(2) of the Securities Act (Ontario), filed March 24, 1988, p. 1.

19. *Globe and Mail*, February 6, 1992, p. B10.

20. *Fortune*, January 29, 1990, p. 122.

21. Rothchild, *op. cit.*, p. 205.

22. *Globe and Mail*, May 16, 1992, p. B1.

Chapter Eleven

1. Colm Kenigan, *A History of Tower Hamlets* (London, 1982).

2. S. K. Al Naib, *London Docklands: Past, Present and Future* (London: Ashmead Press, 1990).

3. Stephanie Williams, *Docklands* (London: Architecture Design and Technology Press, 1990), p. 10.
4. Eve Hostettler, *An Outline History of the Isle of Dogs* (London: Island History Trust, undated), p. 4.
5. Ibid., p. 6.
6. Peter Underwood, *Jack the Ripper: One Hundred Years of Mystery* (London: Javelin, 1987).
7. Al Naib, *op. cit.*, p. 3.
8. Hostettler, *op. cit.*, p. 12.
9. Hugh Clout, ed., *The Times London History Atlas* (London: Times Books, 1991), p. 158.
10. John M. Hall, "Docklands," in *East End and Docklands*, William J. Fishman, Nicholas Breach, John M. Hall, eds (London: Duckworth, 1990), p. 51.
11. Interview, November 27, 1992.
12. Brian Edwards, *Docklands: Urban Design in an Age of Deregulation* (Oxford: Butterworth-Heinemann, 1992), p. 7.
13. Docklands Joint Committee, *Report*, 1976, p. 3.
14. Interview, David Bayliss, director of planning, London Transport, November 30, 1992.

Chapter Twelve

1. Edwards, *op. cit.*, p. 65.
2. Hall, *op. cit.*, p. 52.
3. *The Docklands Experiment: A Critical Review of Eight Years of the London Docklands Development Corporation* (London: Docklands Consultative Committee, 1990), p. 79.
4. Local Government and Planning Act, 1980.
5. Government statement, quoted in *The Docklands Experiment, op. cit.*, p. 22.
6. Nicholas Ridley, secretary of environment, statement before the House of Commons Committee on Employment, 1989, p. 12.
7. *The Docklands Experiment, op. cit.*, p. 19.

8. Ibid.

9. Department of Employment and Unemployment.

10. *Abstract of Greater London Housing Statistics*, London Research Centre, 1992, pp. 221, 231, 232.

11. Nicholas Breach, in *East End and Docklands*, *op. cit.*, pp. 7-8.

12. Edwards, *op. cit.*, p. 8.

13. Interview, December 3, 1992.

14. Quoted from the original plan, an untitled copy obtained by the Docklands Forum.

15. Docklands Forum, *Docklands Forum Experience on Canary Wharf* (London, 1988), p. 2.

16. The Docklands Consultative Committee, *All That Glitters: A Critical Assessment of Canary Wharf*, May, 1992, p. 34.

17. Williams, *op. cit.*, p. 16.

18. Interview, December 1, 1992.

19. *Independent*, May 17, 1986, p. 3.

20. *International Directory of Company Histories*, vol 4, p. 268.

21. *The Times*, July 21, 1987, p. 21a.

Chapter Thirteen

1. The quote is from *Maclean's*, July 9, 1990, p. 33. Luskin was president of the Toronto investment firm of Gluskin, Sheff and Associates Inc.

2. Foster, *Towers of Debt*, *op. cit.*, p. 196.

3. Edwards, *op. cit.*, p. 67.

4. *Globe and Mail*, March 17, 1990.

5. *Maclean's*, August 24, 1987, p. 29.

6. Docklands Consultative Committee, *All that Glitters*, *op. cit.*, p. 18.

7. Ibid.

8. Ibid.

9. Olympia & York, *Canary Wharf Fact Book* (London: February, 1992), p. 8.

10. Edwards, *op. cit.*, p. 70.

11. *Maclean's*, July 9, 1990, p. 33.

12. Olympia & York, Community Affairs Department, *Report*, April 1992, p. 5.

13. Ibid., p. 7.

Chapter Fourteen

1. Interview, November 30, 1992.

2. *Hansard*, Written Answers, July 23, 1987.

3. Interview, November 27, 1992.

4. Association of London Authorities, *How the Cake Was Cut: Ten Years of Docklands* (London, 1991), p. 9.

5. Interview with Eric Sorenson, LDDC, December 3, 1992.

6. *LDDC: Main Bull Points*, memo prepared May 1992, for use of Cabinet ministers in the House of Commons.

7. Docklands Consultative Committee, *All That Glitters, op. cit.*, p. 21. Figures supplied by Olympia & York.

8. Ibid.

9. The road is 1.8 kilometres long, and a kilometre is 3,280.8 feet; × 1.8 = 5,905.44 feet; × 12 = 70,865.28 inches. Divide this into £325,000,000 and you get £4,586.18 per inch, which, at $2.06 per £1, produces a total of $9,447.53 per inch.

10. *Construction News*, December 5, 1990.

11. Association of London Authorities, *How the Cake Was Cut, op. cit.*, p. 9.

12. Ibid.

13. London Transport, *The Jubilee Line Extension And Canary Wharf*, undated.

14. Ibid.

15. *Central London Rail Study: A joint study by The Department of Transport, British Rail Network SouthEast, London Regional Transport, London Underground, Ltd.*, January, 1989, p. 23.

16. *Financial Times*, May 29, 1992, p. 7.

17. Department of Transport, Press Release, July 26, 1989.

18. *Hansard*, Written Answers, January 23, 1989.

19. Interview, November 25, 1992.

20. Interview, November 26, 1992.

21. Interview, December 3, 1992.

Chapter Fifteen

1. (Quoted in) *Financial Post Magazine*, Summer, 1990, p. 169.

2. *Financial Post*, June 10, 1991, p. 7.

3. *New York Times Magazine*, July 17, section VI, p. 16.

4. Rothchild, *op. cit.*, pp. 217-8.

5. Ibid., p. 223.

6. *Globe and Mail*, January 16, 1990, p. B10.

7. Ibid.

8. Rothchild, *op. cit.*, p. 232.

9. Arthur Johnson, "Just Another Deadbeat," *Report on Business*, May, 1990, p. 57.

10. *Globe and Mail*, October 23, 1991, p. B1.

11. Rothchild, *op. cit.*, p. 242.

12. Ibid., p. 240.

13. Ibid., p. 260.

14. *Globe and Mail*, July 21, 1989, p. B1.

15. *Globe and Mail*, July 20, 1989, p. B1.

16. *Toronto Star*, October 18, 1985, p. E1.

17. *Report under Section 90 of the Securities Act (Ontario)*, filed September 29, 1989.

18. Ibid., p. 4.

19. Ibid.

20. Ibid., p. 2.

21. Rothchild, *op. cit.*, p. 249.

22. *Globe and Mail*, January 16, 1990, p. B10.

23. *Globe and Mail*, January 22, 1990, p. B20.

24. Rothchild, *op. cit.*, p. 263.

25. *Financial Post*, May 25, 1992, p. 4.

26. Johnson, *op. cit.*, p. 61.

27. *Globe and Mail*, January 15, 1990, p. B1.

28. Ibid.

29. *Globe and Mail*, October 17, 1990, p. B4.

30. *Globe and Mail*, November 7, 1991, p. A17.

31. *Financial Post*, June 10, 1991, p. 7.

32. *Financial Post*, June 10, 1991, p. 7.

33. *Globe and Mail*, October 23, 1991, p. B9.

34. *Globe and Mail*, March 28, 1992, p. B1.

35. *Globe and Mail*, February 6, 1992, p. B10.

Chapter Sixteen

1. Docklands Consultative Committee, *All That Glitters, op. cit.*, p. 28.

2. Olympia & York, *Canary Wharf Horticulture* (London, 1992).

3. Docklands Consultative Committee, *All That Glitters, op. cit.*, p. 33.

4. *Hansard*, Written Answers, May 2, 1991.

5. Olympia & York Developments Limited, Application under Clause 100(2)(c) of the Securities Act (Ontario), January 24, 1990.

6. DBRS Report #1070, p. 1.

7. *Globe and Mail*, September 21, 1990, p. B1.

8. *Globe and Mail*, June 14, 1990, p. B4.

9. *International Directory of Company Histories*, vol. 2, p. 245.

10. *Globe and Mail*, April 26, 1991, p. B4.

11. *Globe and Mail*, April 26, 1991, p. B4.

12. *Globe and Mail*, January 10, 1992, p. B5.

13. Nicholas von Hoffman, *Capitalist Fools* (New York: Doubleday, 1992), p. 22.

14. *Globe and Mail*, June 24, 1991, p. B1.

15. *Maclean's*, April 8, 1991, p. 9.

16. *Globe and Mail*, June 24, 1991, p. 1.

17. *Globe and Mail*, September 21, 1990, p. B1.

18. Ibid.

19. *Globe and Mail*, April 13, 1990, p. B5.

20. *New York Times*, November 28, 1990, p. D1.

21. Ibid.

Chapter Seventeen

1. Penelope Lively, *City of the Mind* (London: Andre Deutsch, 1991), p. 25.
2. *Maclean's*, April 8, 1991, p. 39.
3. Ibid.
4. Docklands Consultative Committee, *All That Glitters, op. cit.*, p. 30.
5. DBRS Report #11428.
6. Ibid.
7. *Globe and Mail*, June 12, 1992, p. B1.
8. DBRS Report #11458, p. 3.
9. DBRS Report #11460.
10. *Business Week*, June 1, 1992, p. 27.
11. DBRS Report #11458, p. 3.
12. *Globe and Mail*, December 4, 1992, p. 1.
13. DBRS Report #11458.
14. *Globe and Mail*, May 16, 1992, p. B5.
15. *Globe and Mail*, December 8, 1992, p. A8.
16. *Globe and Mail*, December 5, 1992, p. D1.
17. Minutes of Confidential Noteholder Meeting, May 20, 1992, at L'Hôtel, Toronto, p. 11.
18. Ibid.
19. Ibid., p. 12.
20. *Business Week*, July 1, 1992, p. 26.
21. *Globe and Mail*, March 23, 1992.
22. *Financial Post*, March 26, 1992, p. 1.
23. Ibid., April 6, 1992, p. 5.
24. Ibid., April 13, 1992, p. 14.
25. Ibid., April 6, 1992, p. 4.
26. Stewart, *Towers of Gold, op. cit.*, p. 253. The Commission said, "The boards of our major lending institutions are composed almost entirely of persons who have an additional relationship to the bank, usually as the chief officer of a borrower. Inevitably this creates the possibility of a conflict of interest, collective as well as individual, where the directors'

obligation may clash with their duties elsewhere." It was a valid point fifteen years ago, and it is a valid point today.

27. *Financial Post*, April 13, 1992, p. 13.
28. *Globe and Mail*, April 22, 1992, p. B1.

Chapter Eighteen

1. *Financial Post*, April 14, 1992, p. 1.
2. Ibid.
3. "World Bankers Demand Facts," shrieked the *Financial Post* in one warmup story on April 11.
4. *Fortune*, May 8, 1992, p. 82.
5. *Business Week*, June 1, 1992, p. 26.
6. Anthony Bianco, "Magnificent Obsession," *Vanity Fair*, October 22, 1992, p. 266.
7. *Fortune*, May 18, 1992, p. 82.
8. *Independent*, May 17, 1992, p. 4.
9. *Globe and Mail*, December 4, 1992, p. A8.
10. DBRS Rating Report, April 22, 1992.
11. *Independent*, May 17, 1992, p. 4.
12. *Financial Post*, May 18, 1992, p. 10.
13. *Globe and Mail*, May 5, 1992, p. B1.
14. Transcript of bondholders' meeting, p. 20.
15. *Globe and Mail*, December 5, 1992, p. D1.
16. Ibid, p. D3.
17. *Independent*, May 17, 1992, p. 4.
18. *Financial Post*, May 18, 1992, p. 9.
19. *Maclean's*, April 6, 1992, p. 36.
20. *Independent on Sunday*, May 17, 1992, p. 4.
21. *Globe and Mail*, May 16, 1992, p. B1.

Chapter Nineteen

1. *Business Week*, June 1, 1992, p. 26.
2. *Globe and Mail*, January 16, 1993, p. B3.
3. Olympia & York Developments Limited, *Notes to Consolidated Financial Statements*, January 31, 1992 (hereafter, "Notes"), p. 7.
4. Ibid.
5. Laurence H. Kallen, *Corporate Welfare: The Megabankruptcies of the 80s and 90s*, (New York: Carol Publishing, 1991), p. 54.
6. *Financial Times*, May 29, 1992, p. 7.
7. *Globe and Mail*, May 28, 1992, p. B1.
8. *Financial Times*, May 29, 1992, p. 1.
9. Interview, November 26, 1992.
10. *Independent*, May 17, 1992, p. 4.
11. Ibid.
12. *Financial Post*, June 1, 1992, p. 5.
13. *Independent*, May 17, 1992, p. 30.
14. *Toronto Star*, May 30, 1992, p. D2.
15. *Globe and Mail*, June 2, 1992, p. B1.
16. *Globe and Mail*, December 5, 1992, p. D3.
17. *Wall Street Journal*, June 4, 1992.
18. *Toronto Star*, June 5, 1992, p. D2.
19. Court filings.
20. Reasons for Judgment, Teachers Assurance and Annuity Association of America, against Olympia & York Battery Park Company and O&Y Battery Park Corp., p. 26.
21. Ibid., p. 28.
22. Telephone interview, May 11, 1993.
23. Court filing.
24. *New York Times*, July 7, 1992, p. D5.
25. *New York Times*, July 9, 1992, p. D3.
26. Court filing.
27. Olympia & York Notes, *op. cit.*, schedule 14.
28. Ibid., schedule 11.

29. Olympia & York Developments Limited, *President's Message*, July 10, 1992, p. 1.

30. *Auditors' Report*, Price Waterhouse, June 26, 1992, p. 2.

31. *Globe and Mail*, July 10, 1992, p. B1.

32. Ibid., July 23, 1992, p. B1.

33. Ibid., August 15, 1992, p. B3.

34. Ibid., August 20, 1992, p. B1.

35. *Financial Post*, August 17, 1992, p. 9.

36. Court filing.

37. Ibid.

38. *Wall Street Journal*, September 9, 1992, p. B3.

39. *Globe and Mail*, September 16, 1992, p. B1.

40. *Globe and Mail*, September 19, 1992, p. B1.

41. *Globe and Mail*, September 22, 1992, p. B1.

42. *The Times*, September 27, 1992, p. 1. The same issue of *The Times* carried a full page ad boosting the development, with the heading "Are You a Knocker or a Docker." How gauche.

43. *New York Times*, September 29, 1992, p. 1.

44. *Financial Times*, October 1, 1992, p. 23.

45. *Wall Street Journal*, October 1, 1992, p. 3.

46. *Globe and Mail*, October 2, 1992, p. B4.

47. *Globe and Mail*, November 1, 1992, p. B2.

48. *Globe and Mail*, November 19, 1992, p. B1.

49. *Financial Post*, November 21, 1992, p. 1.

50. Court filing.

51. *Globe and Mail*, December 23, 1992, p. B3.

52. *Toronto Star*, December 30, 1992, p. C3.

53. *Globe and Mail*, January 1, 1993, p. B9.

54. *Globe and Mail*, May 13, 1993, p. B1.

Epilogue

1. *Globe and Mail,* February 26, 1993, p. B1.

2. *Globe and Mail,* February 9, 1993, p. B1.

3. *Financial Post,* May 8, 1993, p. S14.

4. *Globe and Mail,* June 2, 1993, p. B1.

5. *Barron's,* May 18, 1992.

6. Foster, *Towers of Debt, op. cit.,* p. 295.

7. Robert Block, in *Business Journal,* May, 1993, pp. 29-30.

8. *Saturday Star,* March 6, 1993, p. A1.

9. *Globe and Mail,* March 6, 1993, p. A20.

10. Interview, August 31, 1992.

Bibliography

Al Naib, S. K. *Discover London Docklands.* London: Ashmead Press, 1992.

Al Naib, S. K. *London Docklands: Past, Present and Future.* London: Ashmead Press, 1991.

Babab, Michael, and Mulroney, Catherine. *Campeau: The Building of an Empire.* Toronto: Doubleday, 1989.

Best, Patricia, and Shortell, Ann. *A Matter of Trust: Power and Privilege in Canada's Trust Companies.* Toronto: Viking, 1985.

Best, Patricia, and Shortell, Ann. *The Brass Ring: Power, Influence and the Brascan Empire.* Toronto: Ballantine, 1988.

Bianco, Anthony. "Magnificent Obsession." *Vanity Fair,* October 1992.

Breach, Nicholas, Fishman, William J., and Hall, John M., eds. *East End and Docklands.* London: Duckworth, 1990.

Bullock, Alan. *Hitler and Stalin: Parallel Lives.* Toronto: McClelland & Stewart, 1991.

Burrough, Bryan, and Helyar, John. *Barbarians at the Gate: The Fall of RJR Nabisco.* New York: Harper & Row, 1990.

Corey, Ford. *Donovan of OSS.* Boston: Little, Brown, 1970.

Department of Transport. *Central London Rail Study.* London, January 1989.

Department of Transport. *Central London Rail Study: A Report on Further Work.* London, 1990.

Department of Transport. *London Docklands Transport: The Growing Network for the 1990s.* London, 1992.

Dewar, Elaine. "The Mysterious Reichmanns." *Toronto Life,* November 1987, pp. 61-186.

Docklands Consultative Committee. *All That Glitters Is Not Gold: A Critical Assessment of Canary Wharf.* London, May 1992.

Docklands Consultative Committee. *The Docklands Experiment: A Critical Review of Eight Years of the London Docklands Development Corporation.* London, 1990.

Docklands Consultative Committee. *How the Cake Was Cut: Ten Years of Docklands.* London, 1991.

Edwards, Dr. Brian. *London Docklands: Urban Design in an Age of Deregulation.* Oxford: Butterworth-Heinemann, 1992.

Fleming, James. *Circles of Power: The Most Influential People in Canada.* Toronto: Doubleday, 1991.

Foster, Peter. *The Master Builders: How the Reichmanns Reached for an Empire.* Toronto: Totem, 1987. First published in hardcover as *The Master Builders: How the Reichmanns Built an Empire.* Toronto: Key Porter, 1986.

Foster, Peter. *Towers of Debt: The Rise and Fall of the Reichmanns.* Toronto: Key Porter, 1993.

Goldenberg, Susan. *Men of Property: The Canadian Developers Who Are Buying America.* Toronto: Personal Library, 1981.

Hostettler, Eve. *An Outline History of the Isle of Dogs.* London: Island History Trust, undated.

The International Directory of Company Histories. Editor-in-Chief, Adele Hast. London: St. James Press, 1992.

Johnson, Arthur. "Just Another Deadbeat." *Report on Business,* May 1990.

Kallen, Laurence H. *Corporate Welfare: The Megabankruptcies of the 80s and 90s.* New York: Carol Publishing, 1991.

Kann, Robert A. *The Multinational Empire: Nationalism and National Reform in the Hapsburg Monarchy, 1848–1914.* Vol. 2. New York: Columbia University Press, 1950.

Kenigan, Colm. *A History of Tower Hamlets.* London, 1982.

Kierans, Eric, and Stewart, Walter. *Wrong End of the Rainbow: The Collapse of Free Enterprise in Canada.* Toronto: Collins, 1988.

Letts, Vanessa. *New York.* London: Cadogan, 1991.

Lorimer, James. *The Developers.* Toronto: Lorimer, 1978.

Macartney, C. A. *Hungary: A Short History.* Chicago: Aldine, 1957.

Macartney, C. A. *October Fifteenth: A History of Modern Hungary, 1929–45.* Edinburgh: University Press, 1957.

Massie, Robert K. *Dreadnought: Britain, Germany and the Coming of the Great War.* New York: Random House, 1991.

Maxwell, Gavin. *Lords of the Atlas: The Rise and Fall of the House of Glaoua, 1893–1956.* London: Longmans, 1956.

McQueen, Rod. *The Moneyspinners: An Intimate Portrait of the Men Who Run Canada's Banks.* Toronto: Macmillan, 1983.

Newman, Peter C. "A Unique Monument to Urban Life." *Maclean's,* March 13, 1989.

Newman, Peter C. *The Canadian Establishment.* Vol. 2, *The Acquisitors.* Toronto: McClelland & Stewart, 1981.

Olive, David. "Owe&Why." *Report on Business,* August 1992.

Olympia & York. *Canary Wharf Fact Book.* London, undated.

Olympia & York. *Canary Wharf Horticulture.* London, 1992.

Rothchild, John. *Going for Broke: How Robert Campeau Bankrupted the Retail Industry, Jolted the Junk Bond Market and Brought the Booming Eighties to a Crashing Halt.* New York: Simon & Schuster, 1991.

Shortell, Ann. *Money Has No Country: Behind the Crisis in Canadian Business.* Toronto: Macmillan, 1991.

Stewart, Walter. *The Golden Fleece: Why the Stock Market Costs You Money.* Toronto: McClelland & Stewart, 1992.

Stewart, Walter. "Good and Rich." *Weekend,* October 27, 1979.

Stewart, Walter. *Towers of Gold, Feet of Clay: The Canadian Banks.* Toronto: Collins, 1982.

Stewart, Walter. *Uneasy Lies the Head: The Truth About Canada's Crown Corporations.* Toronto: Collins, 1987.

The Times London History Atlas. Edited by Hugh Clout. London: Times books, 1991.

Tôkés, Rudolf L. *Béla Kun and the Hungarian Soviet Republic.* New York: Prager, 1967.

Underwood, Peter. *Jack the Ripper: One Hundred Years of Mystery.* London: Javelin, 1987.

von Hoffman, Nicholas. *Capitalist Fools.* New York: Doubleday, 1992.

Walters, E. Garrison. *The Other Europe: Eastern Europe to 1945.* Syracuse: Syracuse University Press, 1988.

Williams, Stephanie. *Docklands.* London: Architecture Design and Technology Press, 1991.

Wright, Carol von Pressentin. *Blue Guide to New York.* New York; W. W. Norton, 1991.

Wurman, Richard Saul. *NYC Access.* New York: Access Books, 1991.

Zeckendorf, William. *The Autobiography of William Zeckendorf.* New York: Holt, Reinhart and Winston, 1970.

Index